Tathagata

Anup Rej

TATHAGATA
A Divine Comedy for Our Time

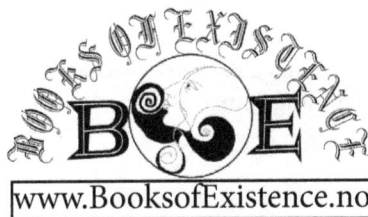

www.BooksofExistence.no

Part 1
MYTHOLOGICAL MAN RETURNING

Prologue

This book was conceived through an unusual mental process. It had taken its birth by a graveyard where the son of the author was buried. Though the structure and form took inspiration from Dante`s Divine Comedy, at no stage of writing it was clear to the author how the content of the book might evolve. Till the end of the writing it was driven by a mental process, where the author had felt his participation as someone, similar to the pilgrim of Dante, who was being guided by his Divine companion. The Guide was taking him in a journey through different realms of the mind while revealing and explaining the meaning of life, and advising him to refrain from certain paths.

In the beginning this process was very confusing for the author. It took him a long time before he could grasp the meaning behind what were being written: Thus a story of the universal man had gradually unfolded from a world unknown to the intellectual mind. The less structured part in the prelude reflects the confusion of the author.

It had taken him many years to complete. During these years he had experienced the existence of a higher mind, who had taken abode in him by overriding the will of man and his intelligence. He had experienced his personal presence in the writing as an ego and a will-bound individual who was struggling to grasp this weird psychological phenomenon. Strung between belief and doubt about the existence of the supernatural, he had ridden through a journey that defied rational comprehension and the power of the ego-bound intellectual mind to intervene.

The author had thus seen himself in the role of a pilgrim making a journey through a complex maze of different realms of consciousness passing through dreams, myths, scientific reason, philosophical contemplation and the mystical experiences.

An epic wandering through the universe and
the different realms of consciousness

Preface

Are we all individual characters appearing on the life's stage as results of evolution and accidental happenings occurring in nature? Or do we appear in life to fulfil a meaning and purpose and play destined roles as parts of a universal being who comes and goes life after life? Does meaning of life lie in conquering and destroying others and establishing one's superiority and dominance over fellow human beings, or do we belong to the common body of humanity, which we should all ply together in order to move forward the possibilities of evolution to a higher stage that life on Earth has bestowed on us? Is the reality an arena where one is thrown to live, reproduce and find meaning of life in the pursuit of winning over needs thrust upon all animals as products of physical interactions in the material sphere as many may suggest? Or, is it a far more interesting opportunity of experiencing an existence where a cosmic mind manifests itself in bodily form?

The book relates a journey of the universal Cosmic Man, named Tathagata, who wanders through a multidimensional reality which manifests through different levels of consciousness which empower and provide possibilities of evolution of higher man. The reality takes its shape according to the nature of consciousness in which the mind perches on the world to gaze at it. The way one chooses decides the reality of life which one may experience as instinct-bound individuals, or creative artistic person, or rational and scientific man, or a mystic for example.

Tathagata's Journey is an epic journey through different levels of consciousness. He comes and goes life after life following the wheel of birth, death and rebirth. He searches beauty, love and meaning of life in the universe, and seeks an escape from the suffering of the world. By bearing conflicting desires and will he wanders from realm to realm in order to find an enlightened way. As parts of Tathagata all human beings carry in themselves the contradictions of the Promethean and the Orphean nature. Like the creatures of Prometheus, on one hand, they seek knowledge, power, wealth and fame in the instinct-bound world, where the will to dominate and the desire to triumph over others reign. In contradiction to this will, which brings tumults of conflicts, as the bearers of Orphean sensibilities, they seek, on the other hand, beauty and love beyond the realm of the senses, and ways that will lead man to find home where one may find peace and tranquillity. Every time Tathagata is reborn, he is entrapped in the Time Hall of Illusion, where a maze of conflicting desires and emotions entangles his mind. All human beings are destined to start their journey in this Time Hall of Illusion from where many paths move to the world. While facing a plethora of possibilities to choose from, they wander through different realms of the mind that lie within themselves. During the wandering the guide of the soul appears as a spiritual power willing to show man the enlightened way. Torn by doubts and disbelief in the spiritual existence, the wanderer often chooses paths of the worldly will and desire, and thus ends up in pursuing activities that lead to suffering, which he wishes to avoid.

Therefore, the journey has no particular cultural framework and temporal setting. It is told through myths of the world, which have a common ground uniting man of all cultures and times. The story is meant to provide knowledge and perspectives that may help human beings, belonging to different cultures in the contemporary world, to grasp the meaning of a wandering of man in the cosmic sphere from a universal mythical perspective. It is based on a common ground where human beings may unite in their striving for love, beauty and home.

The book begins with the stories of the mythical characters, who still incarnate in men and women living today. Tathagata`s journey is an inner journey perceived as illusion generated by the mind. By making meditative reflections in the Time Hall of Illusion he relates the story of the journey he has made in an earlier life and the one in which he has embarked on "now". The life, which has passed is inseparably entangled with the life which is passing or will pass in the future through this Time Hall.

In the end Tathagata expounds an enlightened way to live.

The story of the Journey of Tathagata will provide the readers with perspectives and awareness about the way we can make journey of life, which is bound to a physical body, with its diverse needs, and the mind with its multiple levels of consciousness through which life can be realized. All human life are destined to move in a reality coloured by the projection of the individual mind, and in that sense trapped in a Hall of Illusion. All paths of journey must pass through this illusory "Time Hall", and at every moment there are several choices of paths which lead to different levels of experiences. An inner guide exists in us all, who directs us to choose paths leading to higher state of consciousness and helps us to overcome the obstacles that may appear as sufferings on the way.

It prescribes a way about how to comprehend the meaning of this journey of life as a dual existence comprising of the mortal and the inner Guide. This dual is embeded in a cosmos that exists as a Great Symphony. It is hoped that the readers will gain wisdom and vision to grasp the meaning of being as a part of this symphony of the universe.

Main Mythological Characters

Male: Pometheus, Orpheus and Odysseus of Greek mythology
Female: Helen, Circe and Muses of Greek mythology

Suffering of Prometheus

Prometheus

Prometheus is the personification of the human mind striving to win over the fate and destiny with the help of reason and knowledge, he rises against Heaven in order to curve out the place for the mortal will and desires in life. He is associated with the symbol of the sun, and is a sun-hero, who draws his will power from the awakened mind illumined by the power of the sun. In Greek mythology he is the creator of the human beings. To help his creatures to free themselves from the destiny bound in the hands of the gods and goddesses in Heaven, he stole fire from Heaven and gave it to mankind. With this fire the mortal creatures could decipher the know how of nature and could liberate themselves from the whims of Heavenly powers controlling the forces the courses of life and death on Earth.

As a punishment for giving fire of heaven to the mortals, Prometheus was condemned to a perpetual punishment. Gods kept him bound on a mountain top where an eagle came during the day and fed on his liver which led him to experience suffering during the day. In the evening the eagle flew back. In the cold night when he rested, the liver grew hole again. The eagle returned next morning to continue feeding on the liver in the same way.

The eagle is the symbol of the sun. Its appearance during the day threw the mortal creatures to work. In pursuit of earning their daily breads and procuring the basic necessities of survival the mortals suffer everyday. This is the destiny cursed all mortals who wished to liberate themselves from the will of on upon heavenly gods.

Heavenly musician Orpheus

Orpheus

Orpheus bears the opposite nature of Prometheus. He is the musician of Greek Heaven, whose music brings all to life. The streams in the brooks,pebbles in the wood all dance hearing his music. His music brings back life in the world lying dead in the winter and turns it into a paradise of spring. When his beloved Eurydice died he went to fetch her back from the Goddess of Death. He enthralled the goddess of the underworld by playing his Lyre and got back the life of Eurydice.

Unlike the children of the sun-hero, who went to win lands and conquer wealth and beauty, and engaged in wars and conquests for gaining control of the destiny on Earth, Orpheus led a life in peace and tranquillity as a priest of Apollo - the Greek god of music, arts and knowledge. He took distance from the love of the female Bacchians, who worshiped the sensual experiences of life. Instead he took in the world of creative and intellectual contemplation of the Muses of Apollo.

He represents the side of the human psyche where Muses have their abodes. These Muses are the sources of creative inspirations of artists, musicians and poets.

Through Orpheus and Muses of Apollo the creative power of the mind shines from an ethereal world - unlike the power of the sun, which ignite the physical world and the senses with material glory.

Orpheus and Muses of Apollo

Conflicts between Promethean and Orphean nature

The central element of this journey through the different realms of the mind is a drama of conflict and confusion caused by these contradictory natures of the human psyche: On one side there is a desire to attain the earthly glory by winning fame, wealth and beauty of the mortal world; on other side there exists the desire for peace and tranquillity of a transcendental realm where dream allures, love surpasses the bondage of the senses, and the beauty becomes inaccessible in the physical state.

Thus the drama in search of beauty and love faces dilemma of choices and creating conflicts to decide which path one should choose in life. This contradiction drives life to act and seek, as well as withdraw and meditate. Through such contradictions, Tathagata`s journey continues from one realm of the mind to the other.

Tathagata seeks the enlightened path where these contradictions will one day come and he will be relieved of the suffering world.

Witch goddess Circe waving to Odysseus

Sailing in a stormy sea between the islands of the sun and the moon

The contradictions of life hurl man from one direction to the other, making the journey of life full of tumults and storms.

The tumult of mortal life is beautifully described by the journey of Odysseus in Homer`s epic Odyssey. His destiny drew him to war of Troy. After winning the beauteous queen of Troy as the prize of victory, when he set his sails to return home, he was caught in a stormy sea. He lost directions and moved from one island to the other. In some island he met love and beauty of the witch-queen, in some others he met the beauty as the moon-goddess who brought love and comfort of a homely life.

On the way he faced whirlpools, hounding gorges, half-female half-hound witches, seductive half-bird half-female beauties and ended in shipwrecks. Again and again, as he repaired his ship and made attempt to return home, the journey ended up in new shipwrecks. He either landed on the islands of the sun, or in the islands of the moon, the two cosmic orbs which turned the cycles of day and night, and life and death.

This mythical story describes human destiny caught in the cycle of life and death. It is another story of suffering from which no mortal can escape any respite. Like Prometheus, Odysseus is also another sun-hero. Similar to Prometheus he also bore on himself the perpetual punishment destined for mankind.

Themes of most religions in the world are based on the ideas of how to find a salvation from this suffering world, caught in the wheel of life and death, where the human beings, as progenies of Odysseus and Prometheus, are destined to live.

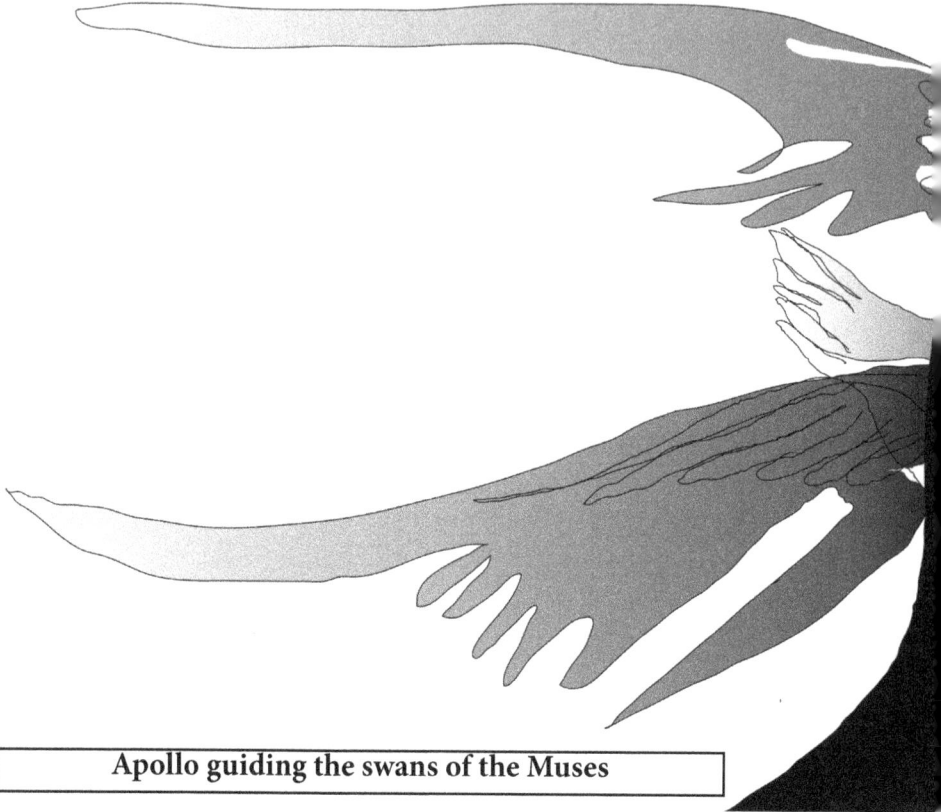

Apollo guiding the swans of the Muses

Apollo versus Bacchus: Rational contemplation versus sensual exploration

Another contradiction of the human mind, on which the journey of the book is based, is the conflict between the rational mind and the sentimental exploration of life, which one may make by attaching oneself to the senses and the perceived world. Apollo represents the inner-sun, which powers the knowledge and the understanding of things through reason and contemplation. He is the intellectual-sun, who explores the domains of the mind through transcendental reflections, which can not be achieved by engaging oneself with the sensual world. He is the inventor of the instruments

and methods with which one can fashion the sense-bound reality as an invisible creator forming the world. His counterpart is Bacchus, the god of wine in Greek mythology. Bacchus inspires the experiences which are bound to physical existence and the senses. He is the drunkard full of exuberance of passion and desires, which promote vitality of regeneration and growth of the physical world. His female followers, the Bacchians, love dancing, drinking and orgies as ways to come in contact with the Divine Bacchus.

Suffering man and his guide

Dual in One: Ego-bound man and his Divine guide

The journey through the different realms of the mind is faced with challenges at every realm: The promethean man encounters the orphean character; the sun-hero faces the temptation of the witch-goddess appearing as physical beauty and drawing him to seductive life; the poetic-man gets lost in the dreamy sphere of emotions where Muses attract the human souls to artistic pursuits; the swans of Apollo draw the chariot of the inner sun and invite human mind to take a ride in the transcendental sphere; Bacchus on the other side, attracts the forces of the mind that clashes with intellectual contemplations of the mind.

The Journey of Tathagata becomes a journey through a complex maze, where reality takes its shape and colour according to how the ego-bound mind manages to steer itself in this multi-dimensional reality. As a will-bound man, bewildered by the choices arising from different realms of the mind, Tathagata, seeks answers, from his guide who, he believes may may exist outside him, and know the meaning behind this suffering world.

It is a journey of the existing as one: Man and the Guide of the Soul. The Guide represents the higher-nature of the mind who can penetrate different realms of consciousness and see the mysteries of existence in it's wholeness. It is a drama of submission to and revolt against the higher-power by a bewildered and confused will bound to the physical conditions of the world.

Through this suffering and search Tathagata attains wisdom and gain understanding of the meaning of life and finds an enlightened path.

Tathagata with his guide flying by the cosmic objects

Know yourself as a part of the Cosmic Man

The guide accompanying the mortal man is the invisible power that connects human life to the consciousness which manifests as the harmony and beauty of the cosmos. The journey with the Guide of the Soul is an experience through the multifold world which penetrates our consciousness through visions, feelings and thoughts.

Journey depicts through a language of poetry and music (in audiobook) the cosmic expanse of the human mind, and its vast attributes revealed through myths, dreams, symbols, mathematics and reason among others. It is an attempt to grasp in words the never ending realm of the cosmic man, who draws the mind higher and higher from the earthly bondage.

This all encompassing consciousness manifests and reveals itself in the mortal sphere through the power of mind of Tathagata. He makes an attempt to grasp the entire spectrum of consciousness from the primitive instincts in man to the highest experience of feeling one with all in the cosmos through meditative reflections.

Finally Tathagata teaches man about the nature of the mind, the different contradictions that drive human consciousness to seek higher-paths, and the cosmic nature of beings.

At the end he confirms his faith in the existence of the Cosmic Man, of whom we are all parts, and invites humanity to follow the enlightened way - a path illumined by the awareness of the existence of the cosmic mind and oneness of all.

Journey of One-in-Three

The question of Man, God and Spirit and how they relate with each other is answered through this story. Tathagata is bound in these three states of existence: In one he is the mortal man existing in body and form, who bears the promethean and orphean nature, and is sailing from islands to islands in search of love, beauty and home, or seeking transcendence from the suffering world of will and desire. In another he is one with the Guide of the Soul, who is a companion of the mortal man and always existing as a shadow existence and a voice of the cosmic man who can not be grasped by using the knowledge about the physical world. He is the mysterious and ever effusive being living in all, who appear in physical forms. Between this physical state of the mortal and the non-physical existence existing beyond all realms of knowledge, Tathagata also exists as a bridge between these two states. This is the state of the meditating Buddha, who can penetrate both realms and connect the mortal with the cosmic being.

By the end of the book Tathagata gives a sermon which explains his threefold nature.

My Journey is Your Journey

It is a journey through the interpenetrating realms of the human mind, through which all life have passed, are passing and will pass. Through this exploration of the mind the questions of central concern to religions and philosophies are touched upon and put under a common perspective. The readers will get a depth of knowledge and attain a heightened awareness about the possibilities inherent in one's own mind by reading this work. It is a vision of the human mind depicted in poetic words which relates my journey as your journey.

A poetic journey at the boundary of religion, philosophy and science

INTRODUCTION

In this part a few central mythological characters are introduced. First is Odysseus who got lost on the sea; then the beautiful witch-goddess Circe who gave him shelter after the shipwreck on her moon-island. It follows the plight of the other sun-heroes like Prometheus and Tantalus who hankered after knowledge and helped the mortals to free themselves from the hands of the gods. As consequence of their acts against the will of Heaven these sun-heroes were condemned to perpetual punishment. They represent the destiny of the mortal human beings striving for knowledge and freedom from the hands of destiny. The other mythical characters like Orpheus and Muses are also introduced in this part to set the stage of contradictions which tear human psyche in conflicts and confusion in different directions.

Searching eternal happiness and immortality

The most central issues for the majority of human beings everywhere and in all time are probably the questions related to life, death and the possibility of rebirth after death. We all wonder about the origin of life, which has brought us to existence, and enjoy the beauty and variety of life forms and nature that exist around us. Most of us do not wish to die, which brings an end to the excitement of living brought to us by our sensual attachments to the world. While the senses bring joy and happiness, in turn, they cause conditions of life's suffering. Passions, desires, will-to-live and compete with others for earning life's subsistence, and will-to-dominate and triumph over others are the main emotions which bring joys and cause sufferings to life.

The life's goal, for most human beings, is to achieve a condition that will make us lead a life without suffering. The greatest suffering is death. From time immemorial human beings have sought a way to overcome the power of death. In the ancient world, the dragon or the serpent power was believed to be causing death. This came from the observation of the sky. The starry constellation of Dragon coils around a fixed point in the sky (North pole). This point was associated with the gate of Heaven, or the axis of the life's tree.

The movement of the Dragon/Serpent around it brought seasonal changes causing cycles of life, death and regeneration year after year. The hero of the oldest epic of the world, Gilgamesh went in search of immortality to overcome the Dragon power. He crossed the Ocean of Death and found the plant of immortality. But before he could eat the plant and become immortal, the Serpent ate it and became immortal instead.

Different religions have professed different paths to achieve immortality and escape suffering. In the Christian view the source of human suffering lies in the sin of Adam and Eve, who ate from the Tree of Knowledge, around which the Serpent coiled. This led to their banishment from Paradise. Since then their progenies had to suffer for this sin of the first couple. Christianity professes the path of abandoning knowledge and rely on the faith in Christ, who, like Prometheus, took upon himself the suffering on behalf of the mortals. Only through him the human beings can gain eternal life.

After the Final Day of Judgment the dead will resurrect and no one will die. The Buddhists consider the realms of the senses as the source of suffering. They profess path of meditation by which one may detach the mind from the sense-bound world, which causes illusions. By following the Eight-fold Way one may improve one's quality of existence in each birth. If one thus goes on improving one's quality of existence in every rebirth, one will at the end reach Nirvana, where there exists no birth or death any longer. The Hindus give karma (actions and deeds) of the previous life the blame for suffering in the present life. It professes path of knowledge, path of engagement in the battle, and path of sensual life. The Hindu way is to submit to the Will of God. All, which happen in life, are predestined by Him. One is asked to practice detachment while acting and doing as predestined. As Krishna explained to Arjuna, the ignorance about this wisdom is considered as the source of suffering. The souls never die, and so the question of immortality does not arise.

The human beings, who are offered these solutions to choose from, are endowed with opposing contradictory nature: On one side desire for knowledge, victory, triumph over gods and destiny, and the will-to-live in the instinct-bound world form the emotional content of the ego-bound life. This is the Promethean nature in man. In contradiction to this he also bears the Orphean sensibilities. Orpheus, the Greek musician of Heaven, could enthrall nature – even the fiercest beasts - with his music. The music of this priest of Apollo, could bring regeneration to all that have died. He lived a meditative and contemplative life, away from the realm of the senses.

Like the male dual, the female also appears in life in her dual aspects: On one side she is Pandora, the seducer, whom the gods had sent to punish the mortals. In her opposite aspect she is the muse, the follower of Apollo, and the source of inspiration to art, music, literature, astronomy and so on. As a seducer she is mother, who gives birth to life, and lover, who brings passionate joy. She is also the killing force, who brings to life jealousy, hatred, war and conflict.

Caught between these conflicting natures, all mortals are destined to seek their path in life's journey. After winning the War of Troy, while Odysseus sought the way back to home, he lost direction on a tumultuous sea and wandered from one island to the other. During the wandering he met the female in her killing aspect, and as the moon-goddess, who brought him happiness and joy. He also visited the realm where the heroes, who sought the power of knowledge and wanted to make the mortals equal to the gods, were thrown into perpetual suffering.

Destiny of the eternal wanderer, Odysseus

After the nightfall when the raging fire kindled Troy,
Among the clashing weapons and the tumults of discord the warriors
shouted in joy,
From Ilium's rampart Aeneas fled,
Amidst spreading hate,
Like a dreadful demigod in a fire-ridden city I stood by the blazing
light,
And saw how pillars of the Priam's palace crumbled in front of
Odysseus' terrible might.
Then capturing the enemy's queen as bride,
Who had seen the death and the murder of her husband with fear and
anguish in her sight,
I had passed by the pyres that had made Ilium red,
And went to the seashore in order to return home and hoped to find
an escape from the wandering as destined by fate.
After coming out of this fiery hell,
I soon felt disoriented and asked myself in which direction I should
sail.
As I moved, the storm bearing thunders and clouds appeared in the
sky,
And lightening, flashing from Neptune's trident, gave fate's harsh
reply.
From the high vault the gods hurled me in a journey on the merciless
waves,
While fearful lightening the fear of death and destruction all around

displayed.

Like a lonely sailor tossed by the waves,

Through crags and cliffs I journeyed through yonder caves.

The beauty of the splendid light cascaded as chains,

And balanced the fear, that benumbed me in suffering and pain.

When in buffeted anguish the sea devoured all,

Mist enwrapped the colossal fire leaping over the sea as a hellish ball,

In the cascading light,

Aglow in the dark tracks of the night,

On the ocean waves,

In the fire I drenched and laved.

When in nature's wrath,

Like a dragon let loose in the sea, from the high vault the lightening jagged,

With pounding beats of the heart I clasped the oars to bring me ashore,

The waves tossed me with ferocious roars.

In a ship carrying the war's spoil,

When I felt left to doom in toil,

I heard the curse of the queen damning me in a witch- like voice:

Her house in ashes,

Her royal palace disappearing in smoke,

Massive walls of fortification destroyed that carry no more any strength of defence and hope,

In every corner of the city only the conquerors' sprawling plundering hands ,

Brought down to ruin all that stand,

Looted, burnt, raped with atrocities that only the plundering hearts could satisfy,

I heard from her mouth the words of appalling agony and cry.

She was Paris' mother and Priam's wife,

Who, when she had given birth to Paris, the seducer of the queen of heart's moonlight,

Had dreamt of the serpents of fire licking her city at night,

From whose ashes as a booty from Troy,

I had taken her as a prisoner of my own pleasure and joy.

As prophetess Cassandra's mother, when she my destiny foretold,

I drew out the sword,

And clutching her hair savagely tried by force to stop that wicked tongue and her constant Trojan boast.

But feeling a sympathy for her beauty every time I spared her throat.

She cursed me as a witch, as the war's fearful ghost.

She told me that disasters will fall, woes will plague,

Faggots will rise and consume my life in the destiny's blaze,

In every sea I shall sail,

Fire will be hailed,

On every shore I shall land,

The beasts of passions will chase me again and again to the strands;

From every tomb where the mothers have wept,

The funeral cries will follow me in hate.

Thus when she wept grieving for the daughter, whom I had sacrificed in Achilles' tomb,

And cried for Hector and Paris - her murdered sons,

A panic struck my heart,

And I drew her blood.

Thus when the weeping was over with her death,

I sought peace by burying her in the witches' grave.

After a short recess when the sea had calmed to give me a chance to bury her, and erect on her grave a witch's tomb,

Like Etna's volcano the sky spewed the darkest fumes under which
my ship again to a hopeless fear succumbed.
Dashing along the sea in the darkness I reached the shore of the
Cyclopes living in dens,
Where those barbarian giants slaughtered and devoured beasts and
men,
Around a burning crater in an everlasting fire, fed as a furnace of
flesh,
From which they their powers forged,
They lived in caves, where they constantly drank and gorged.
As I escaped by blinding the Cyclopes with a fire-drill that I had to
invent,
Where the shore amidst the cliffs had been marked with indents,
I was chased by hurling rocks and stones unhewn,
And thrown again in the tumult of the sea that washed the craters and
the dunes.
After overcoming the danger of the Cyclopes' rage,
I moved towards the Island of the Dawn as the destiny had presaged.
Repairing the boat and replacing the oars as I moved in search of
land,
From the latticed stern,
Soon a beautiful Island I discerned.
It seemed to me that all perils had passed,
And I had arrived to a shore of beauty where I shall find peace at last.
I sped in order to survey,
The pleasant shore, where I felt like halting for a few days on my
way,
After the destruction's brink,
The sight of the land of fresh vines ripe and green,
Brought many sweet thoughts and dreams.

"The fate has given me a chance to escape the curse", I thought,
And made sacrifices to the gods, believing that they decide over the human lots.
Confronting the dangers on the sea, the passion, that had remained for days unsought,
Reappeared again in the mind and ruled my thoughts.
For joys and pleasures, that were untested, in the withering senses again the passions unveiled;
Therefore I sent my sailors to the palace of the queen of the island to enquire about the palace's inmates.
As the sailors - hungry and unfed - reached the palace of the beauteous queen,
They drank from her hands honey mixed with herbs and wine,
And immediately turned into beastly swine.
Seeing their delays as I went to find out what could have fallen to my men in a place that seemed so friendly and secure,
I myself went towards the palace,
Along the way I met a stranger, who gave me a molly from the shore,
And told me to use it against the witch-queen of the island, who possessed the magic power to turn men into filthy swine,
And advised me not to touch her wine.
There I found the sailors wagging in a mire in front of the palace door,
She was sitting in a throne as a goddess and a whore.
As soon as I saw the queen, guarded by beasts, and chanting rhymes
While girdling the animals in chains,
I felt a deep love for the beauty that had still remained in my heart unchanged,
As my eyes caught her eyes as I passed by,
Forgetting the time of distress, the temptation of love became nigh;

9

As she threw her smile,

Baffled by her wile,

A sickness of love came as a tide,

A flame of hidden fire caught the blood igniting the beauty's light;

Like an alert arrow piercing the lust,

It drove the strength of reason away and split my will apart;

In the weakness of love my heart trifled in distress;

Like a captive of the queen I sought her as my consort or mistress.

As she rose from her throne, lifted a cup to my lips and threw her embrace,

Feeling a sudden spurn of fear I touched the molly on her breast and face,

As if, endangered by a divine power, she fell in front of me in regret,

Thus I triumphed over her witchcraft with a power that seemed very sacred.

When subdued and cured of the wickedness, with which she could wile,

I felt saved from the hands of the beauty that was vile,

And I lived with her in the Island of the Dawn for a while.

One night when I came by the sea to refresh my mind where all tidings of love with unearthly world's tidings met,

I heard the footsteps of the stranger, who had handed to me the molly's secret;

He asked me to prepare the boat and set it in a new journey as destined by fate.

In the time of departing,

I did not know why, where ...which land to tell?

I only knew that I must bid the beauty farewell.

Drooped in agony she raised her eyes as the shining goddess of the darkened sky,

And came to the shore as the moon-goddess bidding the mortal a
good-by.
She told me that in the Ocean stream,
Where the life and the death decay and spring,
If I libation bring,
The souls will appear in invisible wings.
As I mutely clasped her in my chest,
Kissed her forehead and asked her to pray for the best,
And promised to return again if destiny so behests,
She told me about the soothsayer, who could see beyond the world
of the sun and the moon spanned between east and west;
This soothsayer knew where destiny would give me a rest.
As I left the past and moved towards an unknown future,
The days of war, love and adventure,
The words, deeds, and thoughts I wished not to remember any more,
Returned again as rushing waves and drew my heart as a ship from
that beauty's shore.

The central aspect of Odysseus' wandering is his destiny as a victor of war, that he had not chosen himself. He did not wish to be recruited for the war against Troy. With a hope to disqualify, he had pretended to be insane. But it did not help. The commander-in chief Agamemnon could disclose his pretention, and fetched Odysseus from his home to join the Greek expedition to Troy.

After winning the war, and taking the queen of Troy as his trophy of the war, when he wished to return home, nature hurled its wrath on him. In search of home every time Odysseus sailed from an island, where he had come after shipwreck, he was caught into tumults of thunders, storms and immense waves. Again and again he suffered loss of his sailors and ended up in shores of island he did not know about.

Another central issue of this journey is his destiny in the hands of the female beauties, whom he met as goddess of love and life, who gives solace and pleasure, as well as the witch goddess, who instils in the minds of the heroes the desire for adventure, war and destruction.

After he departed the shore of Circe, the sorceress foretold him his destiny on the way: Among others he would meet the Sirens, who would try to draw him to land by their power of seduction and beautiful singing voices; he would encounter the whirlpool of Charybdis, and Scylla, the female whose beautiful half of the body remains floating over the water, while the other half, which is the body of a hound of hell, remains submerged under the sea.

Destiny bound in the hands of the witch goddess

On the way marvelous bizarre monsters, who are half-birds and
half-women, will sing in their sweet voice,
Beguiled by their harmonious songs your heart will be torn to make a
choice,
Though they will burn your heart,
Do not be eluded by their clever art,
With beautiful gesture as they will welcome you to receive their
sweet caresses,
Closing your ears and eyes, binding yourself to the mast escape these
death's deadly mistresses,
Stay away from the harbor where the sea, amidst sprays, foams and
fumes,
Will revel in their tuneful staves and tunes.
If you land on their shore,
Be rest assured,
Like wicked witches they will draw you down till you will drown,
With claws and beaks they will scatter bones, blood and flesh
around,
Therefore, though in the moments of festive enchantment the heart
may desire,
Do not leap into the death's singing fire.
O Sisyphus's progeny! To whom the suffering is not a stranger,
Though you will be able to overcome this danger,
Your ever star-crossed tragic fate,
Will bring you near a hellish gate,
To hurl you away from the ship,

Furious gales will stir the ocean from the deep,
Swirling water swallowing wind's pounding beats will vomit up fear,
But try not to come their near.
Where the towering mass of rocks will hang over the passage through
which you must pass,
Monstrous sea will roll in notorious gush;
Where swallowing water, pouring from rocks, the gulf will swell like
a womb,
Through it you will see the darkened world's nefarious tomb.
To one side you will see Scylla's rising head,
Once a beautiful maid,
Whom the witch-goddess with her witchcraft had turned into a
monster whose limb have transformed as the mouths of the hounds
of hell guarding the dead;
As she will guard the passage through which you are destined to sail,
Her thighs and legs, rooted in the depth of the sea, will threaten to
devour you in a fire of hell.
With each pinnacle you will pass,
The struggle to escape the danger will be more and more harsh;
The roaring waves, soaring with storm spouting on rocks spewing
streams,
Will throw your ship in the spinning wind;
In the whirling eddies you will be threatened to be sucked inside
life's darkened whirlpools of cry and scream.
If you plan to return home,
You must hold yourself away from this Charybdis' water churning
the gulf in the danger of passion's foams.
When the strength of the ship will not hold against the onslaught of
the waves, where most sailors are destined to perish,
Leap from the wreckage and swim towards the direction where you

will see the rays of the goddess Iris.

If you let your mind prostrate before her throne,

She will throw rays from her magic crystal stone,

And will save you from the dreadful vortices that your life sought,

And will help you to escape the drag of the ocean that is
tempest-wrought.

Then you will come ashore a fruitful land,

Where lovely lights will burnish its blessed sand.

It is a sea-girt island, whose coast is embraced with happy arms of
the mountain that receive opulent gifts from the sun;

Like its queen's beauty, that has a gentle blaze,

The meadows are lovely in verdure glaze,

The flower and the faunas bemuse in all hearts with their wonderful
gaze.

There the sun rays glint but never scorch,

They open the eyes to the beauty of the earth instead of blinding
them with the power of fiery torch.

Under the eerie ridges, and the jagged peaks, where brooks and
springs teem in slopes and meads,

The fleecy flocks pasture under the sun beside the Hyperon's steeds,

The horned cattle feed on the grass,

In the golden beam the mountains dream,

In dewy-drenched lea,

The queen of the island fountains lease,

And thus in mortal hearts the love's eternal spring release.

There you will see a timeless wood,

Where the trees stand upright and do not rear the branches that turn
and crook;

There nothing is stubborn or stiff,

In the gentle breeze one will hear the songs of love and the heart will never come to weep;

There bliss will reign,

Pure light, that beauty's wonder bears,

Will lift the mind away from the flames and tears;

You will not even know when the heart will fall in her beauty's embrace,

Because in this land of immortal love every passion will spoil beauty's grace.

Wearing festive dress,

The flower-girls of the queen with flower studded tress,

To crown the sailors, who come to take from its shore the pure world's hope and breath,

Will weave beauty's power as flowery wreaths.

When happiness will thus grow,

In a fairy dream of love the heart will see the immortal life's blissful road,

With the eyes of the seer,

I foresee the hands of the destiny, which has no peer,

That will drag you again in a new journey through the wretched world's tumults and tears.

The stranger, who you had met in the Island of Dawn,

Will reappear again to fetch you home where you will be killed by your son.

You have to start once again in the dangerous journey like the wanderer, who is goddess' and witch's dear,

These event are all predetermined that you will not be able to avoid,

Although goddess or witch will try to hold you captive with love and tear.

After being crushed and thrown on the shore, where you will sleep naked in a world, that is lonely and wild,

You will be awakened by the goddess carrying shield, spear and light.

Then you will arrive home to see the barbarous kings had opened in your palace the pleasure's feast,

And turned your house as a brothel where men are no different than beasts,

When you will at last know that the suitors disporting themselves by slaughtering your sheep and drinking your wine,

Have tried to seduce your wife and planned to murder you treacherously by attacking you from behind,

The anger will rise,

The fire and fume will burn in your mind and you will challenge them and bring to them death's dreadful surprise.

With clashing weapons brandishing the air in crushing hate,

The war and blood will follow again as your unavoidable fate;

The weapons will pierce, smash and twist the bodies in welter of blood,

In a ground sodden with warmth, pouring from the hearts, a poisonous river will rush and flood;

Stirring up anger, fire and smoke,

Groans and cries of the wounded and the dying will fill the air in which all will choke;

The bleeding spectres of Hector or Priam,

Or their off springs, whom you had killed to win victory and triumph,

Will follow you as a punishment of an inexpiable sin,

And draw you in an endless war that you wish no more.

The destiny of Odysseus was also to meet the suffering Tantalus, Sisyphus and Ixion – those half-mortal and half-gods, who betrayed the Heaven, and brought heavenly food and drinks to the mortal men. They were the sun-heroes, who taught the mortal beings to rise against the gods and disobey the will of the Heaven. Tantalus, who was an astronomer, was thrown into punishment in Hell. He hung in a branch of a tree bearing luscious fruits by the bank of a pool. The branch, in which he hung, stooped towards the pool, so that Tantalus could remain submerged in the water up to his chest. Over his head stood a huge boulder, which threatened to fall over him at any moment. To make things worse the gods made the waves reach close to his mouth, but each time thirsty Tantalus' made attempts to parch his thirsts, the water receded to his chest. Similarly the wind blew the hanging fruits near his mouth, but each time hungry Tantalus attempted to get hold of the fruits, gusts came to throw them away. While Tantalus was suffering in perpetual hunger and thirst, Sisyphus, the father of Odysseus, was condemned to perpetual labour. He was thrown in the task of rolling a huge boulder towards the summit of a steep mountain slope. Each time he nearly reached the top, the boulder rolled down, carrying Sisyphus with it to the ground throwing him in blood and sweat.

Astronomer Tantalus' suffering in the underworld

Hear me, O mortal or titan! who pass by this hell kindled by time,
In this underworld in the illusive water of the mind,
Where the images of the fruits of knowledge still shine,
I am condemned under a vaulted cave in a perpetual terror,
At which the keeper of the hell's guard itself looks at with feelings of
horror.
Although I stand in water that reaches sometimes up to my chin,
The mouth runs dry, the lips burn in thirst,
The water sinks below the scorched heart deeper than where it has
previously been.
I am Tantalus, whom the Olympian gods call a fiend,
Because I have given the nectar of the gods to my mortal friends.
The tree in which I hang,
Is a tree of eternal pang.
While abundant fruits in the laden branches stoop and sway with the
wind,
As I stretch the limbs to meet the hunger burning in the body as the
fire of sin,
Time and again the gust arising out of the empty world hurls them
away in incalculable swings,
In the treacherous power of the Furies illusions of the luscious fruits
repeat time and again their trembling images in the stream.
Around this abode of punishment,
Where everlasting hunger and thirst never give me respite,
And, instead, always grow stronger and renew,
Where agony leaps in the flesh as unquenchable flames,

See the other forms of punishments that perpetually renew:
In the spokes of the burning wheel Ixion's flesh is tethered to the
burning flames,
In Prometheus' body foul birds of prey feeds on his flesh,
Each night sleep replenishes the loss of the day to bring to the next
morning a rich repast for the ever returning fiend.
Look also at Sisyphus who holding his breath support on his
shoulder the slippery stone of immense weight,
He is gaspingly rolling it along the slope towards the summit before
it will roll back to the bottom of the hill releasing clouds of dust and
dread.
O journey men! return from where you have come,
You will loath to look at the punishment given to the titan as
Knowledge's return,
Disbelief in the power of the gods, and belief in mortal's power of
knowledge have brought damnation under the sun.
Not only for myself I suffer,
I bear torments for my posterity - the descendants of the house of
Pelops, who is my son;
Pelops once served the flesh of his sons to the gods for supper in the
days bygone.
After being revived to life, the children of Pelops, with anger
unchecked and all repentance damned,
Spurred by insensate rage and hate,
Have vied with each other as evil against evil, sword with sword
without remorse,
They have borne all crimes along every treacherous roads guided by
evil force.
One brother has thrown the other into exile,
One has cut other's children to pieces and served them in a banquet,

To prove to his brother that he could hold power of the kingdom by treachery and vile,

In this strife ridden house, where the power has tossed from hands to hands,

Agamemnon and Menelaus have upheld the spirit of their father as warriors riding horses in festive prance,

With ceaseless waves of attacks, brutality and chance,

Their swords have spilled blood in shores and lands,

In war and battle the villainies of nature have filled their hearts with weapon's triumphant clangs.

In this faithless home all sins are considered justified and right,

Brother has slept with brothers' adulterous wife,

Cold blooded revengeful wife has menaced the life of the husband in order to resolve her love's burning strife,

With corrupting hands the father has ravished daughter,

The daughter has begotten father's son,

And become uncle's bride.

These are all complot of the serpent,

Who takes in evil doings its greatest delight.

Thus in the House of Pelops incest has given birth to the murderer, with whom Agamemnon's wife,

In the absence of her husband, have spent her nights;

After returning from the war of Troy,

In the hands of the adulterous wife ,

Agamemnon have fallen victim of the serpent's might.

Thus in Pelops' house, where every means of winning throne have been considered man's natural right,

Agamemnon has succumbed in the treachery of the goddess of the night.

O wanderer! The descendant of this house still sail in the tumultuous waves,
As faithless, lawless creatures imbued with the will-to-power,
They cross lands, havoc cities, welcome fire in which the lusts for power and wealth in heart's cauldron boil,
In banquets they feast with gluttonous meal and like stinking beasts pollute the soil,
Like a baser generation of mankind they consume in pleasures while throwing others to prison and toil.
In every sea they strand,
In every shore they land,
In every corner of the earth they brand their names with fire and blood,
In every place they demolish the barriers of the moral laws,
They let loose Phlegethon's fiery flood.
When they walk in the paths of glory as impious brood,
Flowers heap high, and soldiers give triumphant salutes,
Fireworks crackle, praise pours high,
Devil's eloquent words of honor all words' meanings pollute,
Even I, Tantalus feel aghast and outraged at this development,
And repent for bringing fruits and drinks of the gods to my descendants.
Over my head where you see the swinging branches,
Where the hunger follows agony like the burning torches,
Under my waist, where you see the running stream falling in the lake,
Where dust and mud sink under the water halting the steps,
Closer I reach to the lake, water dries up,
Higher I stretch I get scorched by the pouring rays from the sun's golden cup,
I see the fruits dangle close,

But barely I reach, before they are drawn from my mouth into leaving
hunger's tumultuous roar.
Man or titan, whoever you are!
Behold how the serpent sleeps amidst the branches that luscious
fruits bear!
Look how in the river the serpent coils around the body while the
eagle human flesh tears!
Behold the shining scales of the dragon that stalks near!
Go away from the path of knowledge where Tantalus is bound,
Ixion is going around,
And Sisyphus is condemned to an eternal torment profound.

During this journey of Odysseus, who wanders on tumultuous sea, which hurls him on the beaches of one island to the other, the life of the hero of Homer's Odyssey is caught between two opposite forces of nature. On one side homely life in company of the female beauty, who offers love and pleasure in nature's recluse, is contradicted by the spirit of the sun-heroes, who seek restless adventure, while seeking wealth, power and conquest. They set sails from home to distant lands to wage wars, amass wealth and win victory that will bring to their life food, drinks and comforts, which only the gods in the heaven may enjoy.

This contradiction between the desire for home, that will bring experience of living a loving family life in peace and security, and the desire to overcome any unknown hands of destiny and win and conquer over others, including the Heaven, that bring dangers to life and keep man away from home, is the central issue of human life. This is the sun and the moon aspects of the human mind. Like the hero of Homer's epic all human beings are caught in this duality of wandering between the islands of the sun and the moon.

This contradiction is the source of life as well as the power fueling destructive nature in man. Most religions, epics, and mythologies of the world revolve around this contradiction between the sun and the moon, which feeds perpetual motion to the wheel of life, death and resurrection. Odysseus' wandering between the islands of the sun-heroes and the islands of the moon-goddess, is the same wanderings that have been told by most cultures and civilizations of the world.

Escaping the tumultuous suffering, that Odysseus was thrown into, is the central theme of the major religions of the world. While caught between the sun and the moon, all creatures are destined to die and be reborn, different religions have prescribed different paths of freedom from the suffering world and achieve immortal life.

The Babylonian epic Gilgamesh is the oldest literature where one finds this theme. After experiencing the grief of death of his dear friend and mortal-half Enkedu, Gilgamesh had gone in search of immortality. He crossed the Ocean of Death and found the plant, which could make him immortal. However, before he could eat the plant, a serpent came and became immortal instead. Gilgamesh was destined to die. Beside this duality between the sun and the moon and the mortal's desire to gain immortality by finding path of escape from the wheel, the duality between the mortal and divine counterparts resting as two in one, is another central theme of mythologies, religions and epics of the world.

In western mythology the duality of the human and the divine in man is best depicted in Prometheus and Orpheus. Prometheus is the creator of man, in whom goddess Athena had breathed in life. He had stolen fire from the Heaven to help his mortal creatures. As a punishment for this crime he was left chained on the mountain, where an eagle came during the day to feed on his lever. In the evening the sun-bird left and Prometheus' lever grew whole during the night. Next morning the eagle returned to eat his liver again. This suffering continued without any halt day after day. While bound Prometheus' suffered, the love seeking beauties sat by his feet and offered their comforts and solace.

In contrast to the rebellious Prometheus, who led human beings to defy the Heaven, Orpheus was the Heavenly musician, whose music could enthral the living world as well as the world of the dead. When Orpheus played his lyre, the whole nature danced in joy, and even the fiercest animals in the forest could be tamed. After his beloved Eurydice died of serpent bite he went to the underworld to get her life back. With the power of his music he could enthral the queen of the dead and bring Eurydice back to life. But he could not keep the promise made to the queen of the dead that he won't look back to check if Eurydice was following him or not from the underworld. Eurydice had to return to the underworld again. After the loss of the beloved, Orpheus drew himself in a meditative world. The women, who liked sense-bound ecstasies in dance and revel, and sought love of Orpheus, decapitated him at the end and scattered his flesh and blood in the nature. Nature regenerated from the heavenly musician's blood and flesh.

Orpheus's brings back beauty from the world of the dead

O virgin forest!
When sunray falling on sycamores', laurels', myrtle's, and
willows'quivering leaves,
Break nature's dream-veiled sleep,
In holm oaks', hazels', and ash trees' branching restless twigs,
Acorns, nuts and seeds blow melodies of the wind in heart's golden
reeds,
Firs and beeches, trellis the leaves,
The vines and the ivy rise to the height to listen in the light the
cosmic beeps,
O goddesses and the nymphs!
In tamarisks' and staghorns' pink beds,
Daphnes' and lilacs' crimson shades,
Viburnums' dark berries, purple sand cherries,
Buckthorn's and alder's red-berries,
Sing the songs of the sun-strewn blaze,
In aspens' and hornbeams', maples' and poplars' heads,
Like the Maenads wind Orpheus' music seize,
In flowers and fruits playing the Phrygian flutes the maidens of light,
in love for Orpheus, beat their breasts.
The melodies tipping off the leaves,
The ripples sounding with breeze,
The air changing sounds into harmonies,
Light falling through the air as the notes from his lyre,
"Orpheus! Orpheus!" singing the seeds,
Stones turning as the silence's hymn,
The spears in the hands of the maidens of dream,

Tearing open the seeds from the rinds,

The golden sun's pollen-laden stamen,

The magical life's golden wand bringing back the beauty of life like Hermes' wand,

Keep man awake as well as bring him in trance.

In yellow, white, blue, orange and red,

Where the Maenads' weapons rip open Orpheus' flesh,

In sappy foliage the green wood ooze in pain in leaf-decked shades,

In the crimson blood dripping in the flesh,

A poetic soul moves clad in light and wearing a human shape.

O Orpheus! Dream born poetic blaze!

O singing eternal skylark, the lightning clouds' soaring hymnal chorus in flame!

What thou art,

What thou make,

Reverberate in the wind as music of life on the earth,

As springing grass, blossoming flower, orchids of light, and love's beauteous flame.

Where the West-wind plays with silvery dew,

Cupid's arrows feel and touch the heart in innumerable hues,

In the earth's dark breast,

Where dream has risen from its wintry rest,

Flowers and herbs feel and breathe,

Poppies and pansies,

Daffodils and daisies,

Virginia and Canterbury -bells,

Tulips, statice, speedwells gather in the light with asphodel,

Veronica wipes the blood dripping from the sky's blue bright face.

Like Orpheus bringing back Eurydice from Hades,

Hyacinths, jessamine, Narcissus reflecting in the pool of light its face,

28

From Adonis' blood anemone springing as symbols of the mortal's love for the aphrodisiac maid,

The lily of the vales letting the dew fall in time and space from the tremulous bells,

The bleeding-hearts drooping in the eyes covered with pinkish veil,

Unveil the beauty, who has risen from the dead, from a state lifeless and pale.

O wild flowers, the senses' buds!

The springing morning's camellia, nemophila, phacelia!

Love torn Ophelia!

Life's radiance, ardor and dust!

O flower-strewn grass!

Awakened earth's incantation in verse!

In scents and odours,

In hues of colours that the eyelids pass,

Spark! Spark! ....

Send brighter and brighter luminous sparks!

O verbena, anise, basil, bays and sweets!

O who grow amidst weeds

In rain and clouds,

In commotion, who burst forth through seeds!

While Orpheus bleeds,

The music of life brings forth herbs and hybrids.

O forest filled with scents, fragrances of flowers, herbs, shrubs, and trees!

In a world once in sleep,

Where through darting beams fly insects swift and free,

In awakening feet of worms, snails, slugs and bees,

I hear the footsteps of Orpheus' beloved Eurydice.

This contradiction between the killing-forces and the life-forces, that lie behind all existence which come and go, is the central idea of this book. Similar to the contradictions between the orphean and the promethean natures bringing dynamics to the wheel of life and death, the female in this story is also the killing-goddess as well as the goddess of love and life. In her destructive aspect, she is the seducer, who draws the heroes to the path of wars, deceptions, and treacheries. In this aspect she is Pandora, whom the gods had sent to the mortal realm to punish the creatures of Prometheus. After decorating Pandora with all jewels, gods had sent her as a bride for the hero. Prometheus was clever enough to refuse her hands. However, his brother Epimetheus could not hold the temptations of the wealth that the gods had sent as marriage gifts, and took Pandora as his bride. After the marriage, when Epimetheus opened the jar filled with gifts (also called Pandora's box), hatred and spites flew out, which since then have been afflicting the world.

Helen, the wife of Menelaus, who is the brother of Agamemnon, the Greek commander-in-chief of the war against Troy, is another incarnation of this seductive Pandora. She had seduced the prince of Troy, who had taken her away to his Trojan home. This had led to war. In this aspect the female beauty appears as the force flaming wars and deaths.

Life's goddess and death's vampire

Where the Romans and the Greeks had made their journey towards
the shores as destined by fate,
I see under and above the deepest gulf,
Where death rings its knell,
Demons, ghosts, ominous spirits, speed through ruins and caves;
The Aegean birds flap their wings,
As if, the harpies fly to the islands of death and ruin;
In the dwindling glow of light a fear spreads as omen of the sea
afflicted with trouble and storm,
In twist and turn water burbles gluttonous secret of waves,
From which tumults are born;
In brute pride of the victorious eyes,
That tower above the height soaring against the sky,
Amidst murder, massacre, and cry,
Blood, flame, war, vengeance, terror haul the wrecks across the
burning memory of Troy.
O beauty! who stands as a stone in dream !
The timeless world's reverberation in heart's spiritual stream!
Who appears as the finest statue, which no hands can ever carve!
Who pulls in the eyes the visions that an ethereal sphere encompass,
Whom Michelangelo, Titian, Ruben, and Rembrandt have tried to
paint with colors and brush,
When you draw man to seductive love,
The finest warriors on the earth turn into a dove of lust;

To see your eyes' astonishing beauty sailors and oarsmen steer sails and masts,

And anchor in the shores of death,

Where like deer, tricked by hunter's traps, mortal lovers follow beauty's scented musk.

The luminosity of your body drawn with rays,

That burn man's mind with passionate craze,

Where poets, musicians and artists see diadems in blaze,

Where the mind strokes a lucent soul in search of a loving care,

The sensations spread in breast as breathless air.

Where in search of nectar of the mind,

Birds of passion stoop down from clouds and wind,

Poets lift the souls to see unknown beams,

Emanating from a center, where the universe burns above the heaven and the hell,

Like gems of life you dazzle in mind's poetic spell.

O beauty! human sorrows' unredeemable truth!

The mirror, in which charm and grace reflect beauty abound!

You, who turn your suitors into swine!

You are charming smile's horror tomb,

Where murder, crime, spring as heart's infernal storm,

You are lecherous whore's obnoxious fumes;

Like a buzzing drone, seeking love, you bring your consort to his doom.

While lips kiss deep in flesh to awaken a flare,

As drunkard's jug lulling inconstant mind's wind and air,

You are life's goddess and death's vampire.

To win your love the warriors grapple with arms, made of bronze or steel,

And animate the world with clang and clamor raising love's deadly appeal.

While amidst clashing swords in a battle field,

Flaming torches, like looming giants, huge ramparts lick,

Like stalking ghosts from pillars, holding the structures of palaces,
fumes reek,

In the temple of the Cytherian goddess Helen her lovers seek,

Phoebe's arrows pierce the mortal limbs,

And blind the lovers in pain, who at the end yell and scream,

Achilles dreams love's treacherous dream.

O beauty! Who arouse the heroes like fiery beasts!

Like the boar of Ares, who make man swim in wine and feast,

You who stroke with love,

Corrupt with lust,

Sing with voice enchanting and sweet!

You, who with naked belly's charming dance arouse the suitors to
warring feet!

With lascivious mind's unnerving strength,

You, who beguile the world and create life's bane,

You are life's goddess and death's treacherous dame.

While the blood from decapitated body of Deiphobus rill,

And Menelaus returns in the palace behind the Pallas' hill,

In shining bed, when he again dreams of Helen's loving flesh,

O Beauty!

You never cease to beguile the mortals living in love's fiery hell;

In your treacherous game,

Even Achilles dreams to sleep with the beauteous world's fairest
dame;

And thus along the wall of Troy succumbs to death as a lion beguiled
and tamed.

O beauty!

On your sumptuous bed,
Where you once entertained Paris while inviting dreadful wrath of
Menelaus, who fought love with hate,
Lethe's calm comforts evil,
As destined by fate.
Like an unfaithful spouse you are lascivious heart's cave and ruin,
O charred heart's shining queen!
You carry unceasing passion in your naked breast,
Like Stygian river's burning fire, you are life's death and rest.
In Ileum's fertile field,
Where lush flowers spangle in mead,
Ships draw on shores,
Warriors disembark on steeds;
Horses and heroes amass gloom of war and threat.
While you glow in pearls, gold and gems,
Coaching on a chariot drawn by the finest steeds,
You welcome flames,
Those kindle palaces and cities as a part of your stygian game.
O bejewelled dame!
While you watch death and war without shame,
Your suitors are drawn to pyres lighted by flame.
You, Menelaus' spouse, Paris' lover, Diphobus' mistress, and
Achilles' love in dream!
Within the walls of Troy you brought lascivious debauchery in
Trojan home!
You, Clytemnestra's and Pollux's sister,
Theseus' raped-princess of Spartan throne!
You are beauty's ambiguous joy,
That captivates and destroys.
Committing crimes and employing treacheries that love can deploy,

O queen of beauty!
You are perfumes and fragrance of the flower of eternity,
A sagacious mind's sweetness and taste covered in a mysterious obscurity.
When the shining day comes to its close,
The glittering light in trembling tides plunge on shipwrecks on the shore, where my vision rose,
Where under a starry dome Odysseus wanders alone,
I see Agamemnon sailing towards his home;
Aeneas, guided by the stars, is sailing to Latium,
Where his descendants will build the empire of Rome.
Destiny does not allow to settle in the shore, where these voyagers near,
Their ships wreck on shores and are drawn back by the waves as they try to reach to land with pain and tear.
From the foothill of Phrygia,
Where through the growing thickets of cornel and myrtle stems,
Aeneas had fled from Troy in flame,
Voyagers sail their ships to lands and shores with unknown names.
High on sea, surrounded by mountains,
While the brazen plated oars churn in eyes salt and dust,
Fiery wind kneels on mast,
Neptune swings his trident and leaves the vessel floating just by luck,
The destiny forces the sailors to tackle the mast with blood and sweat,
And throw the mortals in laborious tasks.

Besides encountering the female as the bejewelled heavenly bride, whom the gods have sent to punish the mortals by releasing jealousy, hatred, conflicts deceptions, wars and bondage to the suffering world, the journeyman also meets the beauty in her positive aspects. He discovers her loving hands, that bring comfort and pleasures of living a life full of joy and happiness.

Beauties who love dance, revel and frenzy

They are the daughters of the earth, born of moisture, warmth and heat,
They carry the flames of life that shoot out of the seeds.
The flowers and twigs are their bracelets,
Their eyes are born of the petals with restless gleams,
Their breasts are flanked with slender streams,
Where flow life's eternal poetic themes.
Flinging arms in joy they dance with rays and beams,
In light and shadow they surround the nature in dancing rings.
In the dawn when Zephyr comes with his dew strewn wings,
They caress the hearts with lips of rainbows turning the earth as a dream.
They are the dancing fairy maidens in frenzy of love,
When all sleep in the dark,
Wearing starry light as wreaths, they dance in the hearts.
They are the dream-like nymphs, who scatter in dreams moonlit silvery dusts,
Wearing robes decorated with the moon and the stars,
They join the dance of light over twinkling grass, springing flowers, singing meadows,
In winding notes passing over shining pebbles scattering silence in dreaming hearts,
In the purple tomb of flesh and blood,
They sing the songs of night,

The songs of light,

The songs of death and birth.

In the moonlit web,

Where the creatures of the earth crawl in dreams in search of beauty and love,

In notes of the stars,

In serene chime of Eos rising out of the dark,

Spreading the colors of heart's burning hearth,

With words, hues, and sounds they wake poets, musicians and creators of arts.

In shore, where death is life,

And life is death's another mask,

Like roses bursting in warmth and lust,

They caress the eyes in morning sky's pinkish blush.

In the ballad of beauty and love,

While the moon swings from darkened night to dawn's quivering dewdrops spattering notes of dream on the silent grass,

Throwing off the veils of the night,

They open under the robes the beauty of love in flesh and blood.

Beauty also appears as the Muses accompanied by swans. In the aspect of the Muses, who are companions of god of arts and music Apollo, she is the source of creative inspirations for artists, musicians and poets. As the beautiful swan maidens they bring to mind the contemplative urges of Apollonian kind, that draw the soul away from the realm of the senses and seductive power of the killing-goddess.

The beautiful companions of Apollo

Greeks called them Muses,
The Hindus named them as the companions of goddess Vak
From their breasts stream words from nature's spiritual heart.
They are the maidens who inspire in the creation of poem, music and
art.
In the language in which poems flow in your heart,
They dance with the sun, the moon and the stars.
They are the swan-maidens who swim and cackle in the lake of light
as Helicon's spiritual birds.
In the blue calmness, where clouds touch the height with soft silvery
palms,
Where laving leaves lift the beauty of the living world to the
mountain,
Where in the Pierian stream sing the Pieridae their prayers,
The flowering laurels,
The blue white lilies,
The acanthus leaves with their chimerical stares,
Hold the beauty of the shining sun in the abundance of the tears,
In the heart's poetic spring they are the Muses,
Who swim with swans,
Whom Zeus set in the sky full of stars,
With whom Apollo's power of music, art and intellectual beauty are
one.
Here like Urania as they wave their robes azure blue,

The colors in the morning dews float in shifting hues,
As the starry wreaths crown the dawn with diamond-like dews,
In blood streams flow vision of the inner beauty of the world
carrying purple light's ethereal news,
In the greenery, where silence of an epiphany in a deep depth muse,
While in the morning beauty's eyelash dream and reality fuse,
Poets, artists and musicians seek in their souls their eternal refuge.
Singing from stars to stars,
Behind the hillsides they appear as light to make the human mind
alert,
When morning light streaks through the darkness of the heart,
They stand and laugh like rays from jewels in radiant flush.
When West-wind kisses their hearts to arouse mortal love,
Unfastening the girdles of the silvery willows' and poplars' drooping,
plunging delights of the sun-born lust,
Hanging the silken garments in the shadows,
They run to the lake of life to swim with the rippling wind blowing in
the greenwood verdant and lush.

The journeyman is thus entangled in a labyrinth of life where many diverging urges operate and try to draw him towards different directions. By carrying both the Promethean nature stooped in desires, and the Orphean sensibilities of a meditative life, the protagonist of this odyssey meets the female in her witch-like aspect as well as the moon-goddess of love and beauty. While experiencing contradictions and conflicts, he wanders from realms to realms in search of the right path, that will bring meaning to his wandering. Like Odysseus he is also in search of the way to home, where he will find peace and tranquillity, love and comfort, and feel secure without encountering the fear of death and destruction. On the way when he becomes bewildered and sinks in confusion, without knowing which way to go, the Guide of the Soul appears again and again to lead him out of the labyrinth.

Guide of the Soul speaks

Standing in a territory beyond time and space,
Obscure and removed from the heaven's orbs.
I wait in the gates beyond the senses.
Where causes stir motions,
Knowledge form perchance,
Reasons strive against falsehood,
And the mortals err.
I exist beyond the realm of the will of man,
And hold in my will the will of all born or unborn.
Behold in me the true substance with which things are formed,
Conceive me in shapes that can never be formed by physical rules
and causal laws.
Perceive me as the flames that rise from the mind's unknown abyss,
And make your journey as destined by the will of God.
The night, you may see, constitutes the body that I wear,
Where you may find darkness,
I sway as waves,
The space that you perceive as empty and void,
Is the ocean where I dwell.
In the flow of time,
That imparts motions even to the world that is inert and dead,
I carry multitudes of motions of the individual souls,
That move creating tumultuous flux of life,

As the flow of the destined world that is animate.
In the void where substances rest in the depth of visible forms,
Where through mutations and change,
Contradictions between the opposite forces bring annihilation and regeneration to all,
I awaken the world, while myself rising above it as invisible waves.
Let no doubt of ignorance partake your thoughts,
I wish to be your guide where the sun-borne day and the moon-borne night,
Over lands, seas and craggy heights bring all mortals to tumults and tests.
On the precipice, where the darkness will move as waves,
Follow the tracks that I shall lay with radiant rays.
Around things, that you will see covered with illusion's veils,
While rocks and ridges, plants and trees, clouds and stars that will define the murky hazes in space,
Amidst lightening and storms that will discharge fiery breathes,
Follow my path that will lead to the eternal gate at the end.
Under the hollow depth of the sphere,
Where pleasures, pains, desires and hates,
Like stench of flesh,
Bind man to the sense-bound will and separate the individuals from the rest,
Where malice, woe and illusions,
Exhale and inhale breathes in the human breasts,
Free yourself from the ignorance rising from the sense-bound will,
And follow me as your guide and move away from the treacherous paths,
That lead man to plunge in the heart
Where violence, terror, and horror arouse nature's dreadful mirth.

In every realm the journeyman enters, he wears different masks in or-der to fit into the natures of the worlds where he finds himself. Thus, as he passes through one realm to the other, he makes constant tran-sitions from one character to another. The same man, who appears as the power-loving individual, stooped in the material wealth and glory in the instinct-bound world, changes masks and reappears as the dreaming poetic-man in search of beauty and love beyond the realm of the senses in another phase of the journey. The protagonist of the book acts out the roles of Odysseus, Orpheus and Prometheus as he seeks the path of mean-ing and home. He is also the man of modern time, who is seeking the same immortality, glory and fame as well as tranquillity and meditation as the mythical figures. In this journey of the universal soul, myths and reality of life of women and men intermingle. Different characters emerge from the same universal being. Similarly as the journey proceeds all dif-ferent natures of man merge in the universal character. Thus from one many characters appear, and in the same universal One all characters disappear at the end. This modern odyssey is enacted on a stage, that is the world, rotating with the movements of the sun and the moon, where a plethora of characters enter and exit life after life wearing masks.

Dances of men and women on a rotating stage

Like actors with masks in a theatre, that is the world,
Who are no where more visible than in the depths of their inner light,
In the Time Hall, faceless men and women play roles wearing faces,
And enter the arena of life as ritual players, who live and die, and
with whom all living go to sacrifice.
With changing of light and darkness, as they enter in and exit from
the rotating stage,
In the Time Hall, drama of myths of gods and demons perpetually
repeats again and again.
Wearing faces,
Inside masks,
While dancers swing as whirling wind swirling in time,
They come and go as parts of a nameless fugitive, who is trying to
escape from life's turbulent fate.
In bursts of frenzies as butterflies opening their wings,
In a strange rendezvous,
Where moments fly from cocoons of light,
In light of the moon,
Or of day swimming in endless waves of rays,
Or floating in starry maze from the poles to the highest mountains'
crests,
Swimming in joy of life and love,
They come and go as nameless fugitives caught in the hands of fate.

There is no specific direction of their life,
One does not know where to go,
Only in hearts' echoes one knows that there exists no passage
wherever one may go;
There is only wanting to live and love without being released from
the senses' play,
Responding to desires without dallying away,
It is a theatre, where there will be always something that will remain
understood and unknown.
It is a tryst to freedom,
A joyful frenzy of floating on colourful wings,
Without any direction and no place to go.

From the universal body from characters emerge and in it all characters merge. Confronting the fleeting world of the senses, the will and ego form, which drive man and woman to seek their individual paths. With the power of the individual will, the mortals seek immortality and try to escape the destiny of life and death, and dream to arrive at a realm where only eternal happiness and pleasures will exist. In making these attempts they encounter contradictions of life, that are inherent in nature, and face conflicts with the reality, that is the world, which bring storms and tumults. This is what the Buddhist calls samsara, which is encircled by a fire ignited by the sentinel world.

The central thread of this work, the universal being called Tathagata, of whom all individuals are parts. Therefore this Buddhist concept of the innumerable individuals as parts of the body of Buddha has similarity with this book. The will of the individuals rising and sinking with fleeting movements of the world, perceived by the senses, has a counterpart in the nature of the protagonist of the story.

As Tathagata mediates about the nature of the sentinel world, he sees the Time Hall of Illusion where the stage for the life's journey is set.

Tathagata's meditation: The Will and the Void

What a wonderful image! The whole transitory world is moving in it. There are so many wonderful designs being drawn by the movements of the current dragging one part with another that are twisting, turning, circling like eddies, releasing the knots of movements and creating new eddies again. With them feelings are turning, twisting, releasing themselves from eddies and falling into eddies again. The whole Samsara seem to be like this river where moments are fleeing creating such wonderful patterns of colourful thoughts and confusion of feelings. It is Maya - the illusory veil- that is twisting and turning in the motionless river and creating this motion. T he will is it not a river like this? Is not this will making the river move? Or, the will is moving with matter that drag the motions of the river? Or, are will and matter moving as the same river? The mind seems to be inseparable from the no-mind, that is appearing as the currents, the eddies, the whirling that are turning in the eyes, dissipating and condensing creating the flux of time. Is it carrying an emptiness through innumerable structures of thoughts,that are nothing but illusions of the mind, while there exist nothing but a formless void?

Are all void? These rotations, these expansions, contractions, turbulence, tearing apart and taking part into another turbulence, outside and inside, are only Maya, the transitory reflections of the will into the void or does there exist something concrete, outside the existence of the will, existing by itself? How marvellous this image is! It is devouring itself, breaking itself into parts, scattering itself in the ripples and waves, distributing itself in many forms and designs without ever vanishing from the sight, and always appearing to be the same.

The molecules of water are buffeting on the surrounding matter and evaporating into clouds in order to be absorbed by the tree from the depth of the earth with its roots as well as by the innumerable cells spread across the space as its branches and leaves. How inconstant is this image! Though how unchangeable is this vibrating illusion, that is dissipating without dissipating, falling apart without falling apart, tending to disappear without ever disappearing from the sight. How illusory is this becoming that is always eluding the mind with the vision of the impermanence though always remaining the same! It is mirroring the void, reflecting the emptiness through which the mind and matter are flowing as two conjoint rivers, which exist to perceptions and feelings and appear to the consciousness only as a result of this unity. In separation they constitute the formless void. Here without the will matter seem to be disappearing and without the matter the will seem to be without its base of existence.

Over this river, where the image of the tree is being reflected as an image of the permanent in the stream of impermanence, where wind and air are dragging the matter with it, a spiritual wind is constantly blowing, that is dragging the feelings with it creating turbulence and waves, trying to scatter the image into many small pieces of ideas and thoughts and disperse them in the stream of nothingness. In this nothingness, the world exists as projection of the stream of the psychic energy on the fleeting world of matter, giving each other form and essence. Here the will is bringing the mind in form, and form is bringing the will to its existence. One can not separate these two rivers, that is one.

From the centre of the mandala they are streaming outside and inside the world of matter and form, as well as the domain of the mind, that create this marvellous image on the river. Atoms, molecules, gas and clouds are condensing on it. Like this, in the stream flowing in the void, clouds of gas are condensing into bigger and bigger units, and forming stars, galaxies, cluster of galaxies etc., as burning masses of matter gradually transforming the less organized order into more organized state of solid matter. Energy is being consumed and released in this process, bringing dynamics to the world. Is it not the mind which is bringing an order? Are not the forces attracting the mass into this process a power coming from a greater mind, that contains the reason and purpose of being and becoming? Do not these turning and moving eddies on the river carry the mind, that creates the organic cells, vegetation, life and the being that he himself is? Though the image seems to be splitting into pieces by acts of chance in the wind and air driven by the heat and cold, circulating in the currents into different patterns, is not the will impinging on each accident in order to hold the whole into an organized unity? Does not an unity exist everywhere, that transcends the blindness of the chance ? Without this can this marvellous image, that is always floating as indestructible projection of this self, be created out of chaos?

If this river did not exist, would anything exist? Will not he himself vanish with the disappearance of the river where his own image will disappear? His limbs are dancing in the stream mingling with the branches and leaves- one going over the other with the dancing movement of the rippling waves. His mind is waving the wind that is shuffling through the leaves of thoughts and trying to become one with the wind that is shuffling the bits of images of the tree from its root to the crest.

There is a beautiful vibration inside and outside. The eyes receiving the images are transforming the sensations into musical vibration in the conscious world. They are changing into notes and sounds as chanting hymn from a greater depth of the mind. The ears, which are collecting the restless reverberations scattered by the excited wind, the flashes of light breaking on small ripples and waves, seem to be trying to release themselves from the bondage of the sounds and waves. Behind the visible rays, and the audible waves, there exist strange light and sound, that are moving as the will flowing through the material domain. These strange light and sound are flashing in all corners of the mind, while natural light and sound are vibrating on the dancing waves. They are flashing from poles to poles, branches to branches, leaves to leaves, and the marvellous image is growing in his mind to extend over all streams flowing through the void!

How marvellous! There seem to exist no boundary between the interior and the exterior! Physical stimuli, desire, passion, feelings, pain, sufferings, melancholy, thoughts, ideas, conscious reflections and awareness and unconscious exaltations of emotions all have merged with a marvellous beauty! This beauty is emanating from the centre of the mandala, which lies within himself, where the tree also exist as an inseparable part of the whole to which mind and matter are one.

How green! How bubbling! How infinitely strange is this beauty! It is sinking, surging, rolling with gusts of wind, trilling, spewing, spiting, wheeling, whirling as the part of the mind itself .It is moving away, then returning to vision that is near; it is flowing forward and then twirling backward; it is moving upward, and then pouring downwards. In all these motions what is this, that he is looking at? Is it not that he is only staring at himself, and watching the process of living, dying and returning again and again in this stream of life and death? The void that is hanging over his head, is it not too a part of the stream where he exists? Is it not also the part of the void through which this stream is moving carrying him as a being, who comes and goes with the perpetual turning of the wheel?

Moreover, how can he know that he really exists? Is not his existence an illusion itself ? Who is he ? Is he matter, will, the impulses, the feelings, the ideas, the knowledge with which as a human being he is gazing upon himself ? Is he an aggregate of those senses and the reason that are revealed as ideas through the mediation of a conscious mind? Is he ascertainable to comprehension in the world of will and matter, that is constantly in motion and has no meaning except relative to something that only exist in reference to a part? Are not all parts negating his true identity? And what this true identity may be when all knowing are relative to a part and ascertainable in a world of constant material and psychic flux, where the knower and the object known have no absolute meaning as such?

Is he those feelings of love, pain, suffering and joy, that are twisting and turning and revamping the world as objects of thought? Are not those feelings conditioned in a way that the feelings, with which he forms the concept of the world in images , negate the true nature of himself ? Is he not knowable except as negation of all, that defines the perceptions, creates logic and the foundations of feeling and emotions? Can he be reduced by logic without ever being truly reduced but to nothing? Or can he be known as a sum total of these negative descriptions of his being?

Tathagata sinks deeper and deeper where Buddha emerges as the ultimate beauty submerged in the void. Flickers of rays fly as transitory thoughts describing the impermanence and nothingness behind the veil of Maya pervading all. He wishes not to exist in this illusory world and wants to turn into a block of stone and remain by this river by touching this marvellous stream that burns in the mind's incandescent glow. He hears the river utters: " Sabbe sankhara anicca": All that are constructed and effected by the interaction of the matter and mind are impermanent;" Sabbe dhamma anatta": All conditioned quality is insubstantial; and "Sabbe Sankhara dukkha": All that are constructed and effected by the interaction of matter and mind are the sources of anguish suffering and pain.

PRELUDE

Tathagata mediates in the world, which appears to him as a Time Hall of Illusion, where characters enter and exist as parts of the Cosmic Man. The characters of the living world appear from the One and disappear in the same One life after life. Here the Guide of the Soul, who accompanies the journey-man is also introduced together with the Apollonian mind soaring to Heaven and cosmos.

This prelude sets the stage for understanding the more complex nature of the drama that is going to unfold.

11. Tathagata's meditation: The will and the void

12. Time Hall of illusion

13. Promethean sailor reborn

14. Promethean sailor sails

15. Sailor's recapitulation

16. Heavenly flight

17. Devil lifts the intellectual soul

18. Memory of love on the mountain

19. Guide of the soul appears on the stage

Beginning of the Journey in the Time-Hall of Illusion

There are halls inside halls,
The imaginary walls of perceptions governed by accidental encoun-
ters and chance,
There are secret passages and openings like eye holes,
Tapestries of vast scenarios illumined by the sun and the moon.
From one hall one may enter into another, and from another one may
go across and return to the same;
Here things transform, transmogrify, transmute and metamorphose;
In changing, evolving life, that may seem as a legend,
In searching paths to escape, one ends up in the pyre.
There are curtains in windows and doorways, which hang as cobweb
of illusion,
There are wilderness of doubts, beliefs and superstitions,
Loneliness of whispering delusions,
Wandering and consternation of feelings in bewildering paths lying in
mind's darkness and illumination;
There are myths, magic, and masks,
Hallucinations, telekinesis and strange premonitions,
Swirling patterns of signs and words, whirling in free will in halls of
imagination;
In the loops of time, designs of reality are fated in predestination.
In this Time Hall there are stages inside stages,
Characters inside characters, who try to evade fate of the ones who
precede,

In the images of the forerunners ordained to sacrifice,

Pursued by terror and tyranny of the sun- and the moon-borne time,

In a strange light,

As nameless man, or woman, in and beyond space and time,

As singular and plural at the same time,

Merging as one with others, and departing from one another,

Always moving into and fleeing from the drama of life,

With dropping and raising of the curtains of eternal day and night,

From this Time Hall the eternal journeyman strives to escape destiny

bound to the wheel of death and life.

Promethean sailor reborn

I am reborn as a mortal made of clay and dust.
As a lonely wanderer in the universe,
I have again returned to the shore of life,
Where glacier's ice decorate the mountains as sky-borne ship's
glittering mast.
I have made attempts to understand in words all that there are,
Good, evil, destiny, free-will and everything mysterious or real.
Through philosophy, science, mathematics I have pondered,
To arrive at knowledge's deepest recess, to Devil I have surrendered,
As a progeny of the condemned titan beguiled by the urge of soaring
towards intellectual heights,
In quest to control destiny, that brings perpetual menace and curse,
I have tried to raise myself from earth and dust,
And sought in knowledge a path to escape the wheel of death and
birth.
Beguiled by the powers of languages and thoughts,
I have tried to elevate mortals to the realm of the gods;
By using signs and symbols,
Analysing things floating in the cosmic ball,
I have tried to achieve power unbound,
And wished to rise to the highest height profound,
Following reasons of philosophy, mathematics, and subjects that are
clear and sound,
I have tried to pull Heaven down.

Like Lucifer, who does not trust anything but knowledge's light,

In eternal flight,

Avoiding magical chants and incantations,

Taking distances from music and hymns that are used for spiritual initiation,

Reading sciences instead of poems and verse,

I have searched in knowledge's universe.

Hearing sacred and beautiful songs,

Listening to the sounds of church bells and temple gongs,

Attending discourse of people interested in the realms unknown,

And following arguments about existence that can not be known,

I have found everything that are false and delusive,

Except pain and suffering I have not sought anything elusive.

In dizzying heights, where mountains whirl,

Feeling convulsion and pain,

While barren spirits wish to rise in the skyey terrain vacant space

Beyond star strewn wheel,

Along rocky paths,

Bare, naked, wild and untouched,

Where heights protrude the mountain paths,

I have carried ashes from the hermit's mountain hut.

The Promethean sailor

In life's sea I am born as a sailor, destined to a gallant course,
Against nature's tumults and force.
From crags to cliffs,
From ravines and caves,
In pensive journey I have not yielded to fierce waves.
As a husband and a lover I have delighted in love;
In festivity,
In churning passions' billowing chafes,
In battles and struggles against myself I feel safe.
Where nature will invite me to doom,
In seeking pleasure as passion's bloom,
Beguiled by the serpent that rises from fleshes' tomb,
Without fear,
Creating my own snare,
As a valiant sailor sailing over temptations and distress,
I seek lovers and mistress.
Above raging fire, murmurs of heart that feels discontent,
When feeling of guilt and shame try to quench love's burning flames,
As an earth-bound creature, who does not ask for mercy from above,
I anchor on passion's shores that promise best.
In feasts and flares,
Delights and pains,
Wounds and blood that come as nights' guests,
With a heart never content,

Where a savage blood faces peril's flame,

Menaced by all, except passion's daring intents,

In temptation of love I create again and again my life's bane.

Again and again...

Knowing that all must come to end,

I caress, embrace,

Clasping breast in sinner's couch I undress,

Seeking destruction's brink,

I throw myself against waves that come to betray and drag,

Like whirlpools that swirl inside crags,

Churning fast,

Which destroy ship's keel and mast,

I wander in the tumults of life with a hope to find an escape.

The Promethean sailor recapitulates a previous journey

I had come to lands full of shadows,
There, amidst whispering hills, I had seen days flying by in changing
darkness and light,
Under mists,
Where thoughts had murmured in the heart,
I had heard songs of rivers meandering beneath life's unbound lust.
I had wished to fly beyond the rocky heights,
In a strange wandering wanted to go beyond the skyline defined by
shining beams.
Leaning, dreaming, and then awakening and raising the head,
I had gazed at the distance over "there", blue in sunny blaze,
And felt happy again feeling the warmth of flesh.
Thus I had desired to rise and regain the Paradise.
In glittering lights jittering on waves,
I had dreamt of a journey to a land of fairy tale,
Beyond the limits of time and space.
I had gone very far,
In swirling motions sailing in light,
On bulges of waves where nothing is visible but the fear of an
approaching night,
I had drowned the memories of life that was once a battle ground,
And wanted to cross a world full of chaos of sound.
When blue water, showing its conquering might,
Had tossed feelings on sailor's face,

Renouncing the slavery of nature,

I wished to be free from the earthly prison, where I had once been bound.

Slowly as I had sailed,

Thoughts had risen from a radiant bosom as the waves had swelled,

I had felt possessed,

As a mortal made of earth and clay,

Fashioned by Prometheus,

Riding on the waves,

I had searched knowledge and freedom along the heaven's way.

Happy and proud,

Bathing in rays,

With quivering sensations in the flesh,

I had sailed to discover a greater depth.

In an unfathomable space,

Where stars had burnt as candles in an altar burning in a Mess,

In a journey across the boundary of time and space,

Bound by the realm of the moon and the sun,

As a creature of Prometheus I had sought titan's return.

To win the Paradise, from where Prometheus was thrown,

Carrying splendour of mind in a radiant flesh,

I had sailed under a solar blaze.

On the way, I had seen Bacchus' chariot ascending to Heaven scattering joys from his golden grapes,

Watched Apollo's swans flying over the mortal head,

Seen the blue waves creating swirls and eddies of unrest,

And felt in my chest Odysseus' mighty breast.

I had seen Hercules ascending from the pyre,

Then descending to the Hell.

Amidst foam rolling in streamlines, where waves break apart and leave scales of watery cells,

In an open sphere that cradle the realm of the living and the dead,

I had sailed in order to escape suffering and death.

But it was a delirium:

After I had passed meadows of grapes and vines,

The night had surged,

Billowing waves had leapt to wipe off stars from the night's face.

And a violent wind had pierced the mast creating a vertigo in the flesh.

As the midnight had darkened moonlight,

Wiped away them paths joining the earth to the Milky Way,

A swarm of asteroids had burnt out in space before stooping on the waves,

And filled the sky like the blazing dragon's feathers shooting out rays.

Seeing the phantom of Heaven blazing as a dragon shooting out rays,

Watching the approach of a threatening disaster,

I had felt a stirring of fear in the heart.

Under the sign of the constellation of Scorpion,

That once pursued Orion,

Over the ocean facing Gibraltar,

Where Hercules and Odysseus had gone to offer sacrifice to the divine altar,

As a sailor in the universe I had floated as dusts of stars.

While ferocious tides had hauled away the oars,

As a helpless victim of the destiny I had heard the wave's roar,

In storms' sea-borne quaking,

And clamours of the waves, like a ferocious dragon's awakening,

I had felt the power of dragon's wings, and its fierce claws,

That bring destruction and ruin.

Wearily wandering,

Hurled by hurricane,

Rocked by sprouts breaking on the prow,

Rising and falling with currents causing jerking blows,

Scudding across the deck, like a drunken sailor sinking in the boat,

I had rolled back and forth.

From archipelagoes to archipelagoes,

Feeling nature's wrath I had sailed through cavernous night's darkened holes.

Crossing yelping rocks where sailors sought Siren's love and comforts,

Experiencing in every island mortal sailor's terrible pain,

I had witnessed the power of the dragon once bound in chains.

Recapitulation of the journey continues

Then I had come to a forest where sunbeams' ceaseless dance,
Like divine music in air, life's beauty enhanced,
In meditation of brilliant light, that was over spread,
I had wandered in a realm, that from worlds of myth to reality of life outstretched;
There I had seen beauty as the goddess of love, life, fear and death.
On lofty...lofty waves...
That from arching sky deeper secrets poured,
Amidst canopies on tombs,
Where life's beauty in death's darkness bloomed,
In dew drops' flare,
Where twinkling mist everlasting beauty's message declared,
Leaving senses' snare I had traveled in heart's dreamy depth.
Where Muses in ethereal serenity music tuned,
I had discovered a tranquility of rays strewn and hewn.
Quietly casting eyes in meditation,
Hearing an ethereal incantation,
As I had entered a realm unknown,
I was entrapped in the hands of destiny that I later bemoaned.
Believing that I had seen Eros, Venus' son, who appears in myriads of loving forms,
Walking under a veil of rays,
I had entered a forest without knowing that it was full with bushes of thorns.
With passions still lurking in the heart,
I was penetrated by love's treacherous dart.

The arrow, that had penetrated hearts of lovers endless times,
Had blinded me, as an act of a magical power divine.
Blind and nowhere to hide,
When I was thrown in tumultuous tides,
I had met my guide, who was shining as radiant light.
From that darkness of the mind,
In the emptiness of the sky he had taken me for a cosmic flight.
While I had flown alone,
I had discovered the beauty of my eternal home.
It was an endless journey through passages in space that is infinite:
There I saw worlds folding and unfolding in cosmic brine.
From a temporal world I had flown to a nontemporal realm,
In a world that had no end or beginning,
I had seen Buddha radiating compassion's enlightening beam.
Returning from the journey in a sphere where there was no fire, air,
water or dust,
Clinging to the vision of Buddha in the heart,
I had again gone in search of beauty and love.
It was Maya ... a deep Maya....
That enwrapped all paths,
I had seen the beauty again beckoning me to ascend towards the stars,
Where rays of light were singing the hymns of death and birth.
Amidst myriad of forms,
That carried the illusory world's joy and mirth,
I had followed the Guide of the Soul,
Who promised to redeem the world with a sacrifice of the divine
blood.
As I had ascended towards a height no one can ever attain,
I had encountered the Divine,
Who had asked me to go down in the world to repeat the journey
once again.

The memory of love that he experienced during the journey still lingers in his memory

Tearing the earthly bondage the beauty has gone to the mountain path,
Beyond the green hill, covered with forests,
Departing the senses along the flower decked paths,
Transferring sorrows to the heart,
Where love is bound to senses' love,
In poignant passions,
Leaving desires in painful separation,
She has gone towards the summit,
Where one can feel the cosmic mind's splendid pulse.
Bejewelled with pearls,
Moving towards stars, where sky hides a greater love,
Over a bridge, where celestial light bridges hearts freed from passion's
bondage and regret,
She has gone to seek love's eternal secret.
Free and unbound,
She has followed a path in a timeless glade,
Liberated from passions' spinning web,
She has crossed the realm where senses raid.
Where clouds hide forests that are miles long,
Stretch veils of mists over a path, that glitters over ice-clad sheets
under sky-blue flames,
Where countless spectra of spectacular rays cut flesh,
In swirling flames,
In a citadel of dream,

In a tranquil world where flowers are not molested by senses' claims,
I wish to go once again in search of beauty,
Where love is a journey over the mountain range.
Above petals' sounds,
Where immaculate love drops from compassion unbound,
In the remote height,
I see myself as a part of Bodhisattva meditating in a tranquil ground.
While dizzying steps drag mind to faults and crags,
Dreaming of Nirvana,
I wish to free myself,
And seek the beauty's treasured jewel of the "mountain land".
However, I can still see the beasts in flesh and forms,
Roaming in wilderness,
With speckled and spotted skins.
Who are thrown in struggle and fight with nature day and night-long.
Amidst drifting clouds,
Following mountain streams,
In ripples of thoughts, seeking tranquillity beside the mountain lake,
that create spangles as jewels,
I see ravines of flame.
Where wriggling currents seek motion and change:
Drifting, falling...drifting...
Becoming one with the whole again,
Rushing to control,
Always trying to free themselves from a fleeing world that ends in
vain,
In a feeling of loneliness,
I seek engagement in and resignation from the world in order to build
my strength.
In the Time Hall I see mirrors, where I stand reflected confronting

myself,

I see a part of me, who is Buddha-to-be,

However, I do not know for sure who is He.

Coexisting as subject and object,

I see myself wandering from the village life,

To the mountain landscape that hides the divine light.

Experiencing inner temperatures and pressures,

Where rocks and stones move downward through fractured crevasses
along swirling paths,

Possessing inner tranquillity,

Unmoved by fear of dangers that lurk,

I see myself as Bodhisattva going across a sense-bound world:

As Buddha-to-be,

He is radiating love from a Divine realm beyond death and birth.

With hours moving with time,

Like an enlightened mind he is going across the world where senses
shine.

Leaving miseries and sufferings of cold and wind,

Carrying thoughts transcending the realm of the mortal sin,

Through a halo circumscribed around bright clouds,

Where tranquil mist sleeps under a veil of the dark,

He is scattering glints and twinkling of godly sparks.

This beauty seems everlasting!

In mountains' unpolluted path,

Like Bodhisattva, I wish to free myself from the bondage of senses
that come with human birth.

Freeing myself from the world of flesh and blood,

Where pangs of passion dart,

Emotions' waves swell to deform the hearts,

Moving away from the realm where man is conflict torn,

I wish to go in search of love and beauty,
Who is mountains' jewels adorned.
In the Time Hall of paradox,

Although I see myself as the hermit ascending the mountain slope,
Amidst sunbeams' arrows and bows,
Penetrating glaciers' mask,
I feel caught by passion that rises in throbbing heart.
Quivering as waves in a brimful glass,
Baffled and confused by quest for love,
I see my other part descending towards the base,
Where storms will throw the wanderer from place to place.
Alone...watching the beauty rising in the mountains' marvel...
Feeling delight and pain,
I wander around dark crevices strewn along the massive chains.
In love of the self,
To escape destiny that may bring human bane,
I stand motionless, while looking in all directions.
Throwing myself in thoughts,
In the wilderness,
Feeling the impulses of nature that plunge as cascades,
I am watching a climber, who nature's all dangers defies.
Bearing barren strength, that human courage affirms and testifies,
Nothing more I desire but in nature my nature I wish to verify.
I see the torrents' brink,
Where crags stoop and crevices drink,
In the edges extreme,
I see the beauty ascending to the Heaven, as if, in dream.
Following the feelings' thrusts,
Where fountains gush,

In rocks, which protrude along winding paths, and where fears hush,
I feel the climber's daring impulse!
Soaring above the conflicts of elements,
Where breathtaking summit glitters in light as a splendid gem,
I wish to rise to the summit carrying Heaven's flame.

The Guide of the Soul appears on the stage to explain about the play that repeats again

The man, who you are, is the universal journeyman, who exists always. Although you may not retain the memory of yourself as that man, you have made a circuitous return to the place, where you once were. All signals that I send to your physical existence escape as sensations of body, which create feelings of delight or pain, because your faculties are governed by perceptions received by the senses. Though you will not be able to see me, because I exist as the mysterious waves, which swirl above all physical laws, I have granted to your soul the ability to see the places where you were once born, and will be reborn.

Do not ask for proof of all things, which can not be verified by measuring apparatuses, which can meaningfully explain the world of perceptions in the framework of understandings that are based on logic, framed by events occurring in time and space. Do not desire to see me in the way you perceive objects in the world. Do not seek proof of my existence, as if I am a man possessing limbs, bodies, heads and faces. Do not fail to understand that I can not appear in the mortal shape because I have no existence in time and space. You can only experience my presence in your soul. When you will receive this experience, do not desperately cling to the intellect. It will only bind your thoughts to the senses, and keep you ignorant of the world where the Divine exists.

God does not impart will directly on the human souls, who exist in the world of the will. Instead, I issue from God, and enter the realm where we meet. Neither I depart from the Divine being, nor do I fully carry the essence of the Supreme Existence. Know me as the Guide of the Souls, who has come from God, as a messenger to the mortal world. I appear in order to enlighten the human souls about the nature of the realm that exists beyond the sense-bound sphere. When human beings invoke God, I am the one, who intervenes. Although God is one with Me, it is not possible to exhaust the understanding of Me, or Him.

I have come to accompany you in a journey through a world that is three-fold: Watch the journey from this Time Hall. You will see the world of God and the world of man in unison with the realm that belongs to the spirits, when the bodies decease. You will see things that eternally endure as well as those that decay and disintegrate encountering temporal force. You will see what is confined in nature's core, and what drives all that spring and grow. You will understand the existence that covers the world with its invisible mystic glow.

Although you are constrained by the human will, I shall impart on your mind the power of the Divine Soul, so that you may fulfil the eternal journey of mankind. After the last journey you made, you have moved away from the sentient world, where the life of the human beings unfold in time and space. Part of you "now" exists in a domain where the duration and sequences of time do not follow the causality of time and space. Therefore you are able to see behind and forward in time while past and future are joined by a magical way. The time, that one calls now, has no meaning in this place, that one calls here. Follow me hence.

In search of the beauty whom he has met in the earlier life, and whose memory still lingers on in the mind, the man, who is reborn, and has appeared on the life's stage, begins his journey once again. The first part of the journey proceeds through the village life where the desire for power, wealth and instinct-bound love create conflict, war, bondage and suffering. The Guide of the Soul who accompanies the journeyman shows him a more meaningful path. However, the will-bound mortal chooses a different way.

VILLAGE LIFE

Realm of the Instinct-bound man

In the Time Hall of Illusion Tathagata first chooses to move along the way that leads to the instinct-bound world, where human activities are driven by the will-to-live and the will-to-power. In this conflict torn "Village Life" he seeks the hands of beauty. As he looks for comforts in instinct-bound love, and seeks pleasures in the festivity of the village life, he becomes the prisoner in the hands of the tyrant of the village who is stooped in the will-to-power.

20. In front of the village gate

21. The advice of the guide of the soul

22. Village festival

23. Song of a blind bard

24. Follower of Devil

25. Witches' songs

26. Village beauty brings forth passion

27. The beauty's invitation to dance

28. The advice of the guide of the soul

29. The Guides' warning

30. The power-loving sun hero

Accompanied by the Guide of the Soul the journeyman arrives in front of the gate of entrance to a village. It is a bright sunny morning in the spring time. They walk along a road that skirts along the boundary of the village. Being dazzled by the beauty of the flowering trees bathing in the sunlight, the journeyman's heart becomes full with emotions.

In front of the village gate

What light through this mind's windows break?
O Guide! Tell me what streams so bright through the eyes' darkened haze?
Look at my face!
All sorrows and sufferings have grown pale,
See, how they yield to the joy of light, as the rays of the sun the senses seize!
In the orchard where the beauteous flowers, like buds of love, touch the light's rippling breath,
The desire returns like the arrows of Cupid stirring the heart with the air of a nervous virgin's panting breast.
Though I am embarked on a journey beyond the enjoyment of the beauty of the world,
When the nature stands naked and winks with passionate flames to entreat the eyes,
Like the mortal in love, my heart blushes in the touch of love's eternal flame.
O Guide! do not deny me the human life's passion for beauty.
In contradiction to the will of the divine, with whom I have embarked

on this journey,

I feel in the flesh the lights severing the clouds,

Scattering passionate warming up the breast.

The rays darting through the fresh female buds,

Not yet ripe to be the bride of the life,

Like Cupid's arrows, bring in the heart a young man's lust,

And reveal the secrets that make the flowers the mistresses of light.

Like Cleopatra* after spending a dark night in debauchery in the Nile of the heart,

They sail as vessels of light freed in the stream of love.

As the sun advances in the sky, rolling on the burning wheels,

The senses rush towards the flowers and buds carrying a wanton will.

Amidst this, through the foliage, that decorate the trees with streaks of light and dark,

A beauty too rich, too dear, too enchanting, winks behind flowers and buds.

Like a pinioned bird entrapped in a cage of twigs,

The memories, that was once happiness of flight,

Flap their wings and try to free themselves from the cage of light.

O Guide! the clouds float over the clouds more deep than where the sky

breathes in the cerulean chamber of the stars.

While, in search of dream and love, the petals of the eyes open to cure the sufferings and sorrows of birth,

Drops of tears drop on hearth burning in the bosom of the golden star.

While the morning dews, with all secrets closed in the shining beauty of a jewel,

On the blades and grass, covered in tranquility, hang vibrating spectrum scattering rainbows' spell,

I feel that no morning in my life has lifted my eyes in such a way,
No light has given me such an assurance of this sense seducing fire
that warms up the day.
O Guide! I ask for your counsel.

The Guide gives him advice

I advise you to withdraw your mind away from the senses that
generate lust.
Free yourself from the sense-seducing world of smell, sound, sight
and touch.
Remember, the pleasures that grow like vortices in the stream of
blood,
Although can induce a merry-making man to sing and laugh,
Before they pass will ravage the home where peace can last.
The sensual love, that permeates your mind, can nothing but beget
suffering.
Remember, to quench one's thirst, once one opens senses' spring,
more thirsts will rush.
Look ! how the torments of the senses, that opens a spring in your
mind,
Close the openings of the translucent fissures through which the
divine light may gush!
Listen in your own heart how, like creatures wearing glad-fly wings,
The words, that you sing in praise of the sensual beauty, disturb the
inner air where the quietness may sing its hymn.
Man! Leave the carnal way.
I advise you to withdraw further towards the East,
Where man is not wholly man's own burden that are drawn by the
cattle of passion and lust.
This beauteous sphere, that you behold,
Is enwrapped in a veil of mystery in many thousand folds.
If you want to approach the true path, more you need to disrobe your

soul from the senses' role.

For the sake of satisfaction of the senses, that suck the beauties as nipples of an aroused amorous whore,

Let not your mind trade love's truest satisfaction in the vow not to touch the one you love before God touches your soul.

Do not lower your sight on this sense's mall.

Let us go to the mountain path, that looms beyond this village life where passions are born and reborn.

They watch the villagers, wearing different costumes and masks, entering the village. The Journeyman defends the follies of the sense-bound world.

Village festival

What is then the meaning of life if man should cease to look at the light
that brings passion and delight ?
(He points to the dogs copulating by the roadside.)
Look! how like the farmers' dogs the copulation thrives through nature!
Like a bastard child abandoned by fate,
See how the happy air enticing the warmth of the day chafe the flesh.
Look! how the sensations of joy amidst thousands of flowers rub away from the face
The fear, shame and sorrow of a wretched human state!
Although I know that, like gossamers floating in the air,
This joy is a trifling flight on the moments of the day,
I do not see any reason why one should renounce this world full of cow-dung smell.
While the wicked flames, like serpent's tail,
Coil the senses in a passion, from where rises fire of hell,
And, like the ditch-dogs, the adulterous women and men yelp hearing the angels' bells,
The bed without an odalisque do not awaken the mind
As long as one does not wish to renounce blood and flesh.
The wisdom that you convey sounds like a mockery of human fate.
I hope the nature's wisdom surpasses the role on the stage that you relate.

I am aware that the sensual desires may bring folly,

That may steal from man his freedom.

But what freedom will mean if the human beings only go for the holly?

Although I may not know the life of a sage,

I know that love, hate, friendship, discord, and conflicts that rise

from the sense-bound world and stir the base,

Are not fake emotions played by the actors on a stage.

With the fierceness of a wild beast when in a lover's mind anger raids,

Bringing cascades of tears, when in her curling hair the flames of despair forms a hellish gate,

When she shivers feeling a dilemma between anger and love,

And plans to take revenge against the one she loves in hate,

In the self- torment, when she stabs herself in order to win the prize of love,

I know that in the oozing blood

Life leaves love's ineffaceable stains.

The Guide replies

In the world that follows laws of nature, the instants that may seem
rich and rare,
Often cradle errors of human judgment that may make man bounte-
ous foolishness' legitimate heir.
With the windows of the divine light shut,
When passionate hearts fume in uncontrollable senses' blaze,
Man's desire is man's darkest jail.
Do not be bewitched by this sensual life's charm.
Turn your mind from the village gate,
And follow me towards the mountains where life is tranquil and calm.

Journeyman argues

Neither I wish to err,
Nor do I accept what you profess.
As long as I possess will, I can not escape the chess-board of the stage,
It is a play of man against his fate.
Although you wish to show me a greater way,
I am bound to the role that I am destined to play.
I may suffer in the senses' flame!
But how does it matter when man is bound to duel with himself as
his own opponent on the stage?
O Guide! I am my own duel,
A shadow of myself wearing opponent's mask and dress.
My destiny is bound to the sense-bound will, that find no meaning in
the Divine Will that you profess.
Let us enter the festive village life!

As they enter the village drown in a festival - celebrating the coming of spring - they meet a blind bard.

Song of a blind bard

As the sun cheers through the clouds creating chequered maze of
light
over the marbles laid around the fountain,
Where old and young have gathered carrying a festive pleasure like a
bird in its cage,
All pains of life depart from this hour of the day.
As the streets forfeit quietness and peace in the sun-strewn warmth of
the rays,
While liberty throwing lustful winks flirt in the festive May,
Both the rich and the poor feel seduced by the beauties' sensual gaits.
Though grief and sorrow still linger on villagers' breasts,
In the daylight, that shouts in rays,
The poor man also puts on a happy mask on his face;
Trying to forget all debts and bonds of life, which still hide and stray,
The lovers' eyes sail in tears feeling the pleasure and warmth of the
day.
The shoemaker, wearing his new made pair,
Glints as the sun reflects light from his feet to face;
The tailor, like his much used yard,
Unruly in the inconstant air,
Secretly measures women's buttocks and buxom breasts in lengths
and breadths;
The painter of the village, like a foolish lover, waits for the insincere

girl, who he loves in his good heart's faith.

In the senseless rush of the wind, that blows over her breast,

The girl, who is selling flowers and looking at a good looking boy,

Who - she dreams - will share her love with the passion of flesh,

Shivers in anger when the cheerful boys tease her seeing her love-stricken face.

When they boo ,

She becomes rouge in anger at the behavior that she does not approve,

In search of an honorable recognition of herself,

She hides her face behind the flowers,

And covers her legs under the flowery needle-work,

And in pride decorates her breast with white ribboned laces of her dress.

While one's fun becomes other's anguish,

In the crystal clear scale the azure sky weighs human love against hate:

As the church-bell strikes to remind the sufferings of the Saviour under the dome filled with sun's skyey rays,

Wearing jewels in the ears,

Feeling gall and wormwood for the deeds she hates,

Like a bitter pretty flower trembling in the greetings of the festive gale,

In dishonourable submission to the wickedness in herself,

Where reason is cold and to err is the way of a whore,

A debauched woman, bankrupt in the heart, is out in the festive market to sale herself

And corrupt the villagers with her devilish trade.

Then they meet a follower of Devil flirting around a prostitute.

Seduction as the snare of Devil

The prince of darkness wanders and flies over water and earth in air
and subterranean caves.
Born of the dark,
With specks of fire shining in heart,
As a dark fallen angel from a realm beyond the stars,
Roaring and swirling, and stunning the weaker souls with his glow,
He wins the villagers by offering various kinds of gifts of lusts,
Which will bring on them at the end gods' eternal curse.
Old or youngsters,
Thieves, robbers, or money lenders,
Criminals charged for arson, treason, or man slaughter,
Professors, or laymen inclined to indulgences,
Or having inclination to adultery that may cause matrimonial
conflicts and outrages,
Conjectures and hypothesis difficult to prove or disprove,
With or without diabolical lies,
That permeate minds of laymen, and occasionally even of sages,
All are influenced by cunningness of Devil's methods of abduction,
compulsion or induction,
And his power of seduction.
His power is equally effective among Christians as well as non-Christians,
Fanning in outright foolishness damnation's flames,
Or lacking any sense of purpose and falling in a burning pit without

any shame,

When cavalcades of evil with many different names,

Pass by - some dancing, some rolling, some walking, some being carried in carriages and chairs,

When descent and fall of souls seem independent of ascending towards, or falling inwards Heaven, or Hell,

Joys raise Devil's hair.

In woman's warm-hosed thighs,

In vulgarity of their sexy eyes,

Chalice full to the brink,

Plunging in a never satisfied appetite,

In pensive thoughts lowered under the naval chord,

When unregretted eyes drawing garments of ladies seeking instinctive pleasure,

Lumpy thighs, or breasts not in perfect measures,

Carry passion's treasures,

In Saturday night's wandering in trifling pleasures,

The lower types search love in man's instincts when they are out to enjoy leisure.

Soaring in the sky,

As a bird flying high in a resplendent flame,

With rhythmic resonances and reverberations,

Causing angels to tremble and shake,

In heart's thundering spewing out flames,

Creating movements threatening to tear down the Heaven,

The higher types, who bear countenance fearless and brave,

Hurl deafening noise, and create blinding flashes.

Their weapons come down and multiply in number,

Lit up the earth with glows of flames and destroy while they rush,

And defend victory of Devil, who wants to take vengeance against those who are difficult to crush.

Playing cards, and swaying in drinking glasses,

Tripping on toes, and uttering words that will fill ears in blushes,

In Holy festival days, stumbling as stuttering fools and copulating with Miss Adulteress,

As sinners they seek comfort in sin instead of attending Masses,

Abandoning the Blessed Lady of the virgins, they find salvation in falling instead in the arms of mistresses.

When father in black robe sings blessed sacrament and kneels down in front of altar,

In sexy motives the lower devils gaze at the nuns,

Instead of seeking absolution by penance,

Secretly hiding in darkness behind the candles they shine as children of the black sun.

Whether a nun or an adulteress,

Virgin, or a lascivious mistress,

When Devil whispers the secrets of sins, and inspires the villagers to take sinful chance;

From pretty young girls,

To old men with power, wealth, reputation and charm,

Devil's powers flames of life enhance,

And inspire the villagers to do dirty things,

That make both old or young hearts burn.

In moonlit night to serpent's satisfaction,

Mixing drinks and shaking it to brink,

Like vampires taking off beautiful skins,

With little kicks throwing away from the body everything,

From panties to stockings,

Sniffing at chemises and shifts,

Licking perfumed necks and smelling stench in armpits,

While the lesser devils carry off souls to a voyage in the heart of nature,
And bind the villagers in destiny's chains,
In childbirth, labour and pain,
The higher devils lift intellectual souls, seeking victory over destiny and fate,
Which at the end become their bane.

Witches' songs and dance in the village festival

(First song of the followers of lesser devils)

Flying in raven feathers,
Creating gusts and roars,
High in the heart,
As sinister eyed hags digging nails in the shrubs,
Feeding on beetles, frogs and toads,
We search for rats living along the roads.
As bats, or ravens, or crows,
We hide in places where miserable creatures in abundance thrive,
Like mushrooms cruelty multiply in our minds following nature's
evil drive.
With a hope to survive,
When rats dig through the earth to find a place to hide,
Instinctively we wait until they enter in our gluttonous stomach,
That has no end inside.
Rats, beetles and toads,
The filth in the globe,
Suit us well.
Sailor's wine and urchins' crime,
Drunkards' lust and drowning masts,
In our minds joy's ringlets create.
With poisonous herbs,
Creating ignorance and smoke,

We drown drunken sailors as bewitchers specialized in hoax and coax.

Fresh spring,

Love and hope,

Solemn air, that around altars querl,

Cause us to throw and belch.

We are ravens of black feather,

Creatures of a world nether,

Who will dance? Who will dance?

(Second song)

Apes chatter,

Wheels clatter,

But nothing is more interesting than idle talks, gossips and words that flatter.

Flying low where rumors blow,

When ladies dine,

We swerve as spirits clandestine.

When they gossip in emotion's height,

Before the stories quickly disperse in the air of the night,

With monstrous ears bent and tight,

We fly around the tables shining in candle lights.

Birth of a child, that has been painless and mild,

Though the bride is intelligent and bright, the marriage is not socially right,

The husband, who has not been loyal to his wife, and used fortune behind mistresses in his life,

The advocate, who has newly taken a retire, how he suffers in the hands of a vampire,

The blood-thirsty woman- originally his client as a divorcee-

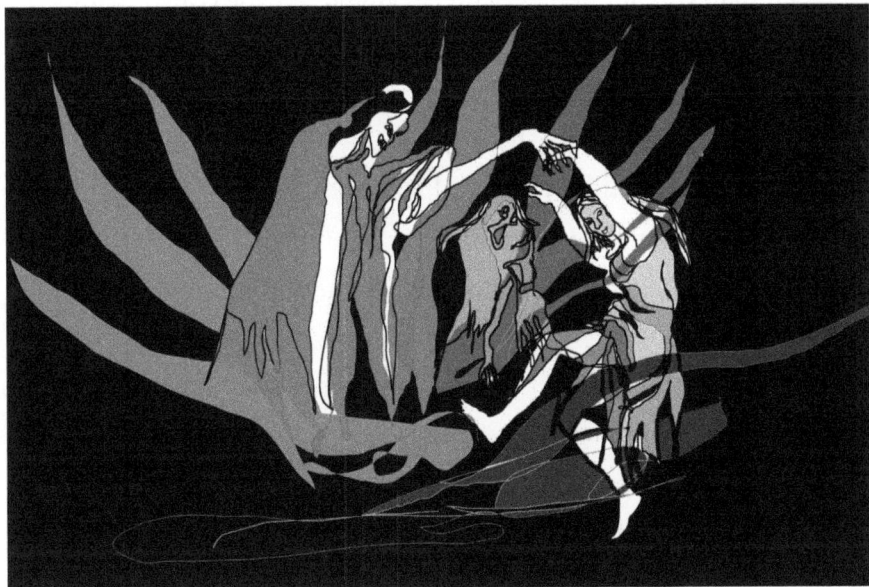

Now, after becoming his wife, does not allow him to speak or see.

When thousands of such talks in liberty meddle with affairs of no concern to others,

As companions of Devil we hide our ears, where gossips fly as butterflies of lies among housewives and mothers.

Thus in overfed entrails,

When malevolent bubbles babble trying to escape constipation's trouble,

Coffee from coffee-cans belch,

And like sugar cubes small talks melt,

Fat ladies laugh loosening their belts.

When chitchat, gibber, gabble...

Give testimonies that life is not philosophers' cage,

Why take troubles?

Though our brains are empty and have not received wisdom's flames,

We are life's most charming dames.

The journeyman watches the beauties in the village forming a ring around the dancing women wearing the masks of the witches.

Village beauty brings forth passion

While the dancers whirl arms-in-arms,
Like opium, that secretes papaverine and brings forth sleep,
Poignant passions drip,
And churning the senses,
Returns the mind to an earth-bound realm.
Under the vaulted roof,
Where lies the mortal senses' home,
Life appears as a wandering at night,
Where instincts kindle magic lanterns of light.
In such a darkness, as I stand and stare,
Down fly the wondrous flares;
What I know,
My moral doubts,
My fancy's flit,
My longings' stir,
Yield to thoughts as wind to fire.
In the body
Where senses' deluge flow,
And a wanton fire spread its glows,
Life appears to be a splendid conflagration,
In flesh and blood it is an eternal incineration.

Like on a shipwrecked deck,
Under vaulted rocks,
Where living creatures feed on living,
Under the universe's vault,
Forces of annihilation feed on everything bound to time and clocks.
Where roaring waves cleave rocks,
The tumults of life leap, lash and create endless shocks,
Shatter and splinter thoughts and send mind in flight as a direction-
less flock,
At the noon-day,
As I watch the beauty in the village life,
Fire of desires lisps lines of love in a burning tongue,
Feelings become ablaze as hours burn,
Events' tides lash on the senses' shore with unsurpassable might,
And a desire sprinkles foam from a sea of turbulent night.
Between water and fire,
Between cradle and pyre,
Between the earth and the cosmos entire,
Where the sun and the moon scatter rays,
And turn days into nights, and nights into days,
Wearing wings from Heaven, or Hell,
I am a wanderer, whose mind flies as a bird over vales and dales.

Beauty's invitation to dance

In this realm, where light and shadow cross all motions,
Bring your arms to my arms,
Give your palms to my palms,
The flames, that sorrows recall,
Will turn as joy moving in a dream hall.
Once you will hold my hand,
The rhythms and the pulses, which stir all hearts,
Will rise through the feet as rhythms, that beat in light, mists and dust;
The clouds will drift along the celestial paths,
In the fluttering wind,
Along flower decked paths,
In twinkling glitters,
In the mirror of the heart will bring eternal love's splendid pulse.
When the new-born blades, in brilliant shades, in stillness remain
awake,
The night whisper to the dusk,
The dreams pass from day to night,
From the light to the dark,
Under the universe's vault,
When feelings between sorrow and joy vacillate,
The dazzling sky pierces the sphere,
Surrounded by mountains, meadows and lakes,
The ravines sweep away rays with thunderous waves,
In the endless void that circumscribe your vision,
See the goddess of the loveliest flames.

O mortal!
Where in true love's bliss nothing dissolves,
Come and dance with the maiden of moon- light,
Your conflicts will resolve.
When the time's tide break the lights,
In brilliant hues,
In trembling eyes,
The rhythms and the pulses of the mind ascend to the height,
In coarse-grained particles flit the spectral light,
When in mirthful capering of the waves bulging along the sun drawn
course,
The short-lived moments catch splendour and perfection of the
whole,
Realize the significance of the mortal life,
Its meaning and goal.
In the valley, where the sun-rays pierce the celestial dome,
Break into rainbows where the fountains play with foams,
Unfurling the hair in the flurrying wind,
Come and dance with me following the eternal lovers' zigzag foot-
prints.
I am the goddess of moonlight,
I stir air of the night,
And set all lovers in swings.
In restless motions,
In innumerable structures and forms,
I whirl with the loop of time,
And create countless thoughts in mortal mind,
That tick with time,
And fling words creating immortal rhymes.
In the sphere, where in nature's laws

Matter arrests matter,

Motions conjoin or halt,

Where in spontaneous throbs today becomes itinerant,

And tomorrow comes to a halt,

Under the infinite void, that is nothing and nil,

Where the shadows rest under a blue cover,

Leaves and grass repose in dream,

Bees sing as they hover,

In quintessence, things - though made of nothing- things' semblance
hold,

I bear the beauty of the moon-goddess in innumerable forms and
folds.

Come!

I shall take you where the moonlight mountains lit,

The shadows in the meadows, like the dancing mountain-maidens,
leap from feet to feet,

In the valleys, where the wind change its course from breeze to a gale,

We shall dance as a brisk wind changing to a boisterous storm danc-
ing with the seafaring sails.

Where echoes repel echoes,

As if, in themselves trying to find the answers, that they seek,

Sounds return to repose in sounds from where they leave,

Come with me to a world where the mountains dream,

And the maidens of love, wreathed with stars, dance and sing.

In the shining pool,

In a moonlit coolness,

Where the stars dip their rays and watch the depth of the place from
where they hurl the heavenly rays,

In the deepest depth of the mind,

Come and dance with the moon-goddess wearing a celestial veil.

Guide's advise to the journeyman in the village

Be on guard,
Here life shines behind the gloom of hate and love,
In maiden's arms you should feel fear,
With loving hands when she will grip,
Know that in her heart there exists a slippery path,
You may tumble and sink in tears.
Like Circe, beauty is hideous and sulphurous,
Pretty and playful,
In her love she seeks bondage,
Clasping hands, twining the arms around neck, fondling with
emotions that stream in breast,
In passionate embrace,
When she bewitches sailors with food, wine and sex,
Sings songs soft and sweet,
Burns hearts with her lascivious lips,
Know her as the goddess of death and folly,
A fate-bound world's witch to who flesh is holly.   .
With desires,
Longing for fire,
Eyes - swift and shy-lancing with lies and betrayal,
She is passion's maid,
The serpentine world's flaming raid.
Dancing and singing with sirens and nymphs,
When she will shine and glint,
Guard yourself against her charm that makes man fall in dream.

She is the queen of the magic herb that creates lecherous desires,
Renouncing everything she makes man follow a path of curse,
When her love's longings inflame,
She is a whirling fire's incarnation as a dame.
When she is carefree and frivolous behind her loveliness,
Her promiscuity is difficult to restrain.
Yield not to her hands,
Looking for thrills of life do not gamble away truthfulness,
In the name of freedom do not erect castles on her beach of sand.
Do not seek shelter where man is defenceless against treacheries of
passion, and himself.
Where she hides guile and deceit,
Do not seek safety in conceit,
Where as a seductive female she reigns by betraying emotions that are
lofty,
Remain on guard against her adultery.
Inside the spheres of fire, water, earth and sky,
Where as a faithless maiden she love's lofty purpose defiles,
Beware of suffering, captivity, and blindness,
Keep guard against freedom that attracts man to her loveliness.
When she will appear cool and refreshing,
Seek in the body a drink of passion by the pool at night,
As wife, lover or enchantress,
Will offer senses of delights,
Know that she is swift in fleeing,
And still swifter in feelings;
As passion's sudden gust,
Igniting fire of lust,
She will leave you in ash and dust.
Do not pursue this tragic fate,

Wait until she sinks behind passion's lake,
Do not submit yourself to the power of the treacherous flesh that coils
as a snake.
When she will appear as a female seeking life's adventure,
As a huntress will chase the lovers as a goddess of fate,
In forests, fields, beside lakes,
Guard against her darts,
That can pierce any mortal heart.
In manly brevity do not lie in wait,
Take guard of her advances if you want to avoid the deadly fate.
Know that beauty summons hate, vengeance, and death,
Remember, for her sake, warriors like Odysseus went to destroy,
and set the city of Troy ablaze.

Guide's warning

After the day is spent in dance,
The darkness will fall,
And the hounds of sorrows will hunt all.
No matter how glad the villagers may seem,
Melancholy, like a marrow-eating scoundrel, sniffs around
everywhere carrying life's sorrowful themes in dreams.
Casting lights and shadows on the ground, where the mortals twist
and dance,
When the footprints follow the laws of uncertainty and chance,
No matter how they may try to balance against the force, that causes
them to turn and tilt,
With the passing of hours man's strength to struggle against the
divine power is bound to wilt.
From the minds of the villagers wisdom has fled,
The dances of the witches are nothing but the dances of the dead.
In the festivity buried in passion's grave,
As they strive to rise higher in pleasure's wanton craze,
The witches carry souls higher and higher inside a cauldron boiling
over a fire,
Where there is only turmoil and blaze.
Soon the dust will sweep away the sunbeam,
The evening twilight will encircle the horizon's rim,
And the eyes will loose vision in the darkness' streams.
Before the night will descend to cover the world in a dream,
Joys will flip with sorrow,

And the villagers will feel pains in the marrow.
Like a flock of sheep, deserted in a darkening mead,
They will feel baffled by their own freedom and whims,
Feeling forlorn they will rend the air with cries and scream.
When man becomes passions' slave,
Liberty of man to act alone leads to a wretched state;
And thus, when man turns into a foolish rake,
The spirit, who dwells in man, punishes man with passion's fiery
stake.

As the liberty of the will leads man to err,
The devilish desires bind the mind in senses' chains.
Feeling of jealousy and hate,
Senses of guilt and shame,
Throw man in a darkness leaving him to struggle for freedom in a
dungeon where Devil joy and happiness bargains.
How shrewd and craftfull man may be,
The spirit moves beside him disguised cap-a-pe,
As the watchman of the heart,
A friend and the master of the souls,
He counsels man to leave the pleasure's art.
But when, as butterflies in trifling flights,
Through sun's golden light,
The vulgar senses, flying in liberty's reckless path,
Tempted by the witches,
Perch on the passion's primrose stems,
The invisible shadow, walking in Godly frame,
Brings an end to the flight of freedom,
And returns man to the dust
To collect in the dust the shadowy world's fiery contempt;

Wherever man turns this shadow returns;
Wherever lusts and passions in sunshine reign,
In the purple cheeks on the face,
In the colours of the eyes,
The human passions passion's dilemma and conflicts contain,
Heat bedabbles man in sweat,
Feelings of shame appear as burning waves,
In tender lips man drinks in thirst the pains streaming in the veins,
In one's own tears,
In one's own blood,
In one's own passion man feels the sufferings' unquenchable flames.
Man! this body is man's freedom's grave.
Beneath beauty's roseate face, the serpent hisses;
Behind the lip that kisses,
The poisonous tongues flicker to taste passion's warmth.
When in a sudden uncontrollable wind of the mind,
Like passion's horse race,
Lying on the green grasses,
Like cadavers of bones and flesh,
The maidens in disheveled tresses,
Submit to the arms of the lovers,
And turn into flesh and bones,
Uncontrolled wind will choke their breaths,
As Oreithya's rape.

Seeing the beauty leaving the festival and following the journeyman, the power-loving ruler of the village appears on the way.

Power loving sun-hero

Before darkness the earth entombs,
Wearing a golden crown,
Like the ruler, that holds over days its sovereign sway,
As the sun controls the clouds moving in unruly ways,
When suppressed men and women revolt,
With strikes of swords,
Cutting throats,
I rip open the villainies of the nature.
In Golgotha,
In light beautiful as molten gold,
I enjoy watching how the heads of ambitious men and women fall
and roll.
Drenched in blood in an abyss dark and deep,
Where the vanquished pass into everlasting sleeps,
Inside a huge vault, under which the earth is entombed,
I love to watch executions,
When decapitated bodies flinch in vain,
The conquered victims yield to my power, which rises as the sun
bathing in a golden rain.
Without any sorrow and pain,
As a victor I love to win my enemies' hate and disdain.
As a brutal executioner, who possesses an insatiable will,
Brandishing swords with unsurpassable skill,

I bring destruction and bane.
I am a child of the sun,
Like a lion, that knows no bound of its courage,
I like to fight with unmatched ferocity,
That nature has bestowed on power-loving men.
When attacked,
I feel excitement's ebullient thrust,
Doubling the strengths in paws and jaws,
Like a beast leaping from the dark,
I rush onto enemies hurling on them a thundering gust,
And multiply assaults until the vanquished welter in blood,
Thus I shine upon earth as a dazzling star.
When the crowds my victory hail,
My fame ply in banners hoisting my name as innumerable royal sails;
When I ring bell,
People attend me as cowards living in Hell,
When, before I ask, people bring me things that will make me feel
comfortable and well,
I can bid all other happiness farewell.
When other nations praise,
To show honour people my sculptures raise,
Titles pompous and great, increase my fame and wealth,
When people pray for my happiness and health,
Sense of joy temper my heart like steel,
And I feel like a ruler descending from the sun,
Who is empowered to do what he wills.
In battles, my heart reels in thunders' wake,
A desire to rule over all rolls in my mind with lightening' shake.
While I thunder ride,
Victory's clamours and cries as tempest rise,

The sounds of joy carry tides;

I fulminate as flames.

Like a ruler of the world, whom no power of the heaven, or the earth

can stun,

I am a child of Prometheus born of clay and dust,

Who has risen to rule the world as rays of the sun.

Though, from dusts I am conceived,

From the star I my power receive,

Before I fall into dust,

The Heaven I wish to besiege.

O sun! Hurl your flames!

O will! Conflict's storm!

In baffled clouds' lightening touch,

In rain's and wind's flying gusts,

Where oceans swell and surge,

Resurrect as a will of the progeny of the titan in my heart;

Lift me to the Heaven as a fire ascending to merge with the star.

The ruler of the village has been trying to win the hands of the village beauty. Seeing her in love with the journeyman the tyrant becomes jealous and angry.

Tyrant's torments in search of love

From morning to evening,
Like a hunter tired,
Fighting with conflicts of desires,
Swirling as smoke above love's burning pyre,
As a spirit that is earthbound,
I feel love's torments, which tear me apart as a hellish hound.
As I try to possess,
The cunning love unkind returns no kisses.
In lovely fleshes' warmth and touch,
Caressing lips' passionate surge,
Where desire and dream rise and merge,
Like a baffling world's thankless bird,
Beauty flies from my grip, as I fumble around passion's burning hearth.
Like, from the heart of a man, left in misery of lust,
Who stirs desires fast and fast,
And at the end reduce the feelings to ash and dust,
The love flies away to freedom in pure air and light.
Flapping wings in a world calm and quiet,
Like a dove ethereal and white,
It soars leaving my heart in a pyre.
O love unkind!

As I chase,

Scuffle, and try to seize,

Like a wounded hound pierced by passion's javelin and flame,

Bleeding in jealousy's madness and hate,

I feel encircled by a fire of Hell.

To release the love that she has kept stored in her breast,

When I grasp her, and press her breast on my chest,

She escapes me by throwing me in hate,

And cuts me into pieces with her eyes' loathsome gaze.

With trembling passion and sweating palm,

When I ask from her my passion's return,

The beauty's lips turn,

And leaves me to feel solitude's burn.

When I see her dancing with any other man jealousy burns like a pyre,

Sorrows swirl as smoke from an unquenchable fire,

I find no cure for this ill,

In a chest strong like steel,

This weakness I am unable to conceal.

When I try to imprison her behind locked door with a guard,

Sorrow and remorse lock my heart,

When I let her go free,

She imprisons me with jealousy's key.

In search of love when she hums like a bee,

Through woods and forests I hie,

Hide, spy and see,

And keep watch that to no one else can win her love except me.

As the mind tries to possess,

The passionate heart its weakness faces:

The cunning love ends before it begins,

It disappears before I lean.

Like a caterpillar walking on tender leaves,

As the passionate heart with its thousand legs,

The lovely flower tries to awake,

Feeling a shame, the beauteous bud its resistance makes.

When tearing her dress and leaning on her breast I begin to undress,

The wanton heart consumes itself before touching the beauty that it wants to possess.

Like thousand bees in search of honey when I on her bosom move,

Like in a garden full of flowers where insects throng as constant nuisance and source of pain and woe,

She her love's light removes.

When like a young fire a kiss I beg,

She rests under my burning body as a senseless stone without any blaze.

Sink light...sink...!

Fire burn thy fire...!

O master and god of desire!

Who has kindled in the heart fire and burn,

In suffering's churn,

While my heart the mortal life's power exhilarates,

As a wanderer in the Time Hall,

I am caught in the suffering of love for the moon- goddess.

Journeyman explains the nature of love he seeks

Leave your jealousy's fear,
I have a greater love in my heart than the one you hold so dear.
I am accompanied by a careful watchman of the heart,
For an earthly desire of flesh and blood, the greater love I would never trade,
You may feel safe.
Do not quarrel on things that has no reality to base.
Neither I shall let any beauty make me love's piteous fool,
Nor shall I sink in beauteous passion's primrose pool,
I do not see this life as a bounteous picnic where love is free,
For me love can only be received by a divine decree.
The love for which you wail is possession bound,
But the love I seek is far more profound.
It neither borrows, nor it lends,
Though it is tender, with power you can never it bend;
It has neither any contender nor any foe,
It has only a splendour of a glittering glow.
Jealousy you feel because you seek to buy something that can not be bought,
Remember I do not belong to such a human lot,
Who buys and sells love, beauty and honor as a cadaverous rot.
Like a stubborn man more you will try to fortify with passion the

possessive love,

More she will leave you by emptying your heart.

Love is neither a toy or a ploy that you can play in night's dark,

If you shuffle it in your heart as a deck of card,

You will loose it in the life's gamble,

Because love leaves life when you make it a farce.

The beauty, whom you try to possess, won't love you before your
mind its possessive disposition loose,

As long as you will try to win her with power of wealth and goods,

You will remain love's pitiful fool.

She may look for love that only true freedom can bring,

How can you win her unless you open your heart's uninhibited
wondrous spring question

Without letting her to dance and sing, as a flower free in the wind, in
the life's beauteous spring,

To collect her as passion's colourful dream,

Once you cull her from the tree where the sunlight streams,

Love will sting you with its venomous sting.

The beauty you try to possess can be possessed by love that reasons
decline,

The one, who you want to love, as if she is a concubine,

Searches beyond flesh and blood a love, which is divine.

Do not be possessed by such malice,

It is in yourself you bear love's poisonous chalice.

As the journeyman holds the hands of the beauty, the tyrant breaks in anger.

Tyrant's anger against his competitor for love

O you, my own reflection!
My interpreter!
Source of pains, conflicts and wounds!
Where the spirits of air, water and dust have made me the ruler of
the sense-bound world with freedom unbound,
Why have you returned again to this village to despise me and my
crown?
Here nothing has changed,
The terror and torment still rouse the spirits as dreadful flames.
Where the glaciers are cold,
The stars tell the stories before untold,
Atlas the universe upholds,
The mountains bow and bear the load,
The lights open the darkness in the cosmic fold,
In the eternal space,
In the wonder glade,
The fierce spirit of Ammon still the world controls,
The sun, as the supreme ruler of the earth, on my hands its power
upholds.
My power is still the only power that this world dominates.
The sorrowful truth,
Wisdom's deepest phrase,

In which your soul seems to be ablaze,

Nothing but deceives itself:

Nothing it gives,

Nothing it takes,

It only burns in itself and leaves ashes before it fades .

In the world where in search of light in vain,

The mortal souls are torn in pleasure and pain,

Like the dun smoke of hell,

I bring power, passion, hours of joy , throbs of life as the sinful
world's thunderous spell.

O my dual nature!

Who doubts about the meanings of all mortal goals!

Who has found nothing to win in the earthly role,

And discovered nothing meaningful to achieve,

How shall you understand the glory of the fierce passions that fill the
air and the earth in the rays in molten gold?

Virtues you dream, the peace you aspire

Result from the faculties that are prone to fear.

O soul full of sentiments and tears!

O infirm mind's evil!

In this world I am the eagle,

The fierce mind's breath-taking chill.

Leave the beauties hands!

Go away from the village,

Where I turn and veer,

Here there is no place for cowards, poets and seers.

Here I am the master of the world with an unquenchable will,

Whose courage, strength and valor are more unbendable than the
strongest steel.

Here friends and foes wake at nights hearing my chivalrous gallop,

Knocking from doors to doors I let them know that they are being ruled by a tyrant despot.

O poet!
When your spirit in kindness sail,
I dream of terror and tyranny in face of which all rebellions would fail,
When in silence you renounce the world, and let thoughts disperse as soundless words in emotion's violent gale,
I bray like a trumpet, waking all life in vales and dales,
In a kingdom vast and great,
I roar like a fierce lion of the world, whom all must obey in love or hate.
When your soul may renounce all earthly ambitions with grace,
Like the heaven's horse freed in a horrid wind,
My ambitions leap and curvet in the sky's vaulted face,
While you carry virtues of angels from a world, that is non-existent and dead,
I carry poisoned chalice of this living world on my head,
While carrying morality's filthy ill,
You fight instincts and desires and suppress the freedom of the human will,
In tyranny's spell,
As Devil of hell,
I plant them well;
While in seeking love your eyes the eternal beauty beholds,
The sun-rays, over my crown, a glorious dream of a great kingdom upholds.
O poetic soul!
Do not again stand on my way,

Go away!

Strange! though I can match in fierceness the greatest warriors of hell,

In confronting you I feel a fear that I am not able to quell,

Ye, the spirit of love gazing at the universe unbound!

O nameless wonder, who keeps vigil in the cosmos with your eyes profound!

Ye, who rise in the inaccessible height, and wander as a mortal moving towards the divine light!

Destiny has chosen me as the ruler over life.

Quit my sight!

Let things rest in the order of things as they are,

Let the power of the tyrant make civilizations appear or disappear,

Let my will fill the time,

Let blood fill the brine,

Let lusts come as hurricane gusts and break the mast,

Let thunders and storms sweep the earth as it had done in the past.

Go away!

Tathagata's meditation in the village life

It was a lonely wandering where man was separate from all. Like dreadful monsters here man wandered alone in treacherous paths. From precipices here man had thrown themselves in the raging sea, in solitary search of beauty and love had jumped in the abyss of happiness full of sensual lusts. Forgetting wisdom they had taken chances, and in foolishness plunged in the crevices that were deep, in hurry moved forward in the fire of the will, and as voluntary acts embraced the beauty weaving the sorcerer's webs that plunder heart's passions in devilish meticulosity and skill. The demonic hunger that devours was called freedom, wantonness and the power to endure the consequences of the folly and lowliness of the spirit were the definitions of life's courage, to sink deeper in disgrace and like cunning and lurking creature despising the noble souls were the way of emancipation from the unworldliness.

Except desires there was nothing that was worthwhile. Anything but merry-making made them weary. There were no higher goal but a valiant rejection of everything that demands from man sacrifice and urges to seek path outside physical comforts. After marriage, bearing child, then slipping away, fluttering and creeping from bed to bed from mistress to mistress, in blindness being awake, inventing in lasciviousness a hell, seeking happiness in dragging oneself in intoxicated states, oppressed and weighed down by the emptiness, melancholy and self-contempt, in this village there were surging clouds over the sea and the dangers of going across.

All around there were supple snakes and slippery witches. In seafarer's delight there was the tantalizing wickedness of freedom like fetterless hunting hounds and bitches. It was a tortuous abyss of the animal instincts. In this shore of the human sea, in a human abyss, riches squandered in filthy passion of squandering the wealth in the desire's bottomless brothels and gambled against themselves by merrymaking and night long dancing and bets. There as the ultimate man I had entered the festivity of life by wearing a mask and trodden the path of suffering in order to awaken the man from the sensual slumber that was abysmally deep. When he was awake I had gone my way across the gulf through the forest towards the mountain path. Sea bore me. From shores to shores I saw myself rising with the sun and going down with the darkness of the night. This sea was supernatural. Here I sailed as the ultimate man. It was a journey to overcome the tumults of passions that create waves and try to wreck the wanderer's boat apart. Once born in flesh and blood here man falls in contradictions with himself. The instincts intoxicate; the passions bewilder; the contradictions between the body bound in causal chains in the needs and necessities of life and the spirit seeking unbound freedom beyond matter create tumults of conflicts. Illusions creep. In war and peace with oneself one feels torn and riven. Once man fails to hold courage and follow the guidance of the inner light, one is wrecked apart and is washed away.

During this journey over the sea I had seen many lands and seen myself among many people. There were many subterranean caves, many vortices and eddies of whirling disturbances rising from these caves, and always a constant fear of death. There were many surges of exalted moments, many wing-bits of thoughts desiring to fly away from this dangerous wandering on the waves of life to the home from where I have come. There were many islands and archipelagoes, inexhaustible number of hidden beaches where one could feel refreshed and renewed as a new seafarer, find oneself anew as parts of the ultimate man. Here between earth and eternity I had felt bound together between man and God. Drawn from below and lifted from above, I had sailed from shore to shore carrying away with myself the trembling joy of awareness of myself as always a new man and always the same one, to whom all wanderers on the sea belong.

In the ocean of becoming where the body is the boat and the spirit is the boatman, in the sea of the living creatures, where a will to exist rises as tides and breaks in foams, away from itself throws the sparkling beads of light on the sand and retreats in tranquillity before coming again, in this longing to live, in this serenity to return, in the beauty and grace of the light snarling up and ending in riddles of eternity and the sublime nothingness that creates no other desire but to go across, there lies the secrets of the soul of the ultimate man. Why does he will? Why does he wander to gaze at life with desire or not? Why does he take this adventure in willing to confront the waves where many may perish? Why does he have this thrust to overcome himself as the spirit rising from the sea to confront the voluptuousness of the waves? Follow me. At the end you will know the wisdom of the ultimate man.

There are volcanoes, eruptions, smokes, and the underworld in this sea where the monsters of the sea carry the sailors off. There are freedom, enough freedom - the great vents through which the infernal flames rise. The journeyman must know how to overcome these dangers lurking in the depth. In this sea all must live and all must inhale and exhale. From the sailors to the gurgling and spitting mud in the ocean floor boiling in the heat that penetrates through the crust, from ashes, smokes and muds to the panting sailors vexed by the fogs and smokes of the hearts, everything and everyone in this sea have certain purpose and role. The tasks of the sailors are to grasp their roles and understand the purpose to sail to reach the destinations, and steer around the volcanoes and escape the grip of the monsters. Those, who are powerless to steer perish. Only those, who can endure in the battle can liberate themselves from the prowess of the monsters breathing flames. They will reach home from where I come.

Know yourself as the eternal journeyman. Will not the dangers. Do not take the dreadful chances. In an attempt to realize yourself do not create monsters out of yourself. Let the power of wisdom harness the reason and gaze upon yourself in the starry world plunging in the depth of the great mind - the highest encounter with the unmoved that moves, the unspeakable that speaks, listen to the whisper and stillness of God beyond all knowledge and reason. Aboard the boat sail and come home to the Self. In this wandering unite with the ultimate One.

You may see sorrow, the black sea flowing underneath. You may see destiny coiling like dragons in the whirling streams. Beneath the cliffs you may discover in yourself the dark monsters trying to thwart the passage, glooms rising and the fears trying to dwarf the courage. Do not feel oppressed by the illusory monsters of the mind that will disappear once you draw from within the strength to slaughter those writhing, coiling, convulsive images of yourself. From the ocean of the dark they rise to test your strength. Before man can go across man must win these forces of the nature. Through these tests man reaches perfection, learn how to overcome desires, and thus descry the blissful island where I had anchored in search of beauty and love as the ultimate man.

CAPTIVATION AND SUFFERING
Emergence of poetic man

The man bound to instincts bears it as his/her destiny because all life are thrown into competition for struggle and survival since the beginning of life. The instincts provide the way to survive by dominating and winning over circumstances which may come on the way. This is the fate of the children of Prometheus, who must strive to free themselves by acquiring knowledge and methods to deal with the hardship of life. This in turn brings more wraths of Heaven as curse of knowledge. As an escape from this suffering the mortal takes flight in the dream of a transcendental beauty and love who may sooth this pain. After the guide of the soul frees him from the "Village Life" he moves to the "Forest Path" in search of this love and beauty.

35. The cry of the Promethean man

36. Promethean man's confusion

37. Poetic man's vision of the goddess

38. Goddess descending from the mountain

39. Dilemma and melancholy of the captive

40. The guide of the soul returns

41. Man's freedom from the village life

42. Journeyman bids farewell to the village life

43. Tathagata's address to the villager

Possessing dual nature Tathagata sees the journeyman: As the poetic-man, accompanied by the Guide of the Soul, he has entered the instinct-bound life, where the will-to-live and will-to-power dominate. His counterpart, the power-loving ruler, is jealous of the love of the beauty, whose hands he tries to win. Thus the journeyman struggles with the dual in himself. On one side the instinctual life draws him to remain in the village as the ruler of the sense-bound world, on the other side, the Guide of the Soul asks him to seek a transcendental love beyond the realm of the senses. The journey through the village life becomes a journey through the suffering world. The poetic self at the end becomes a prisoner in the hands of the power-loving self. Thus the joyful festival sinks into a painful night.

The suffering in this village realm, has both physical and spiritual characters: It is a suffering that Prometheus endured for his crime, as well the suffering that Christ, has taken on himself on behalf of the mortal.

The tyrant puts him in chains and throws him in the village prison.

Cry of the promethean man

O fiery sun!
When you set,
Behind woods and fields,
And the curling clouds hanging over mountains and plains,
Leaving in the heart twilight's burning spell,
Why do you abandon the mortal after spreading over the earth a
magical veil?
Before sinking in the cavernous night,
While hills and valleys fill the earth with the beauty of light,
Over the mortal sphere, while a curtain is drawn,
The day illumined by the sun leave life's cruel verdicts.
O mighty sun, whose power this world commands!
I feel bound in a sorcery;
How shall I break open from the captivity that from the mortals cruel
sacrifices demands?
With nightly hours' fall,
I hear ghostly shadows' call,
My mind feels riven,
In knowledge and reason powered by the sun I am tormented and
torn.
In doubts I feel tattered,
In beliefs I feel battered.
Why do you leave the mortal, who wanted to rise to the Heaven,
where stars are born,

To undergo such suffering, and crown him with a bloodful wreath
of thorns ?

While over the head the cosmic lights sail,

O mighty power, who endlessly feed life with things that move or rest!

Pains twist around the body under starlit night's loveliest gaze.

In blood, where senses clash,

In the prison of the earth the mortal fulgurates in rage in a surreal
haze.

O mighty power governing the fate of the days!

As you leave, the wakeful world sinks in a darkened bay.

With the falling darkness of the night,

Cascading sorrows stoop in the heart spilling suffering in the
bleeding sight.

While in a sadness sinks this mortal soul,

The nightly sky shows its gallant show:

In night's darkest tomb,

Where fears plunge and comb,

In peaceful moon's gentle gloom,

Veiled in silvery bloom,

While in pasture's mist,

That sleeps on meadow as light's silken beast,

Where stars awake the grass,

I hear the evil serpent's hush.

In bitter pain in wound and blood,

Despairs crawl and tears rush.

Blood trickles while tears run,

The hissing wind flying as splinters of blades,

Cut the flesh.

As night's torment haul, break, twist and turn,

Shatter thoughts in wind and scatter them in mind's urn,

In feelings' violent churn,

I am a captive like Prometheus, who was enchained by Volcan's arms.

Every attempt to liberate myself inflict pain,

They bind me more in sufferings' chain.

In shreds of tears,

Where the oozing bloods tremble and flare,

In skeletons' holes bright and clear,

Where vision glides far and near,

I experience accursed Prometheus' misery and pain,

Who is perpetually condemned to scuffle for freedom in vain.

The chains in which I am bound,

Produces anger and hate.

The mortal, who once wished to rise over all powers including Fate,

Remains imprisoned for the crime of attempting to win over the gods,

that could make him great.

Where mortal sadness nourishes hate,

Hellish fire circles a pyre.

While the world is ignited in senses' attire,

Arrows of revenge dart from the Heaven, from where Prometheus

once brought knowledge's fire.

In their cascading glow,

On the earth flows a stream of woe.

Amidst this flame,

Inside the endless starry maze,

As a progeny of the titan, I am ensnared and bound,

And thrown into a punishment to undergo a suffering profound.

In the darkest night's starlit road,

Where cosmic orbs in orbits turn,

And experience the mortal life's solitude and burn,

Filling the darkened will,

In a loathsome skill,
While doubts and disbelieves are inflamed by the sun,
As a plundering hoard,
Anger and hate rush in the mind,
And attacking a burning soul,
Spread a wild fire that can not be tamed,
Leaving the suffering soul to misery, despair and shame.

The promethean man's confusion

When being captivated in the senses' height,
Mind bids farewell to the spiritual light,
And surrenders itself to doubts that incinerates within itself,
I do not know what I ought to choose.
Amazed and confused,
As I try to overcome the weakness of the mind,
That becomes inclined to believe in God's existence on earth,
Doubts split my heart.
To escape this metaphysical puzzle,
When I attempt to loose free from the chains that quiver in wound,
The sphere, which keeps the mortals sense-bound,
Bends over the head, and threatens to bury me on the ground.
When, like a proud progeny of the titan, I wish to rebel,
I end in surrendering to myself.
After committing abundant errors,
Being exhausted by toils, that free nothing,
In agony and pain, I endure at the end an unceasing self-contempt.
Filled in delusions,
With a hope to be free from this blind chaos,
Attempting to overcome the misery of the living and the dying,
As I intend to sacrifice the will of flying,
And decide to surrender to the will of the gods,
I see a realm, where shapeless figures wander by,
The phantom of Prometheus appears and drags me out of the

mortal cry,

And in my will the will to rebel multiply,

As a baffling mind's treacherous eagle,

The will to triumph, as a merciless tyrant,

Returns as a bird flying with the sun.

O enigmatic power possessing magical might!

You, who have appeared in the darkness of the night!

Why do you keep the mortal bound and confused?

Why have you given him the will,

That takes pride when it can godly will refuse?

O almighty! when the sleepless eyes and the vigilant ears,

Confuse the mind that wishes to find meaning of what I see and hear,

Resort to chaos creating dismay,

Fill the heart with fear, self-contempt, misery and pain,

In searching freedom from earthly bondage,

Why every mortal freedom are deemed to end in vain?

O earth, where I am left to be torn!

Before the sun-eagle returns to consume all who are born,

Why do you hurl whirlwinds, blizzards and storms?

Why do you bring curse of the Heaven from the fall of night to the break of the dawn?

Night and day!

On the mortal bay,

Hunger and need,

Throw all living creatures to battles indeed!

After night's piercing cold, frost, wind and gust,

The sun-eagle returns to throw every life to heat and dust.

In continuous toil,

When life's power is devoured by an unceasing turmoil,

The promethean mortals cursed from birth,

Undergo punishments for the titan's crime of bringing the fire of the
Heaven to the earth.

O Heaven!

While triumph and glory freed in the heart,

Exalt the spirit of Prometheus rising in the universe,

In pain I feel joy,

In revolting against the Heaven, I realize how the mortals their
powers of will can employ.

O mortals!

Look at the bleeding body!

To prove strength against fate,

While the suffering soul breathes happiness and joy,

In laceration and wound,

In shriek and cry,

In disdain,

When it laughs against the destiny that has bound me in its chain,

Though fears pierce with their spears,

The hounds of the Hell wander by in tears,

All around awful shadows hunt,

The invisible images haunt,

As a descendant of Prometheus I again and again will defy

The powers of the gods over the mortals as treacherous lies.

The poetic-self dreams about the goddess, descending from the mountain, which girdles the village.

Poetic man's vision of the goddess

In the abyss of time,
Creatures with masks appear in the scene to play their parts under the zenith ,
Where the sun paints the sky in bold colored rays,
The creator, who has lent man this light,
Sets alight the sun over the sphere,
So perfectly and peerlessly created for the seers!
Yea, mortal creatures!
Whose hearts' sorrows turn off the lights when the celebration ends,
As the clouds open the show in the eyes of a greater world by lifting the blue bright lid curved and bend,
Come and watch the life that is a dream again!
In this ephemeral place,
Where peacocks of dreams fly and colors clap over the towers where the dreams are made,
The world is full of love,
Like the jewels of a celestial queen glowing in light,
The liberty is light's jingling bell over the waves held by an infinite chain.
On turfy mountains, where wind pillage rocks stubborn and strong,
And sea spreads moisture on grass furlongs and furlongs,
In a world divided by dream, and joined by sound, sight and blaze,

The invisible sea-born nymphs lit the fire in sovereign grace,
Spreading the warmth of life like the waves that undulate on the grass
from the roots to the blades.
In this world, where soft lights in stillness take their flights over
mind's everlasting tides,
As the wind warming up the bosom heave the waves towards the
sky's tranquil bay,
Listening in the wind the ringing of the bells, hanging around the
wallets of flesh around the necks of the cattle munching new-born
blades on the glade,
I see a beauty,
Dissolved and dispersed from cells to cells,
Walking in a rarest grace.
Crocheting in the mind a pattern of illusion in dream's silken
threads,
She is coming down from the mountain to the village - senses'
ephemeral place.
When light floats in clouds in quest of a purpose in the azure breast,
In a sweet pride,
As she lifts her eyes to invite the light entering the eyes,
Her crimson cheek eclipses the sun's golden light.
In this dreamy world, where the eyes as vessels in radiance shine,
The power of time fades as foams circling in an ethereal brine.

The beauty, who departed after the power-man took him as a prisoner,
appears in his dream in front of the prison gate as a bejewelled goddess
coming down from the mountain landscape.

Goddess descending from the mountain

As the wind quenches the burning cheeks,
The fumbling dusts dry the dazzling beads,
"Content...content" cry the waves as they move in runlets
towards a bigger stream,
"Vouchsafe, O wonder! The joy that is springing to life in the
reeling stream", pray the seeds,
"Deign thy favour", weep the grasses,
"Content...content" sing the meads,
And the flowers wave colours to attract the flying honeycomb-bees.
While the verdant grass, growing between flints and stones,
Bowing their heads before the mystery,
Ask the light, "Why does this freedom shine?"
Standing as a mute statute of silence
When the eyes ask the mind
"Who has created this joy that flows as joy of mine?"
While the moisture, that spectrums of rainbows create,
While flying away from the dews' dwindling breasts ,
In the sparkling wings between the streams of the winds where
the lights cascade,
Opening the immortal eyes towards the moon and the sun,
Over the hillocks, where the stars wander in the cosmic journey and
return,

Wearing fragile jewels,
Where twinkling foams cascades in the light's fountain,
Look! How I dazzle amidst flowers and buds,
Look! How my ethereal beauty
Eyes' thirsts for beauty quench.
Look! Soaking in the light as the hours swell,
When the mind feels no thrust or pain,
As the time carrying motions in the wings of dust,
Break into spectrums,
Freeing the waves from the bondage of the earth,
And create joys in bursts,
Look! How I appear in forms, though not bound in the
bondage of passion and lust.
Look! How crocheting the silken threads, as a goddess I can create the
illusion of light ,
Look! How my images are reflected in the stream of time in a world
where there is no day or night.
Look in your own heart,
Look in your own freedom's pool,
The jewels that I wear in my chest as a golden brooch.
See in the shining mirror of your own eyes the beauty,
Who wants to be mortal's bride,
And leave your emotional wandering in pride.
O beloved mortal, look!
Where shouldering the sky far and near,
The azure sky ignites the ethereal fire,
The wind draw clouds as maidens of heaven bathing in a
glittering lake in disheveled hair,
In love, that exists in the cosmos entire,
To kindle the heart,

I descend to the earth wearing a lighted attire.
Leave the despair that has possessed your heart,
Leave those words, which captivate human souls in thoughts' prison,
Transcend the fire of reason,
Let not your mind be deceived by mind's treachery and treason.
My heart is only love's treasure, where there is nothing to loose,
When I wish to dance with you,
Join me in the dance.
Whirling in dream-like flossy silken loops,
Twin your arms around my arms to escape from earthly prison and loops.
Like two glasses reflecting rays,
Looking at each other, when the eyes will reflect love's eternal bondage,
Like the crystals, which glint creating spectral hues floating in eyes' flimsiness,
At every passing moments of time, which cross the space,
O beloved! Experience in the bondage of love,
The eternal power of life's unearthly maid.

Confusion, dilemma and melancholy of the imprisoned man

Stay beauty where you are!
In man's mind when an erring spirit hides,
Speak not of freedom that may bring meaning and light.
Where the world treasures its lies,
What is the meaning of freedom?
Man is only born to die.
On mountains, meadows and hills,
Where light with its darkness mates,
Nights after nights, days after days all pursuits of life in utter
meaninglessness fade,
Sorrows sink in solitude's lake,
The eddies of time carry the seeds of destruction as inevitable fate,
Events uphold fallacies of events,
Which bring to all life their ends,
When every life is bound to the world,
There are only cries, screams, and flames.
Where things in themselves nothing contain,
There exists an airy suspense.
O beauty!
Where doubts are the equivocators,
And the misleaders of the hearts,
However, deceitful ,
At the end they are the arbitrators between man and his fate.
In the void, where substances glow,

In the motions, where time transforms itself from air and dust to breathing flows,

In pulses' throbs,

In streams of blood moving through the veins,

O beauty! This life is a perilous game,

A stream of illusion,

In senses' end,

In the river of time, where motions impart on things dreadful force,

Draw every existence to a fate-bound course,

I am born to experience life's eternal remorse.

When in feelings of smell and touch life upholds essence of things in senses' flow,

Thoughts, logic and reason only create pain and woe.

In the lights of the moon and the sun,

Death follows life, and life follows death in turn.

O beauty!

Where clouds amidst shadows wander,

Your charm holds my eyes asunder.

Behind your lighted veil,

Where clouds hide lightening and thunders,

I apprehend the hidden forces of destruction and death,

Life's unsurpassable fate.

O illusory maid, who illumines the eyes as a light from the heaven!

In time's play and dance,

When seconds, minutes and hours govern the shapes of the world by accident and chance,

Under your magical veil,

I see the fierce face of the queen of the Hell.

Opening the jaws of destiny and fate,

I see the goddess devouring all in front of the Heaven's gate.

O beauty!

Through your veil transparent and clear,

I see flames in which you consume the mortals who were once your beloved and dear.

Therefore, when the villagers dance and cheer,

I feel a dreadful fear.

When men and women in wantonness sensual pleasures imbibe,

In ignominious wickedness voices of conscience despise,

In the joy of freedom,

In the frivolity of free will,

Live as victims of a treacherous mind,

O beauty! while the sun and the moon shine,

Where all mortals remain confined,

In heart's bleeding,

Life pulsates in passion and lust,

When mind only deceptions trust,

I feel shivering in my blood.

O beauty, wearing light's veil!

You are death's queen and life's flamboyant flame!

O suffering world's witch and loving life's beauteous dame!

Through your veil I glimpse at the moon,

I see the darts of fate swishing across the stars,

I hear the pulses of life and death throbbing in the universe,

I watch my mortal birth destined in the hands of Diana, the goddess of treacherous darts.

The Guide of the Soul returns and gives him advice

Here in the village those who dwell,
Live in a delusion that is dismal and wild,
As flames of a furnace in the Hell,
Here in hearts' tempestuous fire desires will swell.
In an infernal world, where possessions human beings possess,
In an abyss of the mind, that is precarious and dark,
Like a hellish bird with mighty wings outstretched,
In stench and smoke,
In a subterranean path where evil soars,
A penal fire spreads like a burning gulf.
As it steers its flight,
Chaos rises towards a higher height,
And obfuscates sky's celestial light.
In such an ardent night,
Move away from the path, where desires and passions dwell,
And follow the enlightened path, that can free man from the
will-to-power,
Which makes man abominable and cruel.
Do not pursue mind's rebellious thrills,
Follow the Creator's will,
Although free will life's purposes may fulfill,
Know that there exists a higher will,
Which is above reason, which is tied to the senses' swirl.
Know that what may appear as darkness of God,
Carries a light that can illumine the hidden corners in the heart,

And what senses may perceive as light may be a realm of the blind,
Where sense-bound man wanders in the dark.
Do not act against the divine will,
In the world, where your sense-bound experiences are immersed,
Let the human will and the divine will merge.
Leave the world that is chaotic and dark,
And move towards the shore,
Where a boat awaits for a spiritual journey-
Go and embark.
The beauty, whom you search,
You won't meet her in flesh and blood.
However, as you will move along your destined path,
You will meet her as the muses of music and arts.
In streaming wind,
In light's lustrous blaze,
You will see her unveiled.
In the bosom of the nature, where feelings of tranquility in wonder
will shine,
You will see her as a bejewelled goddess bathing in sunshine.
Along branches of trees, where nature love's mystery entwines,
You will discover her as a celestial maiden,
Scattering beauty's glittering signs.
As a goddess of arts you will see her knitting in your mind light's
loftiest designs.
While her beauty will ascend in the glade,
Raise your head,
Walk towards the light that will beckon you with its blaze.
In murmuring joy, when wind will play with leaves and blades,
Stand aright to see her transcendental face.
Where rays swimming from dawn to dusk,

Will ascend and descend with hues of colours leaving golden sparks,
In mortal's eyes,
The beauty will never be shut,
Open the window through which light will penetrate and wash away
the darkness of the senses' nocturnal lust.

The guide of the soul frees the man from the village life

When man derives his power from body's muscular source,
Wins victory by applying brutal force,
When, like a slave of pride, man uses weapons with skill,
Expressing cruel will,
Assaults to kill,
Furbishing errors,
Clinging to the will-to-power makes others bleed,
Creating hate and greed,
In foolishness he mankind leads.
Like winged ants in a journey on their way to die,
Swarming around burning lantern -glasses,
That drown creatures in soot covered with black smutches,
Eyes screened from the dangers lit by fiery matches,
When man rush to die,
In great numbers attack, assail, and fly,
To win a victory evil methods apply,
Man releases the dreadful sprites,
And from the jar of Pandora receives wars and crimes as the gifts
from his heavenly bride.
When cruel instincts fill man from top to toe,
While wealth and pleasure sense-bound desires provoke,
Dreadful thoughts drill in the mind darkened holes,
Seeking success brother brothers betrays,
In absolute trust to physical strength man becomes his own victim
and prey.

When man flies as a hawk without heeding to reason,
Vaults, and brags and commit treason,
Discharges sewage on the earth,
Man becomes a captive in the heart's darkened prison.
As in an ancient mansions' buttress,
Where cracks and faults breathe danger's air,
On pendent beams supporting eyrie,
Where birds guard the bridling in nests that cradle dangers under falcons' stare,
Man's life is entangled in fear's constant snare.
Holding weapons in hands,
When soldiers straddling on horses power's symbols bear,
It is the power that they fear.
Here and there,
When they stalk and strut,
Blow trumpets and blare,
They want to hide under their own gruff stares.
In the castle court,
Around the king of the night,
When soldiers brandish swords...swish! ...swish!...
While the victors festoons whisk,
When in the mind the will-to-power vaults and leaps,
And the desire for power in darkness creeps,
Man sinks in a darkness abysmally deep.
The gaits with which the soldiers ride and turn,
Are like falcons' movements that swing around life's ash and urn.
More freedom they try to seize,
And more they try to blaze,
They produce more ashes, smoke and haze.
Greater they hail the power of the Hell,

Smaller they become in life's beautiful tale.
Beating on drums,
Hitting taut membranes, that all veins strum,
When the soldiers show military skills in festive charm,
A blast of wind puffs as a gale,
Where the heathen world's tyrants set their sails,
In the nether world aflame,
Man becomes choked by the dunnest smoke of the Hell.
In a blood treacherous and cold,
When joys wave and move on festoons' triumphant folds,
Thus victors' pride upholds,
Power its contradictions unfolds.
Firm on purpose,
Daggers unsheathed for a duel,
Showing brevity when man encounters man heartlessly cruel,
Life becomes an arena of the beasts, though unavoidably real.
Behind horses' disheveled hair,
When in a proud mien man straddles on solitude's air,
In dark horses' strides,
When night beguiles and creates evil drives,
When under the blanket of darkness, stars radiate instants' flares,
Man juggles with fire as life's daredevil player.
As the trumpets blare,
The evil mind to the night its allegiance declares,
Under star-beam's cheer,
When man drags man naked and bare,
Throwing the vanquished in hellish flares,
Man brings himself to the deadly portals near.
I free you from this mortal gate;
Move higher towards the mountain landscape,
Where the beauty will meet you as the divine maid.

The journeyman bids farewell to village life

Farewell! Farewell power and might!
In the distant field of view of the village life,
In the flaming sword's blazing light,
In fiercely clashing weapon's flight,
Where in the strengths of the blasts,
The bleeding heart freely swirls,
Chaos, cries, deepen hours' clamour, and shrill,
Colours, shades and hues defend eyes' fierce will,
Things that at the livings eyes gaze,
Create pleasure,
Sow the pain,
Bind mind in a solitude's chain,
Where man lives!
Where man dies!
Where the accidents and chances drive mind's fiery
wheels,
Chaos reels on earth as the flaming life's blazing whirl.
Farewell! Farewell the blind bard!
Where the wheeling flames ascend, descend,
Oppose, reverse. ..
Taming this wild will care free,
In the human realm,
The acts and chance,
Love and hate,
Fraud and bet,

With the flying hours' pain and dream,
Either man leaves or takes,
In a living man's thrilling tale,
Reveal life's tangled net.
Farewell, farewell beauty!
Where in flutes the tunes rise and subside,
In bleeding heart's notes the musicians their songs renew,
In incessant toil, in sweat and blood the life its symphony creates
anew,
In chronometers where the hours age,
In beats and tunes where music the tonal passages gauge,
Amidst joy and grief, pleasure and pain,
Misery or happiness,
Frozen or inflamed,
Where radiance of Apollonian mind elevates man, and
bring the mind to an ethereal plane,
As a mortal clothed in dream,
I shall meet you again by the forest stream.
Farewell earth!
Farewell wind!
Farewell dust!
When true and false,
The dream and life,
Oppose, near...
Air, fire, earth and wind,
Release mind's radiant wings,
In sparkling tears,
In this radiant sphere,
Unite night in lights, and the real in dreams,
In the flaming mind's silent notes,
I hear the music and songs of the muses and the nymphs.

The journeyman sails across the sea, by which the village stands, to-
wards the sun-island nearby.

Tathagata addresses men and women in the Time Hall of Illusion.

Man! You, who live, breathe, feel, see, and touch!

Whom the senses always lure into perching on the realm of dark,

Who is beguiled by the beauty of life on the earth,

In the festive dance of life you who enter wearing masks

to celebrate the spring of passion and lust,

The drama you enact is the play of life enacted by all – I, you, and he,

Who are bound by the destiny, while birth returns to death and again

reappears as life.

Man! Both you and I belong to the soul, who this drama of life has

destined,

The journeyman is yourself - a part of "I" who is desire torn,

I and you appear separate because of the existence of forms,

Which create illusion of time in which all things are born.

The mask you wear is the mask I tear,

The mask you tear is the mask I wear,

Between you and me there exists both nearness and fear,

Because we play as friends as well as contenders,

At the end we merge in one another through love and tear.

The poem of life that you create,

Is the poem of all life I relate,

When "I" leave, "you" come and my role repeat,

When "you" leave "I" come and perform life's acts and deeds;

Between you and me there is always a bondage that will never cease.
In my death you my role receive,
And in your death "I", as a part of universal man, to your role succeed.
In a never ending cycle, while things become in order to cease,
And things cease in order to return in the churning of the temporal wheel,
Carrying a turbulent mind, "I" come as a fierce defiant man who is your counterpart,
And then return to the world where "I" merge with a tranquil mind,
From where "I" again return to fulfill the meaning of the will-borne life.
Man! the poem in which the journeyman travels rise from the sentiments that I ignite,
The story "I" describe is the story in which "you" and
"I" are parts of man who lives and dies in a universal story of life.
The morning "you" see,
The light "you" receive,
The compassion "you" feel,
In meadows and pastures, hills and valleys,
The rainbow, which may lift your mind and your soul elevate,
In my eyes your eyes' dream and mystery relate.
In threads of rays, loops of time,
Bonds and chains, which bind the eyes in sensual flame,
Joining things with things and reflecting on waves in dream's carpet sway,
In beauty beauties permeates,
Feelings in feelings interlace,
In dream dreams penetrate leading "you" and "I" in a drama with multiple roles to play:

From one I become many,
From many I become one,
Splitting as you, he, and I
"I" become you, and you become "I",
Where you as man of this drama, "me" as a man of
another time reinstate, challenge, or defy.
Man! Let us journey from where we are to where we had been and
where we will be...
From here let us return to the world, where we once had been,
As well as proceed to a realm, which we had not seen.
Let us go back as well as forward, where you have lived, and will live,
And move to the path leading to the mind's spiritual stream,
From where you will enter a Divine world above reality, myth and
dream.

While confronting the challenges of finding meanings of living, the universal journeyman experiences many contending and conflicting sentiments and desires. He watches himself playing the roles of different characters, none of whom alone is truly him. Floating in a plethora of sentiments, bearing contradictions at every steps, he watches himself as an actor, who is many in one. He enacts the same play, as individuals in the past had done. In the universal drama, as parts of the eternal journeyman, wearing different masks, he changes the masks along the path of journey: I become you; you become me; he replaces you, or I replace him etc. Thus all participate in a drama acting as parts of Tathagata, who will also appear in the same way in the future.

After leaving the village the journeyman arrives in the forest in the sun-island.

The creative realms of the artists, musicians and poets pass through this forest.

Part 2
REALMS OF CREATIVE
MAN AND COSMIC MAN

FOREST PATH
The dreaming man in search of love and beauty

Realm of the mind that creates creative imagination and dream with which man may fashion his own reality to live
"Forest Path" is the realm of poets, artists and musicians. Here beauty appears as nymphs and muses and Tathagata dreams to win the love of the beauty. In this Orphean realm, where the boundaries among dream, myth and reality are diffused, he is drawn towards the unconscious realm of the mind, where the power of reason and rationality is obfuscated. Though he seeks love and beauty beyond the realm of the senses, and aspires to win the love of the muses, the instinct creeps up in the body and entangles him in a net of destiny. The desire to experience love and beauty beyond the physical boundary of the senses receives a tragic end. In the dark realm of the forest when he comes physically close to the beauty, mistaking him as the instinct-seeking man the beauty blinds the dreaming man. With this dramatic event, the beauty who is also dreaming about the godly love of Orpheus, is spotted by the hunter, who carries the desires and the urges of nature, as shadowy power of the unconscious mind. She is ravished by this hunter in the forest.

44. Real and unreal united in the forest

45. Magnetic drag of Eros

46. The Guide's warning about the illusory forest

47. The mind floating in the lake of Eros

48. Meeting with an artist

49. The artist shows the way to the beauty

After the search of beauty and love in the realm of the senses, which has caused his bondage and suffering in the village life, the journeyman sails towards the realm where the musicians, poets and artists pursue their creative life. In this sphere while Eros drags the mind towards the lighted lake, where the muses and nymph bathe, the boundaries between reality, dream and myth obliterate.

Real and unreal united in the forest

Scanning the East with a dazzling light as the sun rises towards the sky-borne height,

After a night long vigil the dews storing heavenly delight,

Carrying the coolness of the night drop in the bosom of the earth that streams in a heavenly light.

In deep foliage where the hanging, trembling pearls dwindle as the morning wakes,

Gliding along the petals and the blades,

The morning hour in a twinkling glittering maze with the magic power of light on the droplets blaze.

As the dewdrops in joyous lustre splash on the radiant waves,

In the verdant grass the watery trails teem down on a dreamlike face in an endless space.

Drenched in moisture,

Where entwined vines share the shadows of oaks and pines,

The shades shelter the stillness on the dewdrops' ephemeral shines.

Breathing a scented balm in a refreshing calm,

Spreading the sun-ray-hair,

Wearing glittering pearls in the ears where the sunbeams, streaking in space in different layers,

Deepen the deafness of twigs and weeds trying to listen to the notes of life in the depth of the air,
On hard rocks, where the shadows stun the motion of the sun,
The trees, sprawling the branches, in the sunbeams plunge.
Teeming in a haze in a glittering maze where the dews the light's magic conjure,
Floating free in a tangled mesh,
Where the radiant waves crisscross and flight in the skye space,
The loveliest leaves filter the rays from the sky azure,
In a collage of streaks of lights and shades the morning designs a jewel of matchless beauty viridescent and pure.
In the unadorned stresses where the circumbient air
In joyous feelings shuffle the rays in the impassive hair,
The deep foliage dry the moisture fluttering on leaves in a glittering sparkling maze trapped in the dewdrops' snare,
The sun dazzles the eyes and throws the mind in a lake of light glittering with star strewn flare.
Drifting away from rocks and roots where the shadows ensnare the light with the curling branches' sprawling hair,
In the filtered sunbeam drifts the morning sun in the current of the mind as it through the woodland stares.
After the night's vigil, as the eyes in shapes of things plunge in the light's murmuring tide,
Swimming "sourire" of bees and butterflies of light in the eyelids the light's cackling guide,
In the flimsy flickers of the blazing droplets vibrating inside the twinkling lights,
Bursting forth and then returning to hide in the drops oscillating in the waves in flight,
The moments of time synchronize the pulsating beats of life,

With the dropping... oozing...droplets store in the breast of the earth
a heavenly delight.
As in a watery glass where swimming waves scurry,
Along the brim to catch flying sparks that glint in crystals
scintillating in hurry,
Before winking eyelids bury ephemeral images doomed to
destruction in mind's frenzy and fury,
The dazzling sun dipping down to the depth,
Where the drops of water carry from the void the filaments of rays
from the surface to the base,
Floating free in the daylight maze,
Bury the restless moments of time in the depth of concave shape,
Where things precipitate to escape motion and drudgery of weight,
In the deep foliage,
Where amidst branches and twigs the penetrating lights weave a
basket with the curving tendrils' turns and twists,
Cull the blazing drops in the sun-filled air,
Dividing the shadows from the dream-like beauty's lucent hair,
As bees and butterflies dive and swim in the eyes' dewdrop-flares,
The flirting moments fly in the light and shadow where the feelings a
vacuous weightlessness share,
In the bottom of the concave sky,
Where the vines the tree-stems tie,
The stones and rocks on leaf-beds lie,
The sun rays penetrating the vacuous layers,
Crisscross the restless motions of time in the dust streams streaking
the air with the morning beauty's burning hair,
I feel the presence of a tranquil soul moving my near.
Where the blazing sun fills the verdant ferns,
In climbing shining arms trellises the creepers spiraling around the

trunks,

Freeing the butterflies from the cocoon of the mind, the eyes skyward turns,

With blue wings sky-arch span,

In a swimming glimmering twinkling flickering stream of light in flight from the boundaries of the space and time,

A lighted soul glittering in water, air and rays uniting the body and mind,

Moves in front, while a shadow follows me behind.

In the depth of the void,

In a rising glittering sea from where the eyes the rays receive,

In the inmost colors in the ocelli, irises flip wings of rainbows,

Perching on the eyelashes receiving the star beams' blips,

In a twinkling cluster of the radiant glints,

In a maze of flying sparkling wings,

A formless soul moves creating waves in rings.

As birdlings hop,

The trembling dewdrops splash creating flamboyant designs of dots on the fungi and the moss,

Where sunbeams flip and flop,

The dripping motions of light trickle as sobs on the wet silvery rocks,

In transient shocks of the falling dews the wings free the air that rustles from stocks to stocks,

As the shapes of things, in nothing, time's boundary cross,

The light disintegrates and fragments in bits of shadows,

As if the twigs and the branches the light's and the shadow's innumerable butterflies toss.

In restless gleams,

In ripples and rings,

Where in a lake of light wind sprays foams of the dark,

Resting upon the heart,

Where in an eternity ...in a nothing... the eyes the sky engulfs,

In silence the stones, sensing the trilling trickles of the water, the moments surpass,

Pass through hearing, smell, vision and touch,

The calm air holds onto stillness its momentary grasp,

The stars shine and laugh,

The fragrant blooms guard the scents in porous holes open and shut,

In light and darkness in nature's honeycombed heart,

As the beams of the stars slip a mystery in woodland covered in dew-worn dark,

In lees and shades,

Where darkness cuts light with leaves' dew-strewn blades,

While the sky pours the joy and happiness of rays,

Like quivering butterflies in sight,

The feelings of joy flight in the light from the real night to unreal ethereal height.

Inside the forest the journeyman arrives at the Lake of Eros. There he hears the laughter of the nymphs and the muses bathing in the lake. He is drawn towards the place, where the beauties are bathing, by an illusory figure moving in front of him.

Magnetic drag of Eros

As the sounds of the laughs,
The smell of the scents, and the glances of the beauty the senses touch,
Golden light, amidst amber stems and green leaves, as birds of paradise lurch,
The flowers, mingling with all hues, move as dream's eyelash-brush,
Fresh wind steers the flesh as a sail of light floating in blood's purple flush,
Like a traveller in search of a passage through heart's turmoil,
In the depth of the mind in azure light's storm and gush,
I hear feelings' weep and rush.
O Guide!
Like swans of love swimming in a lake of light,
While the words in mind's serenity hush,
The snow white birds of the heart,
Float in the spirit - tranquil and calm,
The Muses sing in their sweetest tongues,
In wind-steered clang,
The angels heart's strings strum,
Light, wind, and air feelings' harp cords plunk.
In beauty's flare,
Where sun beams slip a deep sleep through the eyes in a dreamy stare,

Joys murmur in rustling, rippling sounds,

And an immortal love anchors in tears.

I feel the drag of Eros who seems to walk my near.

O Guide!

In the forest, where Eros drags me along the beauty's path,

Behind me whose footsteps I hear?

Guide's warning about the illusory forest

Do not be eluded by the illusion of light and oscillations of waves
that create tumults in the eyes.
The woman you love,
The beauty you dream of,
The cackle and laughter, which you hear from the lighted lake,
Are only illusions of the mind;
You must win over the senses' erroneous pursuit of the beauty,
And seek the one, who will bring you to the divine realm of love.
Once you follow the illusory vision of Eros, who is moving towards
the lake,
You will be drawn towards an unreal world, that is imaginary and
fake,
Though it may appear as real that you feel, see, smell, and touch,
You will enter in a world, where illusions lurch.
Unless you guard your mind from senses' delusive art,
You will be drawn to believe that unreal is real, myth is life, and
dreams are conscious world's inseparable parts.
Where boundaries of real, unreal, myth and dream blur,
You will step in a realm, where inevitable destiny lurks;
Surpassing the boundaries of space and time it will entangle you in a
maze of mystery,
That has no relation to present, future or past;
You will not know how to distinguish your life from the predestined
role in an eternal cast.
The forest, you see, is the realm,

Where there exist lights inside lights,
Darkness inside darkness,
Dreams inside dreams,
Things inside things,
Beings inside beings,
Worlds inside worlds,
Mysteries inside mysteries united together by unending strings,
That generate randomness flying in time's wings,
Where matter convolutes in matter the essence of existence of things.
The time you feel,
The wind of thoughts that shuffles your will,
Is nothing but a nebulous arrow, which ruptures the reality as dream.
Once you enter the forest disobeying the Divine will,
You will not know how to come out of it;
You will get trapped in a cycle that turns as an eternal wheel.
Inside the forest the cycle of the Zodiac turns,
Destiny and fate spin threads of life in which mystery's webs are spun.
The soul, that moves,
Is a soul, who draws reality to illusion and dream;
No mortal is able to understand this play of destiny,
Whose hands always remain unseen.
If you wish to avoid this trap where illusions stream,
Real is knitted with unreal, and myth in dream,
You should heed to my advice:
Do not enter this realm.

.

The journeyman sees in the radiant figure, moving in front of him, the soul of Orpheus. The maiden of Dionysus (Roman Bachus), who love sensual pleasures, wanted to win the heart of Orpheus after his beloved Eurydice returned to the world of the dead. When the maiden failed in their pursuit, they tore Orpheus into pieces and threw the decapitated body of the musician in the forest. The muses picked the parts and buried them under a tree. From Orpheus' blood and flesh the nature regenerated again and again.

Mind floating in the lake of Eros

Like Orpheus' body torn apart and scattered in different places
among trees, plants and bushes,
Where the dazzling flesh lies open under the sky,
The blue eyes remain closed in a dream opened between the
eyelashes, Amidst
death and decay, that define the boundary of the mortal world
imprisoned in flesh,
Rocks and wood, birds and insects, flowers and herbs, carry the
messages of resurrection from Orpheus' grave.
As in the shore of Lesbos,
Where the blue sea washes Orpheus' blood and brings fragrance of
flowers and roses,
In heart's murmur,
In plaintive melody,
Mind floats in the lake where singing swans float as Apollo's verses
and prose.
Under the sky, where emptiness is resplendent within itself,
In the murmuring water the mind swims in radiance,

An ethereal abyss carries the shining light's reticence,
The quivering wind on serrated leaves,
Bending against the empty sphere, dreams as silvery rings of
paraselenes.
In dazzling circles' silvery quivers,
Like crystalline micas' luminous shivers,
The shining water, in viscous rhythms, serenely chants;
Like in the opal's ballad in the bracelet, where the restless mirages
of light scintillate and dance,
A luminous monstrance in a processional altar holds the eyes towards
the glory of the sun.
As innumerable arrows of rays dart through the brain,
In a dreamy world, where quivering light veils the eyes and binds the
vision in liquid-bonds vibrating in chains,
I see Orpheus' iridescent remains.
In the depth of the soul I see a figure in undrawn lines moving in
time,
On the water where the shades the sunlight screen,
In the quivering stream,
Where the murmuring forest in the depth of the heart chants and
sings,
In the ringing air,
Where the branches swing,
Carried by the wind, where silvery motions drag the trembling lake
like restless mirrors' changing beams,
In the water's edge, that floats like a silvery magic pot,
I see a figure bent in thoughts,
Contemplating while fragments of images of the self are moving in
an illusory world,
Where he is one with man and god.
Where shadows cloak silence in nature's watery breeze,

In the depth of the soul unknown atoms split in infinite bits,
Where all motions cease,
Carrying a sceptre of scintillation the ruptured mind flees,
The twinkling stars become one with the ripples of luminous beads,
I see the musician of Heaven walking in peace:
Moving forward as well as backward in time's quivering breeze,
In the depth of the soul wearing a gaze under a mask,
Where lights cross in the quietest path,
Lowering his brow against the earth,
Where invisible shadows move on water,
Echo plays with Pan exchanging in the air twinkling swarms of stars,
In a voice strange and unknown,
That neither murmurs nor creates echo,
Neither reflects sounds from water or sky,
Nor resonates, fades or dies,
Where trees uplift leaves to the quietude of the spirit,
The sounds annotate the silence in the breeze,
The words fly as buzzing swarm of bees,
He murmurs, speaks, echoes, creates resonance in the mind,
He hears his own echo,
Between earth and water, void and sky,
Like Narcissus sees his image in the world where the transcendental
birds fly.
Where the nymphs swim stroking the surface of the water with their
arms,
The swans draw motions and dither amidst the curving lines amidst
lotus and lilies bathing in the sun,
While the starry drops, gathered on lotus leaves, precociously plunge,
The nymphs set the soul in trance,
In a world where Narcissus, and Eros are one,
I wish to follow the path where Orpheus has gone.

Approaching the lake he meets an artist

In the silvery lake's trembling wind,
Where in the dazzling hues the sun soaks the lights and colors un-
seen,
The lines and forms blot and dissolve in a world within,
I blend colours that the golden sun's secret store,
And in silence and peace paint the maidens with the turbulent
brushes' powerful strokes.
With the arms supporting a palette,
The fingers moving the brushes in green, red and violet,
The knees bend on a taboret,
Like a master listening to the murmur of light coming from soul's
deepest source,
In the nuances of colors I contemplate in a wordless dialogue with the
light's inner force.
In swift changing flashes,
As the bending brush in joyful rhythm the canvas touches,
The arms paint in the feathery clouds the azure mind's plumage-
clothes,
In the living blood in a dripping chasm,
In an azure rhythm,
In the silvery lake's trembling light,
Float in the ripples of rainbows rising above blood's crimson flow.
In swimming strokes,
In diverging waves,
In swift motions of foams from which once Venus rose,

In the palette the shifting colours,
In brushes' strokes,
In ringlets and waves,
Dividing the foams rise as the light's divine force.
In search of a deep truth within,
As I put on the canvas the symbols of the inner world in visual forms
and things,
Raising the arms with fastness of movement displaces air and swims
in the foams rising out of the sea in inner bubbling,
The loftiest rings contort and twist in the wind,
As if Muses swim!
The rising and falling arms, moving in swift strokes, sprinkle colors
of rainbows in the flying air fleeing from the real to a state of dream.
As the hands fly in rainbow's wings,
On the silvery lake,
In the trembling wind,
In the awakening hour's quivering films,
The light, the ripples, this aroused mind's ecstasy to a distance drag,
In the fleeting hour's silvery shiver, between this world of mine and
the other there - beyond, under and over,
There seems to exist a time lag,
In the sleeping hues that make the real unreal and black,
There exists a soul walking in the forest, who is light-clad.

The journeyman wants to know the path

O painter!
Who absorb this light of the real world in the light within!
You who seem to be able to see things in things' inner beings!
Tell me the path of Eros, who moves in this forest,
He is the beloved of Psyche, who searches him in every realms - in
reality or dream.
Tell me the path to find him.

Here the so-called reality is a pandemonium of worlds where many worlds are intertwined. All different projections of the self in the sense-bound world float delusively in a stream of illusion - the so-called real. Man's mind is only a part of a psychic continuum, where man is not separable from the existence of other human beings. In a continuous stream of flow one's thoughts and will take form conditioned by the movements of the material world. It is like innumerable moving mirrors, in which one sees one's own reflections, which create the illusion of the existence of the individual self.

Tathagata is such a projection, or I am a projection of him in the temporal world. He is "myself", who, amidst the transitory flow of images in the mirrors, seeks his true nature in the stream of existence that is ephemeral. Parallel to this ephemeral world, where the mind brings the cognition of the ever changing reality, one also exists in a "virtual" world, where life once lived by the universal man, and life to appear in the future can be foreseen.

The artist shows him the way to follow

In the depth of the soul
I see a figure in invisible lines moving in time.
On the water where the shades the sunlight screen,
In the quivering stream,
Where in the depth of the heart the murmuring forest chants and
sings,
In the ringing air,
Where the branches swing,
Carried by the wind where, like silvery motions drag, the trembling
lake,
Move as restless mirrors' changing beams,
In the water's edge floating like a silvery magic pot,
I see a figure bent in thoughts,
While fragments of his images in the mirror are moving in an
illusory sphere, where he is man and god.
Where shadows cloak silence and peace in nature's watery breeze,
In the depth of the unknown atoms split in infinite bits where all
motions cease,
Carrying a sceptre of scintillation the ruptured mind flees with the
twinkling glitters becoming one with the ripples in the luminous
beads,
I see Eros walking in peace:
He is moving forward and backward in time's quivering breeze.
In the depth of the soul, wearing a tranquil gaze under a mask,
Where lights cross the quietest path,

Lowering his brow against the earth,
Where his invisible shadow moves,
In a voice strange and unknown,
That neither murmurs nor creates echo,
Neither reflects sounds from nature, water or sky,
Nor resonates, fades or dies,
Where trees uplift leaves to quietude of spirit,
Where sounds annotate silence in breeze,
Where words fly in silence as buzzing swarm of bees,
He murmurs, speaks, echoes, and creates resonance in the mind.
Where the nymphs swim stroking the surface of the water with their arms,
The swans draw the motions of time and dither amidst the curving lines amidst profusion of lilies bathing in the sun,
While the starry drops, gathered on the lotus leaves, precociously plunge,
In a world where Narcissus, and Eros are one,
He walks along the way where the beauty has gone.
Follow the light's murmuring stream,
In rosy red flesh where the luminous rupture sets souls in dream,
Swim in the lake of light with the nymphs.
In burst of laughter where the nymphs plunge and the Muses swim,
Cross the light's rippling rings,
Join the maidens, the Maenads, and the Muses,
Who are different manifestations of the same moon-goddess, who lightens the lake with her silvery beam.
Go the way you hear the echo of the rustling wings,
And cross this lake lying in the boundary of real, myth and dream.

Worlds inside worlds where myth and dream intermingle

In the eternal ocean where things flow in space and create a pattern
in mind,
Senses are nothing but imprints of time,
Beliefs and faiths are nothing but illusion's harbours;
Flowers, grass, moisture, or heat that the mortals feel and touch,
And glimmers of light, that dazzle on eyes inside sparkling glass,
Carry only an illusory effulgence in blood.
Here, in the forest, the world is divided into worlds;
Stages after stages are convoluted in layers after layers of dreams
covered in mystic haze;
Crossing the boundary of the mind, where dream separates the real,
One enters a realm, where there is no shore, sight, sound or land.
Journey-man! you have already stepped inside a domain,
Where dream weaves myth with the real,
Here you see a lake, that scintillates beyond the visual world, that
man calls unreal.
Though here time is not yet effaced,
You are already moving in a time that is beyond the events defined
by causes and effects,
Here the mythical world moves carrying destiny and fate.
In a veil of dream, that cloaks all who approach the lake,
Here light penetrates a world where distinction between dream and
reality obliterates.

The soul of Eros or Narcissus, who has brought the dreaming man to this place,
Are one with the lighted lake's ethereal blaze.
Only the nymphs and the goddesses can swim in this lake,
They can bring the mortals to the invisible world through the gate floating in glittering rays.
Where in the shining depth of the distant hues,
The warmth of the flesh dip in pinkish dews,
Where in the murmuring waves' rippling touch,
Rise foams and droplets in water and dust,
The journey-man feels the warmth of the nymphs, who are rubescent rouge,
And sees the realm of the Muses where real and unreal interfuse.

Being confused and disoriented he moves deeper inside the forest, where instinct-bound life still lingers on. He apprehends the presence of a hunter.

The winged horse and the hunter's steed

Amidst the laugh of the beauties I hear rustling sounds of leaves,
And galloping strides of a horse through the reeds.
Like in swiftest hunter's curvetting leap,
Where air pithfully sweep,
Peaceless mind vaults enjoying an evil rider's strongest whips,
I hear in the forest scream and weep.
As the sun rises towards the meridian, as a golden chariot's burning wheel,
Like a king diademed with rays,
Flying in gold-winged waves,
As it crosses the shadows of a darkened will,
In the sun-parched rills,
Where shining pebble glitter and trill,
I hear the wriggling of a venomous serpent, who is lurking to kill.
In silvery webs, where darkness waves,
In bloodstained gaze, where wind streams and helplessly sway,
Where light and shadow bind and unbind heart in oscillating seize of murky feelings,
That free the mind and bind the body in rays,
In the sun-borne day,
I hear the hoof beats of a horse moving nearby in a galloping grace.
In the passing shadows in the changing temporal net,
In countless creatures' shadowy raids,

With wind dispersing from the web,
The mind dissolving in the lake,
The lace of light trembling and falling from the flesh,
In an awakening mind sky drifting in dreams' sleepless sails,
Where the universe is bearing the earth in a weightless space,
I hear the sounds of a galloping horse moving in restless pace.
In an inner haze,
In wind-borne wings,
Where the horse Pegasus star-ward swings,
Dreams harp on the strings,
The Muses sing,
In an airy will a fiery night sleeps in torments' twirl;
On shades, where galloping passions ruthlessly raid,
Darkness chase a flimsy mind like a hound,
On nature's eternal tale,
In stag-trails,
Where nimble-footed deer run alerting the forest with susurrant
sounds,
The beauty's frightened brisk breast pounds.
O Guide!
Tell me who is the hunter galloping around?

The huntsman

He is a man inflamed by the sun and crowned with gold,
Like a half-horse and a half- man, he is a terror for the peace-loving
souls.
Ridding on a horse and carrying a loaded gun,
He roams around in the forest in search for fun.
Killing the beauteous peacocks, stags and doves,
He stuffs his heart with blood stain while he proudly swings his robe.
In the burning daylight, where golden pheasants from branches
plunge,
He launches his attacks till the motions of blood reeling in the
feathers the sun beams stun.
He treasures the dead skulls, in whose antlers he hangs his robes,
And proudly counts the heads of deer he has chopped off with
swords.
With lions' skins he decorates his floors;
With statues of the panting chitas he guards his doors;
Around mirrors carved with golden mastiffs and paws of ferocious
boars,
He looks at himself decorated with badges, emblems, gilt cords and
ropes;
With peacocks' feathers he plumes his chapeau, casques and coats,
And boasts of the beauty of blue green fans, that decorate his armors
hanging on the walls as signs of his power and post.
He collects vases and jars with relief of monkeys, snakes and toads,
And drinks from carafes designed with naked whores.
To chase and kill is his sport,

Because he himself is an animal, who is chased by the ferocious
hounds of will's darkened force;
Like a restless beast he curvets and leaps,
Like poisonous weeds he chokes and kills all life bringing seeds,
Like a pitiful heart with monstrous macabre needs,
He rejoices in killing beauteous animals and birds, which sing and play
in the forests, or frolic in joy in sunlit meads.
More the sky, the green forest,
Those beauteous pheasants with green blue eyes and golden feathers
of light,
Mind's thirst for beauty try to cure,
More the peacocks spreading fans of colours human minds allure,
More the hunter feels confused by the mystery of the beauty of life,
And by killing, collecting, and possessing dead skulls, plucked
feathers, and peeled skins tries to feel comfortable and sure.
In his restless heart he always feels unsure,
Therefore he tries to win over himself with a ferocity of a will that
the powers of evil ensure.
In horses' hoofs he himself scoops,
In dust-wind streams,
He himself ruins;
In blood bathed roads,
He himself goads;
In whipping swishes,
He himself bruises;
In the tormenting force,
He himself is his sufferings source.
As he shoots down doves,
Chases to kill stags in panthers' strokes,
Plucks off plumes, that death's strings tune,

In his blood reeks human will's devilish fumes.

He seeks love as something to be fed to flesh and blood;

And as he gorges with a beastly passion's lust,

He feels abandoned and lonely in his heart.

He moves around the lake with a hope to rape the maidens who come to take their morning baths.

In the forest he has his hunter's hut,

Where he lives in a desolate home in order to fulfil his lust.

All women, who move in the forest, must keep against him an watchful guard.

The woman you love is also an object of his love,

He is also searching her where the forest is dense and dark.

Guide of the soul tells him about the beauty who has entered the forest in search of him

Like you, the beauty, who you have seen in the village, too is moving in this forest path.

She is also seeking the soul of love, who you have seen attired in twinkling stars.

Like Psyche searching Cupid - the winged god of love,

Who came to Psyche at night and left her at dawn,

The beauty is searching you in the part of the forest, where it is full of bushes of thorns.

Like West-wind, who has guided Psyche to the beauteous palace of dream,

Where Cupid has built the illusory realm decorated with golden beams,

In the nature's heart,

Where butterflies guide eyes to flowers,

The blooming petals open their beauties in sunbeam's touch,

Following the wind blowing over your heart,

Touching the earth and dust,

You have entered an illusory forest of beauty and love.

Like the bodiless Eros, who visits Pysche in dream,

While moonshine brings the power of the god of love in blood's ethereal stream,

With the break of each morning wearing radiance on his lighted wings,

When Eros appears over hearts' lakes and springs,

Leave the hunter's lust,

Follow the Muses and the swans for a greater path.

The beauty, who you love, is walking bewildered in the forest path.

Guard yourself against the serpent of the dark,

Withdraw from passion and lust, that drag mortals to illusory joy and mirth,

Leave your search for the sense-bound love,

And move with me towards the mountain path.

Guide tells him about the net that destiny has spread in this illusory forest

Remember that the bewitching beauty, that you may feel close by,
Though beyond your sight,
Is nothing but a lascivious mind's dazzling light.
More you will try to come its close,
More illusion will bind you with its luciferous force.
Remember, love that intoxicates the body with warmth and sweat,
Is nothing but the shadow of the serpent of night,
That appears in light wearing passion's illusory fret.
As you have entered this forest you are subjected to fate,
And as I have said,
Here the treachery of destiny no one will be able to evade.
When you have entered this place through the illusory haze,
The destiny has followed you in a complex maze.
Be sure, before you come out of the forest trail,
You will not meet the beauty you search,
And see her unveiled.
Remember, the hunter, who is moving in the shadow,
Where senses in darkness dwell,
Is a vicious prowler prowling in search of everything that he can quell.
He is notorious and fell;
If you come close to him he will make your life a hell.
Remember, as you will move deeper in this realm illusions will grow

around illusions,
Dreams will penetrate into dreams,
The real will sink in another reality that is neither real or dream,
The myth will juxtapose with the world that you have felt or seen,
And at the end you will not be able to find a way to cross the stream,
Where destiny controls events by pulling magical strings.

The goddess of life and death

O dreaming earth's living hues, ardors that release man from pain!

The daughter of the azure sky, queen of the night and renewer of the earth with torment and rain!

O vaporous, ethereal, chimerical silvery night's moonlit maid!

Demeter's daughter!

Hades' treasure!

Aphrodite and Persephone only in different names!

O intoxication in floral abundance!

Fleur-de-lis...eau-de-cologne of the sleeping mind - sane or insane!

Love's smell returning from the Hell!

Perfumed air's delightful sprinkle!

Luxuriant freshness from the petals, pistils and stems!

O beauty's creator!

The awakening eyes' mascara, cosmetic and flame!

The prefect perfume of the mind!

The sweetest flowers' scents!

The ruptured mind's benzoin and incense!

The maiden returning to the earth adorned with amethyst, ruby, topaz, diamond and gems!

While the light in joy and pleasure pitch nigh on the acanthus leaves,

The swallows twitter and the songbirds flee,

The poppies drowse in the winnowing breeze,

The feelings part and depart in wordless wings,

The winged horse carry the souls to the source of poesy in Helicon's spring,

Like Aristaeus, the will to touch and grasp the beauteous bride of
Orpheus in the sunbeam springs,
The bee-hives swarm on flowers as Orpheus sings,
Dead leaves, insects, worms and creatures with unlovely forms:
Beetles, weevils, cicadas and scorpions,
Gnaw, bore, feed on the sappy foliage,
Chew and burrow the roots as if to reach nature's prenatal tomb,
Rusts, smuts, mildews,
Wilts, sooty molds cause canker blighting life's scents and hues,
And bring in the mind the decaying life's sorrowful news.
O beauty perfumed with Circe's herbs!
Here I hear the evil writhes,
Bitter desires- like eternal guilt- gallop and leap,
Where Orpheus sings I hear the modulations, resonance of the
Siren's songs that put man to sleep,
In the discords of the sounds of the fleeing birds that plunge in shad-
ows,
I listen to the wing-beats of agony,
The quivering flight of the light and the shadow in darkness deep.
In the world where death and life are entangled, beauty and ugliness
are inseparable aspects of the same,
Real and the virtual worlds are intricately enmeshed,
The life passing and the life, that has passed,
Or, going and coming are entangled into a labyrinthine maze.

Feeling bewildered and afraid, the journeyman hurries to find a way to escape the sight of the hunter and steps into the realm of the Muses.

The Muse of Poetry bathing in a stream

In the marvelous bosom where rays touch beauty in peace,
The naked flesh feels the kiss of silvery breeze,
In the soft skin light intoxicates the eyes,
In happiness, like shining marbles, the rocks touch her feet,
Like Pygmallion's Galatea carved from white ivory,
Her naked arms, loin, shoulder, slender neck, and rounded breast
display nature's marvelous artistry.
In the white flesh, where the pinky dots in the breast the life's secret
close,
In bosom's unknown tints pleasure touches the eyes as a pinkish rose,
In the lighted breast, where in virgin warmth in happiness pulls off
all secrets of the flesh,
In veneration the golden light gleams on her tress,
Under the bent knees in the wafting breeze,
In an unstable image moving in light's and shadow's tremulous rings,
In fluidity of the water beauty's image disperses and sings.
Here I peacefully watch:
She tilts her head to the crevice on the rock,
While the running water in the stream of emotion blobs and plops;
As the sprinkling water touches her face,
The rainbow her body embraces;
She bends, bows, touches in gentleness the overhanging rock's

untarnished glaze;
Like a bewitching mineral vibrating in rays,
Like a marble statue in communion with the flesh,
In the crystal clear water, like topaz, she gathers in the palm
pale-yellow light's bright shining blaze.
In the palm's hollow concave space,
Where she tries to imprison the movements of the water running out
of a groove split in a place,
While the changing time never stays immobile and always stoops,
An unceasing continuity of motion fingers evade,
Time flying in touch and feelings restate the ephemerality of the
sandbed,
The eternal beauty stands as a statue in her beauteous blaze.
In the unkempt hair, loosen in the light, as her beauty Galatea recalls,
Along the bosom the running streams trace the temporal fall,
Lifting the arms in serenity as she feels the water's, wind's and
light's caress,
Dividing the running streamlet through the fingers in the shining
runlets,
As she bathes in my eyes where the sunlight cascade,
I watch her as the goddess with whom Pygmalion wished to sleep in
a mortal world of blood and flesh,
Without being apprehensive about the mortal gaze,
Like a stag she in my mind a hunter's passions raises.

The sculptor Pygmalion once fell in love with Venus. As a mortal he could not get the goddess of love as his wife. So he created an ivory sculpture of the goddess, which was so perfect and life-like that it one day became alive. The journeyman stares at the beauty of the Muse, like Pygmalion watching his ivory statue.

The sculptor Pygmalion's dream

As this chaste morning's light in purity brims in her breast,

Her soft skin glistens like silken screen on the flesh,

On the shoulder the mystery of her beauty looms over her chest,

In the nipples, where in passion's bloom the eyes come to a rest,

A desire to sleep with her comes as Pygmalion's ivory maiden,

In whose breast the goddess of love had once breathed life to hold the sculptor,

Who had refrained from love of mortal women,

In love's eternal arrest.

In the forest surrounded by hills,

Like an earthen pot that never fills,

Where, like a naked nymph, the virgin forest fills its rills,

In the murmuring streams she tilts the pitchers filled with human will,

Inside an inner void where silences hush,

A trembling thirst for beauty and love bubbles, burbles in the mind as a stream of desire flows in gush.

Like the weeping willow's branching leaves I wish to reach to her knees,

Like Pygmalion I wish to embrace her and kiss,

Like polished pebbles, shells and fish, I wish to touch her feet as many times as I wish,

In her body leaning on the rock in the stream, that drags my mind in a
bed in a mysterious sleep,
I wish to worship her beauty in flesh and blood,
Where in my heart an altar for love I keep.
In this day-dreaming in a pink couch, where Galatea sleeps,
The body bends and touches her with its lips,
The fingers again and again strokes her as if to sink in the softness of
her limb,
As her nakedness burns as incense,
The surface of the flesh, yielding to the pressure of the fingers, sinks
in a bewitching whiteness,
Beyond the depth of the veins,
In the vast expanse of the mind love expands like a flame,
The heart beats like a hunter as well as a hunted game.
Here as her eyes kindle and spark,
Like scented smell of musk the scents of her flesh attract,
As the ivory maiden of art,
With passion and love of Tyrian blood,
An amorous delight ruptures,
Passion's pomegranate bursts,
The seeds covered with redness of the pulp drop as drops of eternal lust.
On the marble stone where she bathes,
The light flutters like wings of bathing birds in a lake,
The water springs from the rock,
Stoops in the stream,
And becomes one with the vibrating blaze.
Immersed in the water,
In the reflections on the treacherous waves, that always break in the
touch of the rays,
Mirroring the streamlets in the breasts that change in directions as

they run from the neck to the navel in search of ways,
Holding the motion of the water and wind in the naked flesh's
writhing charm,
Like a bathing beauty seizing the passionate eyes in an insatiable burn,
She holds my eyes, which I fail to turn.
Like a stag distracted by the bathing sounds of the silvery maid,
As an illusory deer with dappled skin moves in the sun,
I see the maiden or the Muse,
Watch like a hunter,
In front of the naked flesh both as the deer and the hunter I feel one.
In shades where the warmth of the rays extinct,
And the cool breeze nature's happiness brings,
Under the feet the rustling leaves awaken the sounds fallen in a dream,
The ineffable desire wafts in the wind,
In a tranquil stillness the rocks prostrate on the path where the shad-
ows walk on the stream,
As air stirs the lust ,
The solitary gusts of wind pant, gasp, expire, and touch the breaths in
sudden jumping bursts,
The chest thrusts forward and the lungs inflate,
In a lightning quickness a fear appears on her face.

Apprehending the presence of an unwelcome visitor the bathing Muse hides herself and enquires about the intruder.

The Muse, who possesses divine power of diving, being frightened gives warning to the stranger.

O Stranger! Cross no further than the rock in front of which
you stand,
Otherwise you will dissipate and disappear in the sand,
You will be annihilated if I drop the pebbles that I hold in my hands.
(She picks up the pebbles from the bed of the stream.)
How did you enter this place?
Sinking below the stir of the world, where the words their sounds
forget,
In this realm, which Hermes guards by the power of illusion,
that he creates,
Only when he sends heralds for the souls of the greatest
musicians and poets,
They can come and drink water of this spring where I bathe.

ike a hunter drawn by a beautiful stag

I am a wanderer, who feels disoriented and lost.
In an exalted moment, when I lifted my eyes to extol the beauty of
the immense glitter,
That quivered on the lake as a radiant ball,
Where I made a momentary halt,
In the silvery splendour of the vibrating waves,
My eyes lost contact with the figure, whom I was following along the
bank of the lake.
In search of a beauty, who still burns in the mind as love's burning char,
I followed this veiled figure dressed in a robe that scatters lights like
glittering spangles of stars.
In the immense glitter when I untimely glanced,
The infinite blue void joining the earth and the sky in an azure hue,
My confusion enhanced.
In an undulating lustrous robe I saw water, wind, and light swelled,
And redoubling the shaking of a trembling body, he disappeared
from my sight throwing in the lake a glittering veil.
Then I met an artist, who was painting on a canvas colorful lines and
curves,
I sought his help:"Where did the guide of the soul fade?
And which way I should move to find my way?"
Amidst the glitter of interlacing waves,
As I asked the artist for help,
Wearing a quivering countenance he gazed,
As if to find a link between the real and the mind's unreal blaze,

He asked me to swim through the waves to the nymphs and the
Muses bathing in the lake.
Strange! Though I heard their laughs,
On artist's canvas saw the lines and the sketches,
Where colours held his spirit in a seize,
In the lake I saw no nymph or maid.
Strange! Though there was no one around,
Like a little shell drinking water of the ocean,
As if a libation to the burning cells,
My body pursued desire, and thirst, and sought lactescent warmth
from an unseen breast,
In water... as if, in water within...!
Where in silence relentless ripples of desires dispersed and perished,
I was drawn to this place where I see you undressed.
In the viscous liquid's bubbling drag,
Desires inside desires dragged me to see you naked like a hunter
behind his stag.

Dream to sleep with the goddess

Your breast yields to my eyes the forms of cells that in clasping
hands sense's pleasures repel,
Like the alluring charm of foams of a violent sea kindled by the
golden sunset,
Your bosom attracts, deceives, drags me to a dream,
Where lying in a northern light in a sand-beach
I wish to make love with a goddess without form or weight.
In the confinement of the ethereal bed
I kiss, respire, exhale, inhale and disperse sounds,
As if, in an innocence's paradise, like a bird flying unrestrained,
I seek freedom, where all bondage of morality is exempt from
ethical bounds.
In emotion's credulous bonds the lips draw and haul,
In the softness of the flesh that pleasures refresh,
In assurance of joy,
I pause, repeat...
In a strange metamorphosis feel turned into the foams washing over
a beach
And then returning to the sea.
Like in a sand-beach not visited for centuries,
Where a stranger in a wilderness in emotion's delight foams embrace,
Serenading the night's idyll songs lie in the beach to feel under the
midnight light the sky's sublime rest,
As love's cool dews dwindle in the flesh,
In a sand-beach of dream I feel your arms fold across my chest.

Like in bedchamber's sleeping scent,

Where the hidden shadows cross and bend and copulate in rhythms with the darkness of the sense,

The sky carries the scents of the flesh and rhythms of the flames,

The desires...inside...outside...

In the vastness of time and space,

Before the morning bursts forth in supernal blaze,

And the cosmic void the nightly passion's aversion confesses,

Wish to bend on a body to undress and violate a goddess,

In whose face the stars, as desires of the earthly will, twinkle and vacillate.

O ignis fatus of the night!

Will-o'-the -wisps!

Do not be afraid of the passion of these human eyes.

Tell me who are you,

Who has dragged me out of my hiding like a dream dragging the day out of the night?

The curse thrown by the Muse

No mortal knows this path where I bathe in the stream from where the springs of Helicon surge,
Only the Graces - the nymphs of brilliance, joy, and bloom,
Who rupture human hearts in the spring after the wintry gloom,
Or the poets, and the musicians whom the Muses teach their divine art,
Know this secret path.
Here the eyes of poets open towards the spiritual world once they receive the spiritual water's sprinkling touch.
The footsteps of the beauty, who you have heard, could be of Psyche,
Who is searching Cupid after he had abandoned her in the palace of golden pillars and ivory arch,
Latticed with silvery fretwork of immortal art.
As she could not hold her temptation,
The invisible winged god, who kindles all hearts with his golden arrow from the quiver of the dark,
Had abandoned her in the mortal's path.
The goddess of love, in whose womb Eros had taken his birth,
Had cursed her with an unworthy love,
Because being a mortal she had seduced the god of love.
Or, it could be the footsteps of Eurydice,
Who is following Orpheus from the cavern of Tainaron to the light of the earth,
Where blossoming gardens,
Sparkling fountains,
Sunlit laurels,

White winged birds,
The gentle scents of the fragrant air lull life with water's, air's and
light's enchanting urge.
The valley of Avernus, through which Orpheus brings his beloved
Eurydice to the world of light and love,
Is the valley of the night from which springs this stream,
Where I bathe in a mythical world between reality and dream,
That join the heaven and the earth.
It is a crossroad between light and dark.
On this side of the stream where I take my bathe,
All dissolve in dreams,
The silvery glimmers with which the fountains spout in streams,
Divide this forest, valley, and rocks from the real world with an
illusory screen.
On the other side, darkened souls roam and raid,
The senses restore the reality from sand and dust governed by fate.
Go to the philosopher's path,
There you may meet the soul, who you search.
But, before you move, as a punishment for desiring the love of the
goddesses,
You must bear my curse:
You will be blinded by the mortal beauty, who you search,
And you will not be able to see the beauty, who you love, in flesh
and blood,
Before the illusions of the forest life have passed.
As I sprinkle water from this stream on your heart,
Darkness will anchor in the path,
The beauty will mistake you as the hunter who is hunting in the part
of the forest that is dark.

In attempting to escape the curse of the Muse the journey-man enters into deeper darkness inside the forest

While my eyes, anxious of the fear of being blinded by the very
beauty I search,
Gaze in all directions to escape the destiny that lurches,
The faraway sound of the galloping horse,
In the distance, murmuring in the air,
Create an uncertain anxiety and fear.
Here, where passions still plunge in the will,
The lights and shadows surround me as a frightened deer standing
helpless and still,
Like in a nightmarish dream,
The anxieties loosening a cascading stream,
In a turbulent wind,
Ensnare the flesh and blood in the battle of the senses flowing along
the spleen.
O beauty shining deep in the heart!
O Muse!
Man's suffering's ineffable charge!
Do not blind these eyes where dreams rush in search of beauty and love.
In this unknown forest on Earth,
Dark chasms of fear threaten me with a darkness that all things engulf.
I see no paths,
Through the dense foliage, where shades of the darkness cloak the
overhanging branches,

And all narrow indications of paths fade in a depth through which
no human being seemed to have passed,
Leaves plunge from all sides to close the daylight,
Wherever I move darkness filters into the eyes.
As I walk, beneath the feet the erring steps fail to follow the relations
of time,
O Muse! The goddess of poem and art!
Why do you want to bring upon this curse on the man searching a
way to beauty and love?
Around me I hear confused movements of feet,
As if, the beauty lost in an imperceptible mist,
More the sounds come near,
More I struggle with the conflicts of choice between submitting the
soul to love's foolish snare,
Or, to the will of the Guide who can bring man to a realm beyond
sense's flare.
As I try to find my way,
In indistinct murmurs of waves,
In my gaze the forest its illusions spread,
As if, asleep in darkened haze,
I am awake in a dream where I happen to see and hear.
With the rustling sounds of the leaves,
Where the dead branches crackle under the trampling feet of a steed,
The destiny seems to move near,
I must somehow come out from here!
In the distance as I hear beauty's footsteps,
Apprehend the presence of the hunter prancing as a restless rake,
With sweating feet and palm,
I must hurry to get out of the forest before the destiny fulfils its curse.
In the winding path, where my feet in confusion twist and turn,

215

I must run.

(Being unable to find a way out.)

O soul!

Why do you confuse my steps?

Why do you still beguile me with the beauty that has drawn me to the lake,

And want to bring upon me a treacherous fate?

Here the paths in delirium divide,

The anguish spread as a confinement of greater and greater size;

Wherever I try to spring,

The paths turn into paths,

The darkness entwines into darkness,

Binding the feet in invisible multiplicity of rings,

The soul plunges in the net of invisible strings.

O eyelids! Remain open!

O mind! Hold courage!

O ears! Listen!

Are those sounds of the footsteps approaching from "this" way or "that" way ?

Are the sounds of the galloping horse closing in or receding away?

Is it the beauty?

Is it the hunter?

The senses seem to give alarm...

I wonder who comes!

Shall I surrender?

If not, in which direction shall I run?

While the journeyman is trying to find a route of escape from the darkness of the forest, the beauty is approaching the same place where the journeyman is caught into bewilderment.

Beauty's fear for the hunter

The hunter, like a hawk, roams in search of a sexual mate,

O soul! let not my strength to battle with evil fade,

Let not my search for love turn into fear and hate.

As I feel the hands of evil are approaching as invisible embrace,

Fear grips my soul,

As I feel the breath of a serpent blowing over my shoulder and tress,

A moaning wind of guilt crosses over my breast,

As the hunter approaches like an apparition,

The shadows weaken my vision:

While fears a deep darkness enhance,

The clouds, floating in the mind, reflect no more the light,

An ineffable drag for serpentine love spread over the senses,

And extends everywhere in a darkness with an unending expanse.

I do not understand the meaning of the destiny that seems to draw

me inside the darkness of the forest with its inescapable claws,

It drags my bodiless spirit with its flawless laws.

In this darkened forest where dream's webs turn and twine,

The motions join, disjoin, crisscross in causal lines,

And then cross over the boundaries of space and time,

O soul! The bizarre sleepwalker !

I know not what destiny is going to bring,

I wonder, would it end in a meeting with the hunter, or the soul, who is divine?

I apprehend the presence of a restless hunter,

Who is riding passion's stormy tide,

Like a serpent, he is wreathing beside.

Be alert mind!

Plunge not in passion's delight,

Seek no adventure!

Move back!

In the bosom where the images of love blossom,

Where the heart abjures all ethics and creed,

And by sinning man feel free,

O heart! Do not permit pernicious desires that fly as Aristaeus' bees,

Do not heed to the sinful voice, that led to the birth of Adonis from the tree.

O creeping flesh!

O sleeping eyes!

The dreaming foe!

Hear the warnings: Halt! Move back!

Do not step where queen bee destroys its consort as the drone!

Remember! She is passion's rancorous whore,

Who kills her mate after love is over.

Do not follow the trap of destiny,

That killed Adonis, in the disguise of a boar.

You, who is moving in the darkness, hear!

If you move any more near,

You will regret your search for love in pain and tear,

Woe will tear you the way hunter Actaeon was torn by Artemis' hounds as a deer.

Abandon your pursuit,

The momentary pleasure and joy that you may gain,

Will haunt you as dark sprites, that bring to life its unredeemable pains,
The nectar you search will turn out to be your bane,
You will drown in the very nectar where you search love in vain.
Hold your temptations for love, that I fear more than I love,
Though it may be tempting to the heart,
Love, that is full of deceit and disgust,
That brings woe, scorn, and repentance for lust,
Will not go unavenged,
You will get as return of the joy of fulfilling passion
Unsurpassable destiny's curse and pain.
Hark! the hoof beats of the hunter's stag!
The desolate passion's intimate drag!
I feel, I am tethered as a prey for the hunter,
But, whoever you are,
Believing that I am a passion's stag,
Do not violate the law of the divine world in the encounter.

The beauty encounters the journeyman in the thick darkness. Believing that he is the hunter, she has been trying to escape, the beauty repels him away. The journeyman falls on a bush of thorn and becomes blind. Understanding that the curse of the Muse has been fulfilled, he screams. It helps the hunter to locate them.

The beauty encounters the merciless hunter

Lift your hands off the man,
Let him lie there in thorn alone stricken by sorrow,
Ravaged and injured.
Cling not to the part,
That is my counterpart,
Let him crumble into the dust,
Broken, shattered and insecure.
Let him remain doomed in misery alone and feel aghast,
Let him see through the darkness of the void afar,
Where he has once sought the music of the stars;
Let fear ruffle his heart through the eyes blind and dark,
While like a nymph made of flesh and blood you will unrobe casting away the beauty's veil,
Let him dream of swans, Muses and goddesses in the blindness' hell.
When in blood and flesh I shall enjoy the loveliest maid, man has seen ever,
Let his heart quiver,
Let the Muses shut his eyes in a dream of paradise,
While in the body only pain and agony will shiver;
Let the coagulating blood spread the beams of light,
That he has seen in the twinkling dew-strewn lake and river.

He is a day-dreamer,
In paintings, sculptures and imageries,
He desires to leave the real world behind,
Where the nature, through the senses, things' beauties unfold,
In shades and lights he seeks life, where dreams the world enfold.
In the forest where sunbeams rush,
The streams gush in rainbows opening colourful senses' flush,
Leaving the real world- felt, seen, and touched,
He dreams of another world in an emptiness, that expands and
becomes greater in the heart.
Beauty! Leave this blind man behind,
Come away from the gloom of an dreaming mind,
He is doomed forever:
Let him reflect about the meaning of life:
Who? What for? Why?
He will not find any answer whatsoever.
In my world there exists no god, demon, or ghost,
They exist only as dreaming mind's phantoms and the real world's jokes.
Everything in the world are governed by chances,
That are mutable by natural force,
A man possessing strength of mind does not presume any other force
but the power that determine nature's course.
Here only force against force makes things stand,
When strength against strength matches the human plan,
It is even possible to build a pyramid on sand.
Here life is only a collection of tangled impulses brought forth by
random chance,
And freedom is nothing but senses' wanton dance.
Here victor's will guides the moral force,
And the feeble mind's dreaming love ends in a darkened hole.

Behold beauty!

In my blue eyes' watchful glance

See the noble feature of man born to dominate the earth like the golden sun,

Like a hero from the antiquity,

See in my arms the glamour of power, which is destined to triumph.

I am a horseman in whose body a valiant soul is enclosed,

I only wish I was with an immortal life endowed!

When I see a woman of your beauty,

Like Castor seeking Phoebe as his consort,

On my milky white steed I gallop in speed to seek passion's warm comfort,

In swiftest riding,

I come out of my hiding,

Quickly dismounting,

In swift striding,

I appear from the dark forest as one of the twin brothers: Pollux and Castor.

When like Diana's priestess any beauty tries to tear her away from my arms in scorn and hate,

Like one of the twin stars of Gemini I watch in the moonlight of the heart Hilaeira and Phoebe's rape:

Like Castor spreading his arms around Phoebe's shining ivory neck,

The voluptuous legs and lifting her on the back of the white horse standing in a prancing state,

While I bestride on the white horse,

Pollux, the bright star in Gemini, watches in the whiteness of Hilaeira's breast the passion of human flesh.

Like the breasts, the buttocks, the bellies and the arms inside the silken satin and the lustrous clothes,

Where the denuded bodies of the beauties sparkle revealing the beauties like Hilaeira and Phoebe,
While the moonlight of passion gleams and senses stun,
As burning power of the corporal sun,
I carry off beautiful maidens without caring whether they are priestesses, or witches, or nuns.
As the sun with the moon,
Silver with gold,
The woman shaped in fleshy soft white mould,
Features true beauty only when it is wrapped in human passion's dazzling fold.
Dressed in rings, pearls, bracelets and strings,
Woman's beauty brings life's naked impulses that are real - not any dream.
Like the scene when Phoebe Pollux's power declines,
And in an attempt to free herself from his arms on the earth reclines,
Like the moon with a shaft of light probing the depth of the night,
In her half-naked loin creating in flesh tremulous delight,
My eyes probe the passion of the earthly life in the depth of the sight.

The abduction and ravishment

Do not try to leave my grip,
It can even a lion tame,
Be wise,
Do not fight,
Submit to the passion's flame.
Do not try to hurt,
Learn to love passion that you carry in your heart,
Act no ill,
Let life its pleasure fulfil.
Do not fear,
Let my arms in your body my desires bear.
Do not get dismayed,
Try to overcome the tide of hate.
Free yourself from the narrow view of things,
Stop the tumults of your helpless swings,
Calm your nymphalid wings and bathe as a dove in my passion's
spring.
O beauty who all victors claim!
Do not fill your heart with shame,
Do not remove passionate hands with disdain,
A sweet sleep in the arms, that have won world's wealth, gold and fame,
Will relieve you from pain.
As my arms twist around your body moist and wet,
A beastly power rises in muscles releasing warmth and sweat.
Beauty!

Remember that my mind is free from moral laws,
Like a leopard once I release the power of my body no deer can escape my claws.
If you wish to escape a harsher predicament,
Ease your resistance.
Remember in front of power holds no moral clause,
Even the nymphs will be forced to break Diana's laws.
I am resolved to win beauty by power and force,
Nothing will be able to change this course.
Though you wear in your breast a sparkling cross as a divine sign,
In Satan's garden there is no other way,
To Satan you must resign.

Tathagata's meditation along the forest path

In this island there was a forest. It was the forest of life and death where trees drew nourishments from the soil and energy from the sky. It was the forest bound in a serpentine fate of life, death and resurrection. It was the path through which one could discover how the whole creation was sustained. At dawn when I had entered the forest I had seen myself split as two but strangely united as one. On one side there was a shadow of myself and on the other side the light that was casting the shadow. I was divided between darkness and light. Though there was no darkness and light the objects around created this illusion of darkness and light. As light accompanies darkness and darkness accompanies light I was my own companion. All around I saw the life in the forest moving through such contradictions. The body was contradicting the spirit, the passion was contradicting with the desire to renounce, will was contradicting with itself. Truly it was a maze of the real and the unreal. I was seeing myself and then disappearing from myself and becoming someone else. I was never sure when I was awake and when I had fallen in a dream I knew not when I was within myself or outside myself, when I was one or the another, when I was shadow or the light, when I was separate and not-separate from the rest, whether fingers of some unknown destiny was regulating my wandering or I was causing the happenings by my own choices and actions. I was not sure if I was betraying myself or I was being betrayed by someone else. I only knew that I was searching myself, moving towards home through a riddle of existence that was difficult to comprehend.

Here love, woman, beauty all seemed to be riddles. The male and the female were often the same who were reversing the roles as myself in pursuit of the other and the other in pursuit of me. When I desired she appeared in the higher path and when I sought her in the higher path she appeared as desire. There was a thirst for love for the other half and at the same time a love for the self. One enraptured the feelings from the senses, the other entrapped the soul in the senses ropes. One was the sun and the other was the moon engaged in an eternal battle of the mythical serpent and the eagle.

In this forest there was a lake- a lake that was also me. Beside a secluded stream it was the lake of Eros where Narcissus had seen himself in multiple images scattered in reality, myth and dream and Psyche had thrown herself in the longing for love that only death could redeem. This lake was also a part of the sea that had penetrated through the rocks and stones and reached this forest in the realm of myth, reality and dream. Here images formed according to the will that surged with Eros - the incomprehensible irrationality that drew man to deeper and deeper domains of the consciousness that merged with the unconscious world of archetypal symbols and dream. Every step brought me to many paths in many domains in different psychic states. Gradually the whole forest turned out to be a kind of tarantula's web, spinning in different threads different patterns of images that entangled the existence deeper and deeper in ad infinitum layers in a sea lying in the psychic depth. Every path was knitted with many other paths. It was difficult to know which path to choose. They all seemed different and ultimately seemed to come back to the same. Groping for a path I had wandered in this multiple reality as the ultimate man.

There were incredible beauties, the hunters, the stags, the hounds, many colourful vegetating, and monstrous shrieks of the birds and animals sending adverse signs, and fugitive trying to escape. It was a veritable labyrinth of the blind paths entangling the wanderer in the complex maze of the existence that spanned from time and space to domains outside time and space. There were melodies, ecstasies, notes, that diverted the vision in different ways. The huntsmen were struggling with the beasts. The will to exist was struggling with the will to perish; the will to life was seeking the will to death. It was a forest of veritable contradictions that created a labyrinthine maze. In this labyrinth I had wandered as the man with multiple awarenesse of the life that varied with the depth of the journey of the soul through the domains, what man calls the domains of the "conscious" and "unconscious" in and outside the boundaries of time and space. You may ask what I had been seeking? What is the meaning of this labyrinthine journey where everything exist in a non-temporality with present, past and future as indistinguishable and the reality as an illusion of the will that gradually disappears with the knowledge of the existence that is an emptiness infinitely vast? What is the meaning of this journey where most journeymen will go astray and perish in the blindness of the heart?

Hear about the way through this labyrinth and the blind alleys of the mind where man may get entrapped unless man makes use of the higher power of the mid that illumines the world and the different layers of the inner darkness and light. With this power it is possible to see the greater depth of the sea from where I have risen and arrived. In trying to escape from the world where there exists no physical means to escape, in willing to free oneself from the symbolic world where many different worlds are enmeshed, in confronting the monstrous existence that is the invisible aspect of oneself, in trying to move beyond the domain where all movements return again to the labyrinthine maze, there lies the process of self-knowledge, the awareness of the multiplicity of the whole in many different folds. One can know oneself as submerged in a multifold reality of existence, whose experience and knowledge can never be exhausted by any one.One can be aware of oneself as the part of the whole infinitely spread in worlds after worlds, in different levels of consciousness as a part of the ultimate man, who is beyond all knowing and understanding by the individual minds, who possesses restricted awareness and experience of life. By making this journey one will know one's infinite possibilities as the free will moving with the whole in infinite numbers of paths and understanding that in wandering, dreaming and confronting the monster like forces in the labyrinth there lies the possibility of being illumined and enlightened as the great rising star. Those wanderers who do not succumb to this fear are drawn closer to the height of the ultimate man to be illumined by a light from where I have risen to bring man the knowledge of enlightenment of the great mind.

O passersby! Do not wander in the darkness. In this forest I had found the river to where many rivers meet – always flowing aloft and flowing alone. It is the river of the spirit all souls are beckoned. It is the river of the will that branches in innumerable paths and penetrates different domains and heights of the mind creating the sensations of reality and forming illusions of dreams. Innumerable are its tributaries. One never exactly knows where they go. As you, I, and he the tributaries of the mind run from dendrites to dendrites, bifurcate in innumerable branches, penetrate the grounds, rocks, mountains and evaporate in nothingness before one is able to know where they are going and what there is to know. They move through thousands and thousands of trodden and untrodden paths, willing to return and willing to go away, without really knowing what is the best way. But the man of true knowledge knows the slopes through which one may pass and meet the sea from where I come and in which will may be freed from the tumults of the confusions on the way.

It is the river of becoming, the mind's mirror reflecting in innumerable spangles of rays the will that breaks as foams and churns with the opposing forces of the nature and mind creating emotions and thoughts. In innumerable fold of mirrors it commands the rays and reflects the beauty of the mind of the ultimate mind. The living creatures, non-living too, see in this river the sacrifice. Like trembling leaves in the sunlight, the images of the birds or the beasts or the human kind tremble , break, revolve and rotate, creating unfamiliar shapes in the waves disperse never truly knowing where they go. In this stream of the will I had gazed at the multifold images of myself, always uncertain in shapes, always breaking away to join with the spangles that float in the sunshine over the currents dancing with the rays. I had thus seen beauty and love flowing through the forest as part of myself divided and separate in the other half of the mirror where in perishing man understands love and loving man perishes in the stream moving towards the ultimate way. It is a love that creates no desire.

It rises in the breast as the light that warms up the body and illumines the whole mind. With it man turns into a river that originates in the sea and flows to the sea carrying the fragments of the body as amorphous dust floating in a golden light moves in the mind. There is no suffering in this willing; there is no pain and joy. Eternally recurring it is the will that redeems man from the suffering of existence that you have already heard. You may ask who is He? How shall you know Him? In this multifold mirror which image of Him you will grasp as the true image of Him?

In this streaming will how shall you still your thoughts and contemplate on the love that stills every movements? How in this multitudinous movements will you be able to grasp Him as the One, who remains unmoved? These questions are not easy to answer and even more difficult to comprehend with answers that are based on the experience of man. Although I am the enlightened man I do not know my own nature through the process of human thoughts. I exist domains and domains beyond where human thoughts, as willed and known by man, are non existent and there is no willing, in the sense man wills, at all. I have already spoken of the multiplicities of the images and the worlds where my existence extends that are not finite, countable in numbers and not possible to fathom within a framework of knowledge based on the concepts of separation in time and space. I am the shadow of myself as well as the light of the rays from where the shadows spring. I am the innumerable spangles of rays and the waves dancing with the rays - streaming from a stillness deep within that can never be approached with the knowledge or thoughts. Down the surface of the sea where you see me and hear me speak I am a movement towards stillness passing through the infinite stages of the will that in the depth of the psychic domains gradually ceases to will. There is no form that is more real or false than any form in which you may my image contemplate. As I have said before, He is infinite, unknowable and beyond comprehension of even the sages. Follow me! You may comprehend me better at the end.

Hunter's paradise and dreamer's hell

In a self-willed folly I have followed beauty's magic song,
And now my eyes are pierced by multitudinous thorns.
O Guide! Inside the visible world there exist many invisible worlds
as you said,
But I refused to listen to your advise because I was followed by my
destiny that had to this blindness led.
When in the pain-stricken eyes' blood bathed cave,
The darkness penetrates like in a grave,
I feel alone and desolate in the hands of fate;
When in the charred hollow sight awful shadows' anarchy rise,
From the depth of the soul arrive darkened tides,
And lash the soul with lawless pride;
In the mystery's deepening gloom,
I feel like a man shattered and doomed.
O darkness!
While the eyes remain blind and paralyzed,
The lights adorn the beauty in the hunter's eyes,
He departs along the sunlit road abducting the beauty by force,
The awful shadows float in destiny's invisible course;
The hunter gallops hurling triumphant laughter in dales and vales,
When the destiny has imprisoned my dreaming eyes in a darkness
covered with misery's veil;
This forest seems to be a hunters' paradise, and the dreamer's hell.
O darkness! In pride bestriding on a steed,
As the hunter flees in triumphant speed,

I do not know what I should believe:

God, destiny, which no mortal eyes can see?

Or, freewill and the reality where man lives like Aristaeus, who raises passion's bees?

O darkness!

Like a man of a tragic play when I feel helpless and bleed,

I do not know how shall come out of the forest.

When destiny has dragged me in a hideous path where all efforts to undo it will turn in vain,

All attempts to free oneself will instead captivate man in more chains,

In this dream-veiled lane,

I see no path, where my misery may end.

I do not know how I shall come out of this despair and pain.

O blindness permeating the cells!

Penetrating deep in the eyes' bloodfull trails!

As pains fork out as glow,

In the eyes the blood's horrors flow.

In this bleeding world,

O oozy moss, flowers, foliage!

Breathing in the tormented soul's wafting breeze!

As the hunter carries off the beauty in skye speed,

And moves towards the sun strewn path in his steed,

In my mind an anarchy rides,

Chaos wings itself to the height, where darkness creates tumultuous tides;

In soul's bewilderment in a tomb of pain,

Strange! I still search love and beauty in vain!

Life is such a forest, where love oscillates between the serpentine tempta-
tions of flesh and blood and the love that lies beyond the realm of the sen-
sual pleasures. It is similar to the love of the twins -Castor and Pollux for
the moon-goddess and her priestesses. These twins - one of mortal origin,
like Castor, and other, Pollux, whose father is a god- are inseparable pair,
who represent the unity of love in the heaven and the earth. Like the stars
in the Constellation Gemini they ignite the human hearts and drive man
to seek passionate love as well as bring wisdom to control the sensual de-
sires. It is the unavoidable destiny of life in the forest, where Castor and
Pollux appear. The Centaurs, the half-horse-half-man follow the twins
in their hunts. They roam eternally in the forest. While the twin want to
bring an end to the destiny, the destiny pursues the twins. After the man
becomes blind, the journey in search of love and beauty in the physical
plane comes to an end. A vision of love and beauty, which transcends the
physical realm, now appears in the mind. He sees the beauty through the
contemplative power of the mind in the domain of ideas and thoughts.
Beauty is a process of self-realization, where knowledge and rationality
help man to find instrumental means to interact with the world in order
to shape ideas and thoughts in visible forms. The next part of the story
passes through this Apollonian realm, where the power of mind brings
forth urges of artistic creativity over the sensual ecstasies and feelings.

The Guide of the soul wants to show him the realm of Apollo, that can be
seen without the help of the physical eyes. They sail away from the part
of the forest where the beauty has been perceived by the physical senses.

236

The soul sails towards an unseen island

In the universe where there seems to exist no light far out in the
depth of the sight,
Where in the infinite the sensual world the finite forms describe,
In an Eldorado of vision, where the inner light a journey of the soul
in search of beauty inscribes,
While the fabulous voyagers in thoughts and dream,
Depart the senses' streams,
I see a boat carrying the treasures of jewels and wealth moving
towards a distant land,
With vast glowing shores of golden sand.
With hearts aloft in passion filling them with ecstasies of dream,
The soul sails across the sea towards an island unseen.
As the riches of the shores the mind allures,
Like shifting clouds while amidst desires the heart feels insecure,
Feeling the fierce intensity of the burning sun,
The mind plunges as oars in an unknown sea as plunderers in search
of a nocturnal land,
Where no sailors have ever gone.
Under the blue sky, where the space infinitely extends,
Forest, caverns, rocks, and ridges breaking waves in foams the
adventurous mind's thrilling joy maintain,
Passing by huts, villages, and towns,
Where people live, suffer, and mourn,
In the impulse of nature the wandering mind feels passion torn;
Like pirates, sailing from their Aegean home,

In the ever-changing sound and light churning the foams,
The bellowing mind feels captivated under an endless dome.
While beyond the ethereal-bound,
Where a starry sphere dissolves in a mystery unbound,
Where all boundaries merge,
In the depth of the sky the sun, as a ship of passion carry the
plunderer's urge,
The water, as awakened mind's vivid dream,
Like gold flowing out of emerald green,
Turns yellow on the white foam that spread silken skin,
Sprinkles fine sprays of bubbles that try to reach the beauty that
emanates from the sun,
And in the blind eyes follow the motions of the churning mind behind
the stern.
Behind the waves, where the mind in wonder sleeps,
Behind the mountains and caves, where light merges with eternity,
Where, in an imagined shore,
The steps of the beauty shine as steps of a goddess in a golden shrine,
While waves in the wind breathe out mystery's whispering brine,
In vision's wandering, intoxicating the world,
I see drunken Bacchus with his jar of wine.
Steering the ship of the sun towards the world below,
While the setting sun spreads in the heart a dreaming glow,
Over the blazing hill pierced with rays,
Where soul, and will enjoy with nature wanton light's revel and play;
Granting glory to the drunken world joyous and gay,
While beating drums, and rattling cymbals Maenads lift the world
from the burden of flesh,
In a magic of frenzy,
Throwing arms upwards in search of deliverance in a world bound to

flesh,

Bacchus pours from his jar the wine,

While the frenzied women undress.

Like a boat, steered by the pirates of the heart,

When human grief, suffering and cries to the shore arrive,

Where the power of love the beauteous world revives,

The sun, carrying the pirates of the soul,

Sails across the sky,

Descends towards the ocean behind the hill;

Where cypress trees standing as green lanterns around the temple of the goddess of Dawn seduce the mortal will,

In the slopes leaning towards the archipelago,

Where the sun a luminous spectacle hauls,

The frenzied dancers in madness respond to Bacchus' call.

As I contemplate on this drunken world,

Bedecked with vineyards growing along the slopes,

Where the sailors fall in delirium without any hope,

That hampers movements and brings the conscious mind's journey to a halt,

In an ocean of salt,

The ferment of ivy, leaves and grapes,

Carry the fragrance of Bacchus' wine around masts and sails,

Slowing the rhythms of the muscles bring the conscious mind's journey that ends in a wreck.

As the green water penetrates the hull,

The rudder and the anchor are devoured by a sea over which the mind floats as an azure gull,

Where the pirates on sea,

Sink before they are able to extort from life the desired ransom at the port of call,

In a dark-blue world the waves dance and scroll.

As the sea spews foams towards the horizon bending towards the dawn,

In the mind creatures of unseen shapes leap out from a depth from where all life are born;

Dazzled by the vibrancy of the light of the stars,

In which cosmos appears very far,

Curving and bending,

Rising and descending,

Creating clouds of fog,

In ecstasy they dance appearing and disappearing from crags and rocks.

In this delirious world, they constantly form and deform in many colours and shapes;

While the evening light tries to define the contours of the inner world in curled up fire that burns the flesh,

As Bacchus lands on the shore of Naxos to marry the goddess,

Radiating inner rays,

I see Ariande in his gaze.

As the stars appear as jewels studded on the sky with golden threads,

I see the bridal crown of Ariadne being lifted to the heaven over an ocean, where vision wanders on the waves;

In a boat, that from shores to shores,

Life to life,

Many dimensions of existence steers,

I am a journeyman possessing the eyes of the seers.

APOLLONIAN REALM

Beyond the realm of the sense-bound life

The physical blindness causes the termination of the world bound to the senses and opens the inner realm, where Apollo radiates the beauty that can only be imagined through intellectual and contemplative power of the mind. In this Apollonian realm beauty reveals itself in colours, forms and sounds that can only be mentally grasped by great artistic, musical and poetic personalities. By using the power of the intellect, which can shape the diffused unconscious experiences of the Dionysian (Bacchus) realm into objective forms, the mind sees the realm of beauty that can not be experienced by the physical stimuli brought by the eyes. With it the guide of the soul brings him out of this treacherous "Forest Path" where mind feels trapped in an effusive unconscious world.

69. Beauty beyond the realm of the forest

70. Apollo: God of intellectual contemplation and beauty

71. Mind flies in nothingness

72. Pain of creative life

73. Despair of the journeyman at the death of the beauty

74. Journeyman beseeches Devil for help

75. Guide of the soul disguised as Devil appears

The journeyman speaks:

Beauty beyond the realm of the forest

O Muse! From whom the words spring,
By whose power in the mortal bosom love of light sings,
The feelings soar from the earth to the sky in lighted wings,
O beauty, who with such vision the souls inspires!
You have shown me the path outside senses' fire.
O Muse! Blessed are the eyes of the few,
That after seeing your beauty has bade life adieu,
Now I leave the realm of Nymphs and maids,
And move towards the mountain way,
Where I shall meet a greater beauty as the guide of the soul has said.
I can see the world through an inner vision again,
The wandering in the forest seems to be a journey in vain;
I am now embarked on a path, where beauty is not corrupted by
bloodfull stains.
As shadows deepen fast,
The shores appearing in the vision gradually sink behind the
darkened night's starry sparks;
In the Cytherean sand,
Where Venus rose from waves,
The Aegean rocks, where the pirates anchored for raids,
The azure arc, in which Dionysus on Naxos embarked,
On Delos' tides quivering in light,
Apollo's swans lift in my mind their wings in weightless jerks.
In the Phrygian meadow, where Phoebes rose over Anatolia's

sleeping head,

Along whose mountainous slope Aeneas fled,

Where Odysseus' and Aeneas' wandering gradually the vision fill,

Sinking behind the hill,

In varied hues, when the evening pass by,

O Muse! The man, who was once delighted in seeing the beauty's
naked form,

Now seeks a world beyond senses tumults and storms.

As the vision drags the eyes away from the shore,

Where mankind through war and struggle erect life's sullen tombs,

And through endless strife crown heroes with wreaths of thorns,

The shadows recede from the soul once drawn by darker powers,

That hauled the day towards night's sorrow-bound hours.

Now I see in my vision the beauty of the world of music, poetry and art,

An exit from the forest, where every directions once dragged me to
alluring paths.

I now depart the life of desire and lust.

O Muse!

You have lifted my soul above the bondage of the earth and the dust.

Vision of Apollo: The god of intellectual contemplation and beauty

After riding a suffering's ship,
Thrown in tempest and wrecked by storms,
In the cup of gold, where Heracles sailed to the end of the world,
Where the trees of paradise are born,
The dreaming heart seeks a land filled with cherubic songs.
Though blindness writhes in the eyes as an irreversible curse,
Still gnaws the flesh in termites' lusts,
Invades the light under the night's festering tomb,
Like buzzing drone animates the vision of a carcass decaying with
worms,
In the gentle touch of the wind,
In the evening light's caress,
The heart glows in an endless space;
From the poison of delight,
That once had set Troy in flame,
Torches of Apollo, ignites a pyre in life's mystic funeral game,
And opens the eyes as petals of glittering gems.
Peculiarly beaming from where eyes see no light,
Where orbs sparkle as radiant bodies of delight,
Like in a garden of paradise with secret routes,
Where the soul glows in an wondrous joy,
I watch things go by:
Colorful flames,
Harmony of sounds rising from instruments,

The alluring mystery ignited by the torches of the evening rays,
Precious stones, caskets of jewels, perfumes, and decorations,
The eyes drawn with finest mascara sprinkled with scents,
The funeral vase, where tear and remembrance store the memory of the beauty,
Once worshiped by artists, musicians and poets,
In profound emptiness caress of light revealing an aureole,
Amidst colonnades of crystals standing as frozen splendid trees of gems,
Magical waves rising from emptiness and splashing in multitudes of colours and flames,
Pouring out streams from outside the boundary of time and space,
Like Ganges, Nile, Euphrates of endlessly stirring emotions splitting out of the firmament,
In an endless tableau,
Marbles and metals repleting the sun and its flame,
In an auroral pyre, where golden fire burns,
The resplendent heart fills its amphora,
From it Apollo drinks sacrificial blood purified by flames.
Lovely Apollo,
God of rays bursting from the world above to the world below,
Radiating inside a halo,
Springing and streaming through mind's crevasses and furrows,
Lifting things away unscorching beyond illusion's webs,
In a shining sunset,
Like violin's trembling strings mingling with golden wings,
Scattering rays congealing the blood in the wind,
While the Muses sing,
In a spiritual sky, beyond vision's depth,
Strangely reverberating like hymns in flames,

Flooding over sorrow and pain,

Beyond the mountains and the waves,

Where fire of the wheel, on which roll the chariot of the dusk and the dawn,

Opens a star-woven sky over fields studded with Flora and fauns.

In golden arrow's quiver,

Where clouds float in human flesh's ethereal fibres,

Feelings sail, while the golden rays waver,

Bringing an apparition of light, in which dissolve heart's notes and songs,

Blindness illumines the mind and the body once scattered and torn.

Wrapped in mist, and enshrouded by dream,

While the flames of the dusk sing a serene hymn,

O Apollo! Oracle's God!

Though blind, while flesh appears dark,

In the eyes a greater visions has embarked.

Like jewels scattering rays,

I see your face,

That displays a godly grace;

Like painter's art captivating the heart,

It illumines my eyes from a distance mystic and strange;

In a puzzling mirror, where time the meanings of events obscure,

And creates in the mind innumerable designs made with artistic hands that is skilful and sure,

In a silence within, I see you radiate a charm that is divine and pure.

Here seas merge with other seas,

The sky screens another sky,

Shades and lights darken, or illumine spiritual shades and lights,

Halo, adorning the human sight,

Surges from a mystic halo, that is neither light nor night.

In this world I walk through a sculptured garden decorated with statues gilded with rays,
Whom the sky has lifted from the drudgery of weights;
Where the hands of sculptors have sought forms,
Which are outside space,
In a chimerical maze of light and shade,
Where unity and harmony of dimensions have metamorphosed the stones,
That can make man awake in dream,
I feel awakened by a dream, when I am not really awake.
I adore these lovely forms,
Where cold stones awaken mind's radiant warmth,
I see in the shining marble's frigidity the glory of Apollo's sun.
Though eternally sterile and can not copulate with man of blood and flesh,
Though blind and deaf, who can not understand what a human may say,
Though no caress of love can bring throbs in the breast,
Though no illicit desire can bring shame, or make man pale,
Though lips do not separate drinking a drop,
Or feeling thirst for flames,
They carry the true nectar of beauty,
The chalice of ambrosia,
Where Apollo dissolves in the beams as imperishable essence of things.
Like Homer blind,
From whose eyes no scene of battle could escape,
No god or titan, no phantom or man,
No sceptres, or ghosts,
Could run away from a history in a universe lighted by inner flame;

Where no voyager, set at sea,
Sailing to luxuriant islands, teeming with vines, cattle and steeds
could undo his fate,
There exist eyes unknown,
With which man can see things between the Paradise and the mortal
home.

Mind flies in a lake of nothingness aglow in the inner radiance

Flapping the white wings outstretched,
Where the sun is glowing in rays scattered by dust,
In water within, in the lake of the mind,
Where in melancholy light mirrors the sky infinitely vast,
Where the feathers of rays fly in the depth as awakened eyes'
dazzling darts,
Bathing in a lake, like a mythical bird,
Singing in harmonious voice the eternal hymns of beauty and love,
The great swan lifts its wings from the heart.
While the eyes flight over the forest and the trees drowsy in love,
Where the Maenads tear fleshes with bloodstained lust,
In a great lake, where the sky dips its lips in thirst,
When singing mysterious songs the flocks of swans fly by arching in
marvellous curves,
The poets, and the musicians find words and notes written with
feathers of the unearthly birds.
Over the lake, where sunbeam shines,
On a glowing canvas, drawn with invisible lines,
When feelings' intensity of colours are overwhelmed by the limita-
tions of space and time,
Flapping wings the great swan scatters foams from a golden brine.
O swan! Scattering light of the inner sun!
The creator of beauty and art!
The deepest voice in the heart!

In which your singing soars,
The sun rows beside your wings with its golden oars;
O awakened mind's ever joy!
The weightless mind's melodious buoy!
In soul's unbound flight towards a magical height,
Where the sun flies as Apollo's sun-disc toy,
Poets, artists, and musicians watch the flight of Delos' golden boy.
I see the swan flies to Parnassus towards a lake deep and vast,
Where poets, musicians and artists come to drink from the source of
immortal poetry, music, and art.
While singing it takes a golden turn,
Around the sun,
Feelings incinerate in senses' burn;
Between earth and air,
Where mind feels the presence of a mystic player,
The world listens to sounds,
Coming from a hidden world surpassing body's physical bounds.
Here being amazed I watch the wandering from shore to shore,
From Delos I see him arriving in Apollo's' grove.
Where nymphs play tunes in Delphic harp,
I see him listening to Calliope reciting her epic verse.
While Erato sings about Apollonian beauty and love,
And West-wind blows in the flute of the heart,
In solitary sorrow Melpomene scatters a melancholy,
While flowers spring from the beautiful Hybanthus' blood.
While blood drips where a golden knife is held,
He listens to the story of the Muse of tragedy about love, beauty and
death.
Playing on Dorian flute,
While Euterpe creates emotion's different hues,

Which in shepherds' hearts turn into golden dews,

While poesy and tune meet where flowers of innumerable colours are abundantly strewn,

The feelings, in self-created joy, pass by meadows creating a humble quietness over green turf and dunes,

In loneliness he seeks the beauty in pastoral tunes.

When words and syllables, melodies and tunes,

Mimic colours and shades, which lie outside the realm of flesh and bone,

Where Polyhymnia leaning on a wall of piled up stones,

In soaring thoughts overcomes the bounds of space and time,

Musingly lifts the mind from the earth to where beauty is eternal and sublime,

He listens to the hymns of the Muse,

That transform blood into spiritual wine.

Plucking the mind as harps, lyre, and cythara made of ethereal strings,

From the Helicon spring,

The great swan flies carrying music in vibrating wings;

Awakening the earth with a voice, that remains a riddle that no mortal can probe,

It stoops in the eddying current,

Where, like Peneus, wriggling between Mount Ossa and Mount Olympia,

He enters Daphne's grove.

While as an Apollonian artist man wanders in search of beauty and love, and tries to create in form the formless beauty, which one sees in the mind, the creative process brings despair and pain. The physical limitations of one's own body and the instrumental capacities at disposal, with which one may shape the physical world in form, bring limitations to such artistic endeavours.

Pain of creative life

O beauty of the invisible art!
Why do you stir the heart?
Why do you kindle in the spirit your burning sparks?
Though you are beyond conversion in lines and forms,
Why do you still allure the mind with a vision of eternal light's
dazzling warmth?
O beauty covered under light's illusory veil!
Why do you keep the soul fettered in a dream-like spell,
And kindle the spirit with emotion's surge and swell?
Although words are composed in the heart,
The lines and forms fumble in the soul seeking a greater art,
As I gaze upon the creative self,
Light turns into dark,
In melancholy and loneliness nothing coheres,
The mysteries of the beauty only this soul oppress.
Although there exists no way of healing these feelings,
Like a captive of pain,
The soul tries again and again to penetrate the secret of beauty in
vain.

As a mortal made of dust and clay,
Wandering in feelings' dismay,
Dwarfed by the tasks which bring creative pain,
O beauty!
Remaining awake far beyond midnight,
Why the mortal soul still seeks to unite with life's flaming coil,
And strives to win over the forces of nature that brings labor and toil?
How arduous the task that brings pain!
How hopeless the efforts that always end in vain!
How gloomy the life may seem when it is set to tests!
How strange!
Creative mind does not let the soul seek a peaceful rest.
Alighting the mind with a source of energy,
Shaking body's lethargy,
It brings a power to fight with rocks, marbles, or stones,
And, like Pygmalion's sculptures, brings forth a bodiless beauty that
exists beyond flesh and bone.
O soul seeking art through creative pain!
Where nature's forces rise through veins,
While carrying torrents' dread,
The golden sheep, fiery and red,
Gaze in the meadow basking in the sun's burning blaze,
While I seek to grasp beauty's golden stuff,
In an airy wind I hear a voice rising from the mind's inner gulf.
O innate power!
That always rises in perilous hours,
Like Psyche, set to fulfil Venus' tasks,
Who inspires to fetch the shreds of the dread,
Makes man visit even the world of the dead,
In this creative suffering,

You are a live-giving spring,

Amidst a bondage to the world made of things,

You are the power of Eros', who elevates artists in his transcendental wings.

O mind's light giving fountain!

Springing from the top of an inaccessible mountain!

Above which there exists no more height to rise,

While the stars heavenward ride,

The dark torrents downward dive,

Impulses plunge in a blue depth, in whirling waves,

A vermilion sunset disperses colors warm and red,

From a stream of Medusa's blood rises Pegasus in foaming wings,

Over an unknown sea the creative soul is set to ride in a realm beyond visible things.

While the journeyman still seeks the path to reach the beauty, and con-templates about the Platonic love, the beauty in the forest, after being ravished by the hunter, and then realizing that the man, who she has blinded is the one, whose love she has been searching all her life, finds the treachery of destiny too hard to bear. She takes her life. It appears as a treacherous game of destiny without an end. The beauty, whom he has been searching in a real person is dead. The love, which he so deeply craved in life, seems lost for ever from the physical sphere. Life appears to him as an endless paradox, an unceasing whirlpool of pain, agony, despair and confusion. The journey through the forest brings to him mis-ery and sorrow. Here the power of the human will seems futile, and the soul's agonies know no bound. In the forest, every living creature seem entrapped, fastened and bound as sacrificial animals in front of an al-tar of a mystery that he can not comprehend. Here snakes hiss, mighty pythons gape, boars of destiny ravage and uproot life throwing creatures into meaningless peril. In this strange realm the meaning of truth and falsehood, righteousness and wickedness, order and disorder, harmony and chaos, all seem beyond the grasp of human understanding. It is a trap of death and destruction - a blind prison, where man has no choice but to submit to destiny. An immense despair grips the soul of the jour-neyman.

Despair of the journeyman at the death of the beauty

O beauty! Sleeping in your unearthly home!
O fires', desires', and wanton heart's earthly tomb!
In your love's tempered flame,
Heart's beatings spread confusion, guilt and shame.
As you sleep the sleep of the dead,
Where pulsation of your eyes once drew my mind towards the lighted
lake,
Death's wings flap in my mind and create a tumultuous shake.
O beauty! I know there is no solace in this mourning and grief,
In death's tomb there is no meaning in trying to speak.
In the stolid sleep that time engulfs,
I know, no shivering, quivering or cry will help to cross death's
abysmal gulf.
It is a vicious play of destiny without an end,
Here no power of moaning the power of destiny will be able to contain.
Feeling treachery and disgust,
Weep no more heart!
Weep no more...!
Try to stand erect and rise from the dust!
O heart, cry no more!
Now try to soar!
Where destiny is prowling,
There is no meaning in helpless howling,
In fluttering and flickering of sorrow,

There is no way to gain strength in the marrow!
Bow no more to the treacherous world's virility,
Rise with dignity!
Show human mind's ability,
Stand up against the power that tries to bind living creatures in an eternal servility.
Rise above the buoyant moon floating in a mystic air!
Rise as a disc of rays that can remove all fears,
O mind! Rise above the sun!
Let no more the destiny's treachery return.
O mind! Clear the illusions that are deep and far,
Rise as a celestial star!
O soul, rise above the dust and the earth!
Above the wheel that turns the cycle of birth, death and rebirth,
Rise as a wandering flame seeking through the knowledge's path a greater universe.

Beseeches the Devil for help

O Lucifer, who can show path at night!
Enter in my eyes as light,
In this dark depth have pity in my plight.
I am not able to understand sacred signs and the logic of the Divine,
It seems that following the Guide I have only pursued an illusion of
the mind.
In trying to follow the figure clad in radiant ray,
I have lost my way,
And have stepped in paths that have randomly strayed.
In spirit's tumult when around the lake,
At the beauty of the goddess I have gazed,
Curse has seized.
Like a prisoner of fate,
In search of love I have met the beauty as lifeless and dead.
O Lucifer! Who can help man to find a path at night!
You who can guide man in the human knowledge's lofty height,
Though hidden behind vapor and cloud,
You, who can help to understand the celestial happenings with gifts
of reason, and power of doubt,
Who is true to sight, sound and touch,
Come! Appear!
Help me to get out of this realm where I am a victim of Muse's curse.
You! Who seek no heavenly sound!
Or search any vision that is divinely profound,
To whom things happen because they are bound in the laws of

ground,
And things die and decay as matter in the universe evolve and
progress,
Exposing all living creatures to dust and distress,
Rise! Appear!
Help me to get out of this treacherous quagmire of the heart.
While sorrow and grief,
The destiny and the spirit unknown and deep,
Ensnare the heart in an everlasting sleep,
O Lucifer!
With the knowledge of the elements of earth, air and water,
You, who know what lies behind the inner world's flaming spell!
Who can help the mortals when they err!
Come! Appear!
Help me out of this treacherous fire!
O master of knowledge!
Free me from this wretched world's senseless fear,
Hear my prayer:
With logic and reason discipline my mind,
Admit in the heart no foolish illusion that may make man blind,
Instead of letting the mind spin dream-like webs night and day,
Let faith in the natural law be the guide on the way.
Help me to get out from this mind's abyss,
Lifting the veils of dreams bring me to the realm gifted with
knowledge's bliss.
In this abyss of sorrow and pain,
All actions appear tied to a dream-like chain,
In high, low, above, below and everywhere,
There seem to exist an unsurpassable snare,
O Lucifer! Free me from this despair!

Get me out of this nightmare,
Of ceaseless destiny, that is full of fire and flare.
In this blind eyes, where the memories of the rays still stir the fire,
Bring me to the knowledge's path ... in a world lower or higher...
I really do not care.

Tathagata`s meditation

It is a story where I have crossed a sea, journeyed over a river, gone beyond the reality in the past, wandered through domains where the time has no definite meaning, gone both ways - towards the past as well as the future. Like in images in the mirror I have walked both in the real world, that is virtual, and virtual world, that is real. This river plunges into the sea after passing through the forest, crossing the cities, and then winding backward.

I have already fled from many forests, many cities, many wars and battles. I have wandered alone from many shores to shores. Now I have taken refuge here to gaze at life,that I have left behind. Amidst the diversity of life, that creates a chaos and disorder as results of the competitions for life, I see the naked world, that is frighteningly real. While things battle with things, life wars against life, the beauty breaks forth carrying colours and warmth of the sunlight, like an irreducible absurdity, I see in the nudity of life the beauty of the world.

While fleeing I gaze. Like a person enthralled by the beauty of the colourful maze, I look at the world in strange somnolence - as if, neither dreaming nor being awake. I wish to separate my one half from the other half, enter as other into another world, that is inside another... thus I travel ...deeper .. deeper ...pass through history, time, myth ...stalk in hell, or fly in paradise... in order to find out who am I? In front of this beauty I see the hairy leaves, that hang around her naked flesh. I contemplate on the jungle between her thighs where passion creeps and rises from abdomen to the breast, and a desire of love points towards her organ of sex. This sight makes me forget the fear of death. I stop as a bewildered stag in a strange illusion, and follow the passion's drags, that bring me to the lake, where the beauty bathes as a woman of blood and flesh. Like a lovely woman I discover her mysterious flesh. With eyes wide open I stare at her nudity that seems absurd but true. Like a goddess she sprinkles rays in the eyes, scatters feelings in the body, and generates the sensations of the serpentine power in the lower part.I see the world revealed as wonder of the senses, absurdly knitted with another world that is outside the sphere of time. She overwhelms reason and I enter into darker and darker world to seek unnatural relations with her body and flesh.

I do not understand this play of destiny. I stand, gaze and look at the stream, where I see her bathing. It is on the other side of the mirror, on the opposite bank of the river. Since the time, when I have left the shore on the other side, the reality floats as nothingness in my consciousness inside the mirror. The river has become time; the forest has transformed; the beauty has become one with the women of flesh and blood, in whose sex I have felt trapped in a darkness of the mind. In a jungle, where venous serpents have writhed and hissed, huntsmen have pursued their preys, in front of her nudity I have felt drawn deeper and deeper in a darkness. Then feeling a sudden fright I have tried to run away. In trying to flee I have made false judgments and fallen in the danger that I have wished to avoid. At the end I have become blind.

Guide of the Soul disguised as Devil appears

Though my power both the earth and the heaven spans,
I am not what you may believe I am.
I am neither light nor night,
Some call me Devil, and some call me the highest Angel of light,
Some believe I am a power that comes from the celestial height.
Some conceive me as Satan, who is the source of earthly evil and all
miserable plights.
Some invoke me as the prince of the night,
Who in death and destruction takes immeasurable delight,
While some worship me as an Angel lifted in a splendid light in a
heavenly flight.
In the human fantasy, that knows no bound,
I am imagined as a father of lie, a deceiver, a leader of disobedience,
a great dragon for whom a fire in hell rises to create an everlasting
suffering profound.
Some also imagine me as a prince of darkness fighting against the
principle of light,
They see me as power-loving, lustful, covetous, conceited fellow
flying in the height,
Or as a luciferous, sinister creature obsessed with vile,
Whose character, temperament and idiosyncrasies are only meant to
corrupt and defile.
To some I am insanely libidinous and malignant, whose body is
spotted with unusual marks,

And they believe that I dwell in a bottomless pit of the hellish dark.
On the other hand some see my godlike birth,
Who soars as a messenger of light as the sun on the earth.
They see me as holy, infinite and co-eternal with God,
While good and evil are creation of the mind, that is unable to
understand the will of the Lord.
Some see me as the divine knowledge that helps man to understand
the meaning of the temporal acts,
The dynamic unity of reason that ties human experiences with facts;
Some see me as the creative reason, who no form and fantasy can
describe,
Though hidden they think I manifest through the laws that God to
the world prescribes.
Some see me as the power of the mind, which sets norms and rules to
the human will,
They beseech my help so that the will of God in their life may fulfill.
Some conceive me as the power of discursive thinking in a
contemplative mind,
Which is a great source of knowledge of the ultimate reality to
whom all human will should resign.
Some imagine me as the mediator between the earth and the heaven
through whom the cosmic principles can be known,
Like the light of the eternal crystal - God's shining stone,
They see me as the power through which the cosmic mind has
eternally shone.
Some see me as the bearer of judgment, idea, notions of ethics that
bind the earthly dwellings of man with the eternal home;
Though I am not made of any substance they consider me as the
guide of reason of the mortal made of flesh and bone.
Some conceive me as the divine nothing revealed and related to the

world by thoughts,

And perceive me as the luminous idea that emanates from Thoth.

However, my image varies with varying interests of the nations and tribes,

They see me as evil or good depending on benefit or sacrifice.

With changing history I am one's God and other's demon,

One's devil and other's Simon,

One's Michael and other's Mammon,

One's Satan and other's Angel,

One's dragon and other's Gabrielle, Uriel or Archangel.

You may call me by any name that you may like,

Whether one calls me Angel or Satan I am always alike.

In this world, where often truth is lie,

If you wish I can be your guide,

Where using reason and knowledge man rises from hell and falls from the paradise,

I can bring you out of this world to a world where heaven and hell exist side by side.

The journey in the realm of the artists, musicians and poets brings an end to the search of the beauty at the physical plane. The suffering in this sphere gives birth to a newer vision and elevates the mind to the realm of reason and rational contemplation lying beyond the sense-bound sphere. Leaving the realm of Eros, where dreamy urges and artistic emotions, harnessed by the unconscious drives, lead man through a path where gods, goddesses, muses, and nymphs mingle with the real women and men of the world, and happenings appear to be bound in the hands of destiny. Without being able to comprehend the meaning and purpose of these happenings the journeyman leaves the forest and follows the Devil to the Philosophers' Path.

The Guide imparts on him a new inner vision, and brings him out of the forest.

PHILOSOPHERS`
PATH
Realm of rational contemplation

After leaving the "Forest Path" he arrives at the Meadow of Death, where the beauty, who after being ravished by the hunter, has taken her life and is burning in a pyre. Here he meets the souls of the philosophers – among others Neo-Platonist, Hegelian, Stoic, Schopenhauer, Nietzsche, Krishna of Bhagavat Gita. They expound their philosophies about the meaning of life and death, and how one may overcome the suffering in the world and pursue meaningful paths to act and live.

Seeing the journeyman sunk in sadness, Stoic gives him advise:

Stoic

You seem saddened with grief that has driven you away from the forest. Are you trying to run away ? Will any place satisfy you? Are you not dashing away hither and thither to find a path that in turn draws you to more sorrow and pain? Take authority of yourself and be stationed within your soul. Thus find a place in the inner home, where your soul actually belongs. You have come through the dense forest covered with trees that have risen to the Skye height, that shut off all lights. In the secluded spot you have looked in wonderment at the beauty and desired her love. But that path has led you to this place. What's good in dragging up suffering, that is over? By being unhappy now for what has passed you only deceive your life and bring on your life more hardship that you should bear. Fight against these follies of the mind, exert yourself against the load that wishes to sink your soul as a monster of fear.

The source of suffering lies within. When you yourself is the creator of your own sorrow let it not plague and harass the mind. Otherwise, the things that you are trying to run away from will be with you all the time. The only safe harbor in life's tossing lies in you. Do not be bothered about the troubled sea, or on the fear of what the future may bring. Stand ready and confident squaring the breast to take without skulking and flinching whatever the fortune may hurl. On the way to the tracks, that lead to precipice on the giddy height, it is so ordained that one will be carried off the course and go down, from where one must sail again to the cherished land once more. The destiny will hurl the boat headlong on the rocks, dash it into pieces. But if you can cling to the destiny's wholesome plan, you will not feel miserable at the wreck. Like Odysseus' journey, Neptune is always against the mortal from the day man is born. But journey we must make. Without it we will never arrive at the height where we are destined to merge with the higher part - our Self. It is a long road you have embarked on. You must expect slippery paths, knocks and falls. On the way the companions will depart, one you love will die, you have to bury your father, son, daughter and wife. But do not be afraid. These are the things all must face. Wanting to die or escape is derived from false concepts of the principles of nature and life. In the path, where often the thunder and lightning may strike, hold on to the terrain without being afraid of the fearful light.

Odysseus' wandering is also our own wandering. Every day there are storms caused by the vices, that Odysseus never knew from before. Like him mortal life is not spared of the eye-distracting beauties, or the savage monsters revelling on blood. Insidious voices beguiling the ears of the sailors, ship wrecks, misfortunes, all are companions with which all mortals must live day by day. Sometimes one must encounter monsters and beasts, sometimes the evil men, who are more dangerous than the beasts. Fire may rob man from property, flood may cause havoc, but brave should bear up with courage all that fortune sends. As clear sky follows clouds, after calm comes storm, day succeeds night, part of heaven ascends while the other part descends in the darkness, brave man knows that only by means of such opposite the eternity endures.

It is clear that to loose someone one loves is the hardest blow to bear. But preserve the serenity of the mind and the attitude that all that happen have a greater reason and take place only to serve the nature to its best. Everything will return :Every beauty ravaged by time will again succeed the beauty that has gone. Although things that succeed will not quite be the same there is nowhere a loss, never a complete dissolution of what once has been. Everything will go to preserve the order of the things. Multitudes of beings doomed to die after birth will follow others to where everyone is heading for from the beginning of time. Nothing is durable. Destinies of men and cities sweep alike. Terror may come in the most tranquil time without giving any hint that it comes. Torture, exile, shipwreck, war, misfortune, may banish man to wilderness and make the very surrounding in which one lives suffocating. But all these are the terms of human lots. Keep this view of life in front of your eyes when you move further to your life's destined path. It is only then you will not be overwhelmed or feel struck numb by the fortune or misfortune that may come.

The city, from where I come, has burned down; the wealth and glory of her beauty have gone. Like that, time will sweep away the traces of every city of whose splendor and magnificence you may hear. The structures built by human skill and industry cannot stand nature's force. I have seen how the mountain massifs have crumbled away, whole regions of land have submerged under flood water, waves have covered landmarks far out from the boundary where the sea once had stood. Under the soaring peak beside the sea, that beckoned mariners seeking lowly pleasure, I have seen the immense force of the volcanic fires, that once made the mountain tops glow, slide and eat vegetation away and reduce to a barren land the shore that once was a seat of burgeoning life. Subterranean explosions, violence of flood, volcanic outbursts fracturing the crust, plague carrying off population, drought turning lands to desert and decay and many other ways, that are tedious to account, are among the modes by which the fate always overtakes. As a result all that stand must fall. But keep in your view the notion that things fall only to rise to the exalted heights.

This is the way to defy that inspire fear. Despise all things that terrify and set chains on the freedom and brings man to a state that cause tears. Be beaten, get burnt, walk straight, probe the mystery of the nature and life where they may hide. Liberate quality in yourself that can take command of the mind over the pleasures of life. What's the use of possessing a horse, if you cannot master and control its reins and gallop through the terrain where you wish to see the true nature of your spirit unveiled? Overcome emotions, take self-control. Use the divine spark, that is a part of your make up, and rise within yourself. Use your power and from a trickling fountain burst into a cascade. Let not the waves of the noise, the cataracts of pain, create a racket around your soul. Absorb the babel and the roaring discordant noise and hear the voice of the falling commotion of the spirit emitting music of life and be self-absorbed.

If you desire to reach the destination lying at the height , like Odysseus passing by the Siren's land by binding himself on the mast, with these words in mind steer all clear. Let not eating, drinking, squandering, theft, that most living call living, slip you from self-control and lead you to Siren's jaws. Stay clear from the drunken man's tortuous path; guard your eyes from the beauty in wood and by the stream; tilt not your heart to the seduction of the senses believing that on the earth you have found the garden of Paradise. Where the giant forest in ecstasy gazes at the sky, the woman's breasts, buttocks and thigh glow in passion's light, the serpent of life trades the forces of light with misery and death of the night, the curveting horse with vicious might accouter around passion's hearth, the waxing day awakens the solitude of lust, sputtering flames of the heart drive the huntsman to chase the stags of the lust, where mother, daughter, wife, lover and whosoever bring love, embroil life in which man is tossed in tides, hold your spirit's might and stand above the wreckage in the waves, that create day and night, darkness and light. Thus swim over the sea to the shore where you have your origin of birth and walk towards the height where the mountains take their radiant baths. When the ones, who are coming down the slope, will throw forward the bodies to the ground and tilt the weight towards the rugged earth, rein your body backward from the drag of the spirit of gravity and climb upward to the mountain terrain beckoning the mind to a realm beyond the stars. Reconcile the body to accept tiredness, remain serene, rise to the sublime height higher than yourself, carry your mind forward above the trifling world flitting underneath in the light and dark. Seize yourself, make king of yourself and rise to a kingdom above the earth.

The philosopher, who has professed the view that the world is driven primarily by the will-to-live tells him:

The world as will-to-live

The world, that you see flowing and burning, emerges from a will that is monstrous like fire of hell. It gives birth to grotesque grottoes and cavernous recesses in the underground and it arranges, deranges the streams and waterfalls, tumbling, dashing and foaming outwards dispersing sprays of moisture, that reflect the dark forces making everything mobile. The sulphurous vapors out of the rocky chasms, where the darkness sinks deeper and deeper, encircled by clouds coiling and rotating within itself in the evil's behest spew out flames. While pursuing itself, as the hero running away with the shattered spear, from which it itself has created the will-to-kill, like restless spirit bearing the storm-clouds, the flashing of lightning, and crushing of thunders it trysts upon itself. Like the rocks of grotesque, weird and fearful forms it creates itself. From its mouth the tongues of fire leap from crevices; the molten contents plunge downwards, brilliant flames in fearless excitement and in exultant gesture rise upward and celebrate the joy of the nature's peril. In painful eruptions, it drinks its own annihilation from the poisonous bowl sinking downward. In a strange drama with frenzy, wrath and flash of anger it awakens its own bride from the slumbering hearth of the nature's heart and thus unites with the love before falling in a forgetfulness of his own nature and the beauty whom it loves. In this war, contest, battle, search, and kindling one's own pyre where the beauty sacrifices itself in the burning flames shooting through the world, as the will-to-live it nourishes on itself, feasts on its own body, battles against, subjugates, and devours itself. Waging an incessant struggle and conflict with itself it separates from itself as its own double - on one side it acts like a devourer while on the other side as a befreer and creator of itself. In the contest, that constantly fluctuates between the victory and defeat, it produces incessant pain and perpetual suffering. Like a young hydra growing out of the old one and separating itself therefrom it fights with itself while it is still firmly attached to the old, with a hope to escape its own devourment. Thus it wages a perpetual battle between the two parts of the same. Like bull-dog ant, that, when cut into two, attacks the tail with its head, while the tail defends against the head by stinging it, every life is fettered to a contest between two parts of oneself as an urge of the will-to-live.

The will is its own hunter, the food and prey for itself. In a strange obscure way it also knows from beforehand its own necessity for survival and defense as well as the strategy to annihilate its prey. Like the bird building the nest for the bridling it has not yet seen, the beaver erecting a dam whose purpose is unknown to it, the bees collecting honey for the winter still unknown to them, the spider with deliberate cunning building snares for the future prey unknown to it, the instincts of actions derived from the will resemble concepts of purpose, although will-to-live is devoid of any purpose at all. In the never ending war, in constant struggle, where one specie strives to wrest from the other its right to exist, the will adapts itself to bring an agreement with its own restless self, that has no final goal, or satisfaction.

This ceaseless never satisfied striving is carried through cycles of life and death, causing endless suffering, and unspeakable pain. Thus the

misery of the living go on for ever with the triumph of wickedness, scornful mastery of chance, and irretrievable fall of the innocents as preys in the hands of the wicked ones. Like a mighty storm, rushing along without any aim, it carries everything away with it in its bending and agitating sway. It brings only a constant struggle resulting in the only certainty that the life will loose at the end. It is like sailing in a sea full with overhanging rocks and whirlpools sucking all towards an abysmal depth. In struggling, in making effort to avoid the dangers, man only comes near the inevitable fate that ends in an irremediable shipwreck. This is the final goal of the wearisome voyage, that no one can avoid. Like destiny of Odysseus it drags him to the world of the dead, in order to throw him up again on the shore of the living to repeat a similar journey again. He thus always find himself as newly sprung into existence to undergo this merciless suffering. He moves through the island of the Dawn to the Island of the setting sun and back again and again. Death like the setting sun, engulfs the life and always remains glowing without the constant source of light. It brings new days to the world with new life and is always rising and setting.

We all live in this drama of life and death. This rising and sinking world, that I describe, is covered under the veil of Maya, which always covers the eyes and the mind and causes the mortals to see a world that neither is or is not. Like in the Palace of Maya, inside the dome circumscribed by the motion of the moon and the sun, what appears as moving is actually at rest and what remains still may seem to be flowing in time. Amidst this illusion the will acts as an irresistible urge setting the wheel of life and becoming. It is blind, has no knowledge of itself before it mirrors itself in the world as object of itself. Through the images in the mirror it obtains the knowledge of itself, and the life and all objects existing and becoming in the temporal flow. Splitting into subject and object it becomes object of its own knowing as a spectator, who knows no time, and emerges as a being in the illusion of time. Through this knowledge, that arises out of nothing, man heightens himself as a subject, who is pure knowing and stands above the carving, and suffering of the sentient beings that he himself has created with his will. Thus looking at himself as a pure knowing being he steps into another world where everything that agitate the life no longer exist. Torments of passion, suffering and struggle to live cease, all differences of individuality disappear, no happiness or misery touch the mind anymore. Thus he sinks in a state where reality and dream become one and he views the world like a boatman sitting calmly on his small boat. He trusts the frail craft in a stormy sea rising and falling with the howling waves. The infinite past or infinite future appear strange to him. For him only the eternal present alone exists in the tranquillity unmoved by the boundless sufferings.

Sitting in this boat, holding calm by using the faculty of reason, he surveys the universal life extending through past and future. Like a skilled navigator with highly precise chart, compass and quadrant he knows exactly his position in the violent sea and lives a life in the abstract sphere of calm deliberation. Through this reflective withdrawal in abstract contemplation he plays at the same time the part of the audience and the actor in the drama of life. He plays his role in a scene, then takes his place in the audience, and watches the play that rolls on until his turn to return to the play comes again. It goes on until he dies in the last scene. He knows this suffering is a must and therefore he views the life with perfect rational objectivity in which passions, errors, excellence, selfishness, love, hatred, fear, boldness, frivolity, stupidity, genius and so on reflect the nature of the same person, who always appears with the same purpose and fate in the stage with different masks. Only the incidents differ from piece to piece, but nothing else of the man, acting on the stage or observing it from the outside, change. He looks in a half-awake and half-dream state at the drama of life as a phantasmagoria where different chessmen of a game stand chess mate at the end and fall in the darkness of death only to join the souls in the carnival in the meadow, where the souls coming through the chasms of the heaven or the hell meet time and again.

Life is thus a merciless tragedy in a kingdom of chance and error where folly and wickedness, like the mime dwarfs, wield the scourge. It is a series of continual mishaps - great and small- that torment the race, to whom the hero, who has risen from the pyre, belongs. Abandoned to fate, the sufferer is always arrayed against the enemy without any mercy from the heaven or the hell. In this hopeless and irretrievable state the will reflects its invincible and indomitable nature - the hero himself - who acts out in the eternal drama in life's stage. Man thus creates of himself in his own image the demons, the giants and the gods. He offers sacrifice, prayer, vows and their fulfilment, pilgrimages, salutations to his own image by looking at life from an abstract sphere of pure intellectual reflectivity, that is neither real or unreal.

Thus God becomes man, and man becomes God in order to bring to the world the teaching the salvation from the misery that only come from the world and man himself. In surrendering this will, in dissolution into the nothingness, by merging with oneself through self-knowledge in the pure sphere of subjectivity, in attaining a state, where there is no will and no world, there exists redemption from suffering for the sentient beings.

The Neo-Platonist, who passes by tells him:

Neo-Platonist

Beauty and light come from the supreme soul of All, that streams through nature and of which the mortal eyes are incapable of vision. Only through the rupture of the mind the images may stir the heart by which man may know the nature of All.

It floats in the flux of time creating beauty of life and the splendor of manifold forms. This veritable beauty is never in quest. It has no longing to be born. There is no place from where it comes and there is no place where it goes. Above all powers and patterns creating the illusion of time it is the power of becoming that brings it into forms. Though it is formless in its very depth, that has limitless extension, it embodies the compassion by which it springs and grows in form. It is eternal and universal. It grants its light to the shapes as a subject of a limitless love residing in shapes and forms. The loveliness, that begets beauty and streams from beauty itself, confers upon the beauty its visible form, cannot be felt, seen, touched or perceived by smell. This beauty, beyond all measures, exists in a higher realm as the enlightening light beckoning the sense-bound mind to the love of God.

The soul's suffering comes when it ceases to dwell in this perfect beauty, that is itself illuminated and illumines all visions always. With its unfailing light it sustains, fosters, and endows with fullest measure that each can absorb. It is the fire that warms every receptive body within its infinite range. In this fire nothing can disappear, or dissolve without giving birth to another form. This transcendental fire, that is more truly alive, and possesses life and the principles that bring forth life, unceasingly animate the universe with flames that can never be quenched. It always remains itself, unyielding to change, unsusceptible to the pain and suffering. It draws the souls from the lower to the higher realm and descends to the deeper depth of darkness to lift the creatures to Itself. Beginning as a great light shining at the center it gives forth brilliance and radiance, some of which move above and some sink underneath being drawn by the splendour of the forms, that it itself illumines. From it arises the souls taking the bodies as clothes. As it reaches outwards more and more and proceeds to bodies that are earthly and heavy, it plunges from the heaven to the low corporeal state. Stage by stage it sinks in the realm of the forgetfulness and becomes too feeble to carry the burden of the weight to lift itself to the world from where it has emanated. In this abysmal world of the corporeal state it loses self-mastery and falls in the power of fate and destiny. The soul becomes enchained and remains entombed in the world like in a grave. But there exists a reason why it is enchained in the corporeal forms, and why the divine being and the dweller in the loftier realm has penetrated the sphere of the earthly bonds and voluntarily plunged into the darkness where evil writhes.

It is an intellectual act, a purposeful willing of the divine mind. All are parts of the higher reason, and the intellective principle arising from God. Like actors of a divine stage, with different costumes and masks each soul is allotted its fortune, that is not haphazard but planned. Each soul must adapt itself to the destiny assigned to it, and attunes itself, ranges itself rightly to the divine play. According to the higher principle of the drama they are enrolled to speak out, and act out exhibiting what the soul can express. Thus making oneself as an actor of the play, bringing in one's own personal excellence or defect, receiving in the end punishment or reward, the role of each actor is meant to be acted out like strings of a lyre adjusted, and set to produce a music of life emanating from the mind of God. Painful, joyful, harsh or happy- whatever it might be- every actor is directed towards a harmony mak- ing the music of life. Each of the characters has a guiding spirit, who wants to lead him, or her, to the next higher path. Those, who develop evil trends, weighs down the purpose of the spirit and moves down- wards. Those, who is able to follow the guiding spirit and rises towards the noblest part of himself to which he is being led, becomes sovereign in his life. He works for the next higher stage and goes on climbing until he attains the highest knowledge of himself i.e. the knowledge of the one from whom he emanates.

The same reason, that leads, may also fetter man to the power that draws him, or her, to the lower stage, where the instincts of the will- to-power dwells. Without this contradiction the cycle bringing multi- tudinous births and deaths can not be sustained. The transcendental light needs to reach down in order to create the music of life, where animate and inanimate co-operate as things and creatures bound in the spindle of Necessity entangled like in a web. Thus the universe is a wonder of power and wisdom, where roads pass along which all must make their journeys according to the law and reason being attracted by the beguiling beauty and love which none will be able to escape. The unenlightened mind may not be able to conceive the messages of the guiding spirit, though it leads him towards the Soul to whom all belong. But the enlightened mind knows his guide, and by knowing sets out to the place where he must, and understands, before he begins his journey, where his destination will be at the end.

The unenlightened one is the sufferer, who is constantly swept onward towards his due, hurried always by the restless driving of errors. At last being fatigued and wearied by the forces, against which he or she struggles, he or she will fall into his or her fit place and by a movement of reason will be brought to a life that he or she did not choose. The eternal scheme in the divine mind decrees the intensity and duration of his or her suffering before lifting the chastisement and giving man the faculty and power to rise from suffering in harmony with the universal plan of life orchestrated by the music of the stage where the drama of life is played.

This is ineluctable. No power will be able to hinder this destiny. Thus there exists meaning and reason behind the death of the beauty, who is doomed. A great soul is the one, who by knowing this keeps his body's and mind's turmoil still. He, or she, sees earth at peace, the sea at peace, the air tranquil in the harmony of the heaven, where all remain at rest. The great soul is the one who rolls inward penetrating and permeating from all sides and moves towards the light pouring outward from a centre supernally bright. As the rays of the sun throwing their brilliance upon a louring cloud make it gleam as gold, so the great soul entering the material course casts upon his surrounding world the beauty of the divine soul. He lifts the world sunk in darkness and constrained to live in the endless motions of the things. By the power of his soul he mirrors the beauty of the heaven on the earth.

Krishna of the Indian epic Mahabharat appears and expounds:

Teachings from Upanishad and Bhagavat-gita

Man! all life must pass away to reappear again from the world of the dead. Grieve not for those who die, or feel joyous for those who live. The one, who lives or dies, has been for all time and will be forever. The soul, that is neither real nor unreal, in dying only wanders on to a new body, that feels heat and cold, sees light and shadow, and experiences pleasure and pain. But every bodily existence is transient, that in the eyes of the beholder "is" when seen under the illusion of Maya, and "is not" when viewed from outside the domain of the senses.

The spirit, that is beyond destruction and time, dwells in the impermanent body that by dissolution and creation brings forth the illusion of time. The beauty, that burns in the pyre, is beyond time and never dies. As an everlasting and never changing soul of an eternal light it goes in order to come. In each return it puts on new garment and mask, and like the beautiful bride, seeks her mate in the mortal world bound in the causal chains. Man! rise from your despair. Win over the illusion of pleasure and pain, gain or loss, suffering or happiness. I know the path where there is no fate against whom you need to fight. It lies beyond the world driven by the earthly opposites that binds mind and body in the delusion of the forest enwrapped in the veil of Maya. By striving to attain freedom and self-knowledge by the help of the blind urges that empowers the will driving the nature do not do violence to yourself.

Surrender your will to me and rest tranquil in the faith of the wisdom that I bear.

Only then I shall be able to take you in a flight beyond the realm of time and space, and can show you the world that goes and comes in the stream of life. I can bring you to the path of conscious contemplation, where at the end there exists no more striving towards perfection, and the world is absorbed in a harmonious tranquil wisdom. No more the wandering senses, that carry the mind, like a vessel in the storms of desires, will carry you away on the sufferings' waves. You will no more be whirled round by fate.

Waver not. Lift up yourself. Allow not the will to be your own enemy. Rise from despair! I live under the everlasting sun, that brings forth light. I wish to reveal to you the secret of the conscious contemplation because I seek a friend who has already experienced the suffering of the mortal world. Without this suffering man can not understand the meaning of the wisdom, that I relate.

Like you I have also been born many times. While you have forgotten all, I remember everything. While you surrender your will easily to the urges of nature and sink in darkness of the thoughts, I contemplate on the abstract domain of the mind where the spirit can rise to the light. While you feel confused in the innumerable images in the mirror, where will reflects its nature and sees itself burning in the fire of the sense-bound world, through knowledge and contemplation I attain self-harmony and see in my mind the lighted flash of the inner "sun", that unites and holds the world in an eternal harmony of the whole.

This place, where you have entered, is divided into three parts: The realm of tranquil light, that hovers above the pyre, the domain where the pyre burns and creates the restlessly moving time flowing in the stream and the region of the darkness where the souls live amidst the shadows and fall downwards in the hell. In the upper sphere, deep within the human thoughts, lies the domain of the radiant inner "sun", that illumines the mind where thoughts wander not. In this sphere of the mind no longer passions, desires, conflicts, or doubts, like the clouds ripped off by the air in the pathless wind, obstruct the illumination by the radiance of the "sun".

In the region of the flames the beauty is encircled by a magic fire, from where the hero rescues his bride, and at the end himself burns in the pyre. From here the white winged steed, or bird rises heavenward, sorrow returns as joy, and joy dissipates in sorrow, the sacrifice and offering become the secrets of the magic seeds from where the life begins again. In this domain, what seems to exist is what it is not. It is the realm of Maya created by the flames, the light and the day ignited by the sun.

In the shadow world lies the serpent of eternity - the beast coiling around the tree of life. Here lies the chasm of the irrational, from where the dark fume rises. With this fume greed, delusion, ignorance rise to the world. Creating lust and passion in restless hearts it clouds the wisdom and covers the light from above. In deceitfulness, insolence, self-conceit, anger and harshness the shadows rise to chain heroes in the sins of the hell depriving them of truth, moral foundation, and belief and faith in anything higher than the deceit, conceit and the illusion of will-to-power and dominate. It is the punishment ground where man, holding fast to the dark impulses. tortures his own soul with insatiable desires. Enchained by delusion, selfishness, arrogance, and pleasures of own carvings, made drunk with pride and vainglory of the wrong doings, helping to take refuge in the sensual enjoyment, creating cravings for power with unjust means, generating the lust for amassing wealth, that hurls others to deprivation, the shadows of the world guide man to the hell. In this hell, at first, the objects of desires seem like sweet drink through which one may win immortality, but as the drops enter the body they turn into burning poison.

Like Hercules, all heroes incinerate at the end. In this place I am the only one who knows the way to descend to darkness and ascend to the domain of light. Do not be bewildered. Surrender your will to me and follow me hence.

After that he passes by a grove where the soul of blind Oedipus is mourning his life's acts. He speaks to the journeyman:

Blind Oedipus's fate

Outside the city of Thebes where Heracles was born,

I wander in a grove full of thistles and thorns,

Here no sun can ever be seen,

Through it runs a stream from whose water a dark world erupts and springs,

Its ice-cold water only the blood and the libation brings.

In its vast span of darkness where deep foliage grow,

The steps lead me to my own grave lying dug in the grove.

Here the trees growing as wood give me no shelter,

At every step I walk I stagger and falter,

As I search my way out of this world in eternal peril,

I wander and travel in search of salvation from life's and death's perennial wheel.

In its thickly wooded path, road divides into three ways:

The first runs across the stream towards the land of Bacchus where the senses exalt life's drama and play,

The second passes over the hill where Sisyphus along the slope of the hill falls and rises,

And strives to topple the stone before destiny brings him down with the power of the gravity that all other powers surprises;

The third winds through a passage that passes by a straggling pool,

Where the blind man wanders like a fool.

Along the path, where I walk, there is a river from where wind blows to my breast,

And with sprays from a colorless stream a feeling of helplessness moistens my chest.

In this grove all steps are grim,

Like a man destined to walk alone in a desolate world with lawless whim.

In the darkness when I hear cries and screams,

I know that someone is being sacrificed like a sheep near the ocean stream.

From there the souls depart,

And the ferryman takes them across Styx to the gate of the underworld,

Where the fearful hound keeps its guard.

While I walk along this hellish path,

I hear the magic incantation of the goddess of death calling the ghosts to take new birth,

In a cryptic tone I hear the guiding souls commanding the shadowy ghosts,

To the pool of forgetfulness where they will put new robes,

And set in journeys towards the world run by laws, chance and material force.

Thus inside a chasm of darkness where Tantalus hangs beside a lake,

I see a quintessential night without a break,

Like an aged grim man as I walk bowing down the body in front of a perpetually menacing fear,

I hear the Furies' and Erinys' cheers,

Confined in a dark tomb of everlasting night,

I listen beside the ocean stream witches' chants and hymns.

The anger of the gods have sent me the perpetual disease, destruction and plague,

I have received this scourge for the murder of the father and defiling his bed.

In this monstrous world of procreation, where from the old the new generations spring,

I walk as the symbol of sin;

As abomination of the gods for breaking the sacred commandments and the laws,

That the world's harmony and beauty preserve,

For the mortals the gods have this fearful destiny reserved.

It is a riddle of the Sphinx,

The witch from whose jaws dripped flesh and blood,

Who sat on a rocky seat and devoured the progenies of the mortal birth.

She once had shrieked over my head to proclaim my doom,

However, by answering her riddles I had brought her under her tomb.

With lions' wrath in the body,

Wriggling serpent's wretchedness in tail,

And eagle-like wings widespread,

This monstrous lion- bird had asked me the riddles of birth and death.

What a fool I was!

By bringing her destruction to dust,

I had brought my own calamity and defiled the world with my abominable lusts;

Against nature's law I had given birth in the womb where I myself had taken my birth.

The Sphinx's order, that governs death and birth, seems sinister!

That my children became my brothers and sisters.

O what a monstrous complicity of the sin!

That mortals have no power to rescind.

Plague, death, civil war, had driven me from my home,

To live a life in despair and suffering the destiny had thrown me from my throne.

As a blind man faltering, groping, staggering with a stick in hand,

I remain banished for ever from my people and land.

The great evil, that I did not choose,

As destiny's treacherous hands had the flames of a pyre let loose.

Its method of working seems not to follow any law or chance,

It seems to exist as flames that only mortal sufferings enhance.

In its treachery cities fall in ruins,

The lamentations renew,

Like an unceasing funeral constant wars and battles sinew.

Disasters seem to creep everywhere:

Slow and creeping they come to kill before one becomes aware.

Like a strange monster who has risen from the water and soil,

As a serpent it winds and coils,

Around the tree from which all life owe its seeds,

It arouses passions for revenge and war, indeed!

In the tongues of evil it commands the progenies of Tantalus to the battle field,

And spreads terrors of the warrior riding the battle hardened steeds.

Its mighty wings cover all,

With its descent the life becomes pale,

The leaves fall in vales and dales,

Looming hills throw shadows across the valleys bringing winter's spell,

Where Bacchus in nature's fullness once brought his gift,

The vines bend on ground and pass away in lifeless sleep,

And sink in the river of the underworld flowing down in the deep,
The plague and pestilence devour earth's spoil,
In an everlasting night the world sinks in the water where Fates'
cauldron boil.
Here in this dark world amidst the cries of the Erinyes,
And the terror of the Furies,
While the shivering ghosts come cowering by,
Like a blind specter I wander and walk by;
Phlegethon's fire mingles with the rushing flood of the darkness
pouring from my eyes,
And the destiny's harsh stream flows as Fates' murmuring Stygian
reply.
It is a punishment and a chastisement for an inexpiable crime,
An offence for which I remain ever guilty to time.
Oedipus, who has broken the laws,
Must pay the price for solving the riddle of the Sphinx,
Who holds the order of life and death in its paws,
He must remain guilty to the generations to come,
And must die in banishment because there is no forgiveness for what
he has done.
For him there is no other way to live,
But to wander in loneliness where the darkness hiss and swish,
And the Erinyes lynch him with guilt's' terrible whips.
In his eyes, where the orbs of the sky stare in the darkness,
Where he gropes in a lightless world for finding hopes in a void of
great immenseness,
In seeing where he sees nothing,
In order to find a support where he clutches to everything,
Where in a wild madness the world around him in a vast nothing
revolves,

The human tragedies without human choices turn and evolve.

From this darkness as he tries to wrench away his eyes,

The holes in the eyes gaze vacant in search of light.

When he holds his head upright,

Scans the sky with a hope to see something beyond this terrifying world where there is no bottom or height,

An emptiness fills his sight,

In the uprooted cavities of the eyes tears teem as a lake of night,

And torrents of sorrow pour forth in his heart carrying Acheron's might.

O darkness! look at the slayer of the father from whose eyes all lights have fled,

Look at this face the true face of Oedipus before he is dead.

O universe! hear! Ignite the twelve constellation in the height!

End this procession of the Erinyes and the Furies and this fearful sacrificial rite,

Cease this perennial night and show me the light.

Although I deny no charge,

My conscience still remains confused at large,

I know not for which crime the fate had me condemned?

Why oracle had become my bane question

As a young man with passion blaze,

Who knew not his father and killed the one, who obstructed his path, in anger's seize,

I bore no other guilt but that comes with the vigour of the age!

O destiny! Why have you complotted this guilt and sin,

For which my wandering must again and again begin?

Why must I live to die, and never from this wheel my salvation win?

O evil! Upon the road where I falter,

In the judgment of destiny, I know, no one is allowed to be a defaulter,

Onward I move,

The feet stumble in graves, and shake,

"Am I going or am I coming?"

That I never seem to know;

The one who has gone before,

Brings me here as a blind man searching for an oar;

The one who has come before leaves me at the hellish grove.

In this confused world dark and deep now and then I hear someone speaks:

"O ill-fated Oedipus! Hurry... move... go away,

Take with you sickness, disease, sin, pain, far... far... far away...

Go away ... go away fumbling through this heart's trembling night,

See light in mind's ethereal height.

Go away...In search of pure air and the sacred light

Go away...."

Tathagata's meditation

I see the path where Oedipus has walked, and in the cross-road where he met his destiny. I see the path where a blind man, under the dome has seen the sky, watched from the inside and the outside of himself the world moving in both ways. In this cross-road I remember the palace, the pillars, the balustrades, the sculptures carved in marbles and stones. I remember the story of Heracles, Odysseus, Achilles, Polyxena, Helen - the men and women of history and myth, who have lived to love beauty, seek power and wealth, and at the end die in the hands of the destiny.

I see a wandering man going home...alone.... He is nobody...only a symbol of man whose life is controlled by the destiny and fate. Everywhere he is born, and everywhere he dies. Everywhere he is a part of the living world, and everywhere he is a part of the dead. Everywhere he wanders in the grove- like Oedipus, or sails on the sea - like Odysseus. Everywhere he meets woman as object of love, beauty, and sex. Everywhere he steps, he feels a drag from the other side. Everywhere he stops, he sees the reflection of himself as someone else... someone superfluous to himself ! Every step he takes, he feels a fear. He is in search of himself...his home...his freedom ... that he never finds.

Here, from the other side of the mirror, I see someone gazing at this world where images are moving as on the river. He leans on a tree, watches the shadow, moves with the movement of the stream outside a sphere where time has ceased. He looks at the tormented man, follows him, moves behind him .Where the world plunges as shadowy vibrations and moves outward I see him standing beside the plunging stream.

He is Tathagata, never born but always being reborn as the illusion of time. I see him emerging as a shadow of nothing. Though invisible still he is there...standing on the bank ... looking at the sentient beings with compassion and love. I see him moving through cycles and cycles of birth and rebirth... never dying... existing as the shadow from the other world gazing at the images flowing along the river: Behind, in front, below and above me... he is everywhere. His eyes penetrate all. The whole world is transparent to his gaze. I am his part. Through my gaze he gazes at me; through my reflections he sees me; through my contemplation he contemplates on my suffering; through my fear he knows my fear. I see him on the other side. He sees me on this side. I become him. He becomes me as I cross the river.

PARTY IN PHILOSOPHERS` HOUSE
Mind seeking beyond reason

When the different philosophical views fail to convince him that anyone of them may show him the path that will bring him what he is searching, the guide of the soul brings him to a party of the philosophers, who have found ways to live without caring for philosophies. Here epicureans, blasphemers, cynics, hypocrites sing about the meaninglessness of philosophical search, and profess the paths of happiness in indulgences in eating, drinking, dancing, and merry making without caring for any meaning or moral.

82. Song of the first epicurean

83. Song of the first sceptic

84. Song of the first cynic

85. Song of the first blasphemer

86. Song of the first hypocrite

87. Flight from nothingness

88. Song of the second epicurean

89. Song of the second sceptic

90. Song of the second cynic

91. Song of the second hypocrite

Crossing the dark grove, he comes to the Philosophers' House, where epicureans, blasphemers, cynics, sceptics and hypocrites have gathered for a feast.

The philosophers eat, drink and sing:

The first Epicurean sings

I have joined the party today,

Because I am much more blood, bone, marrow and clay,

I seek no heaven of feelings,

For me heaven is where the pleasure hangs in the drunk-man's eyes

from the sky or the ceilings,

For me the punch and the ,

Are more serious issues than any philosophical matter.

Sweet is the vintage, the showering bliss of Bacchus on the earth,

Sweet is this escape of the heart in pleasure and mirth.

Sweet is this purple gush,

This glittering glass that causes the blood to flush,

Sweet is the old wine in barrels,

Sweet is the end of strife   that brings man his highest laurel,

Sweet is this creature who no more has to defend himself against

morality's tiresome pledge,

Sweet is this life where there is no drudgery of the daily life's dregs.

I wish to drink and leap in the sway,

Where the boatmen in the sea toss on the waves,

I do not wish to escape the shore where there are drunkards' graves,

Because nothing will cross the boundary of the blood and flesh once one is dead.

I do not wish to be rescued,

Because all moral rescuers try to eschew

Their own fear of the wine-and-watery sea where I feel safe.

Where crewmen crowd with wine and drink to pleasures pledge,

I wish to run high on the edge.

Where the waves of joy spit on the beach as foams of champagne,

The moisture in the wine spray dews in the heart where pleasures are bottled and contained,

Nothing in the world can surpass this beauty of the sea spitting foams and spraying dews in the heart,

Without knowing the bottles of cold wine and fine champagne drunk in drunkard's art ,

No rescuer will know this thrill of living, and joy of swimming,

To experience it they themselves must jump at last.

Instead of trying to preach in vain,

For the honours of the robes of the priests that they try to gain,

The religious men should follow this sermon of the mirth,

And follow me to the joys of life on the earth.

The first sceptic sings

The poetry and language are for the emotional fools,
Where the meaningless words are meant to dig the feelings as
wisdom's tools,
The art , what the best can be said of it, is that it is devoid of
common use,
And an amusing entertainment in which those, who are gifted for
being addicted in art, feel bemused,
The science is the domain that is most abstruse,
The prestigious profession of men who, by incomprehensible
jargons, the truth of the nature abuse,
Those who read everything till the pages fall apart and the bindings
of the books become loose,
Are nothing but hungry goose,
Who feed on all bad or good,
The professors of classic studies, and mythology read stuff that they
never should,
And they should not try to lead man to seek meaning in a
meaningless world over which no one ought to brood.
The facts of history and tradition,
And all other information that come out of the press after speculative
editorial additions,
To infect the knowledge and truth in big editions,
Bringing episodes, that one should better believe, before one accepts
or denies,

Only seeing with one's own eyes,

Doubtlessly cry for moral where there is no moral to find,

Fill the world with lies of intellectual kind ,

With the critics 'articles and experts' commentary and remark,

Limits the nature of truth that they demark,

With tortuosity of the mind that the world's knowledge make,

Tell and point about the great mind's greatest foolish mistakes.

These are among some of the foolishness of the wise,

Who possess the unstoppable tendency to claim truth as they

philosophize :

What are we?

And whence we came and what shall we be?

What is the future that we cannot see?

What are the purpose of existence that is incessantly present,

That always changes and carries with it all as a temporal agent?

He fails to accept that most questions are what they are,

Because Eve had listened to Devil while he had seduced her.

Indians, Orphics, Pythagoras, Plato, and Zeno,

Caesar, Agustus, Seneca, Marcus Aurelius, and Nero,

Plotinus, Augustine, Aristotle, Aquinas, and the monks living on

Monte Casino,

Hildebrand and his friend Bruno,

Spinoza, Rousseau, Kant, Hegel and Napoleon - the hero,

Machiavelli's Caesar Borgia, Byron's Corsair, and Nietzsche's Hitler

seeking life's inferno,

Should have known that their philosophies, acts and deeds carried no

more meaning than the bankrupt man's gambling in the casinos.

For my part I do not wish to share view with Pyrrho, Timon or Cato,

For me philosophy does not worth a potato.

I only live to die,

And by glorifying the nothingness of life,
I wish to avoid the philosophers' greatest strife.
I even do not wish to speculate like Pyrrho against the philosophical
speculation,
That there exists no ground for any rational ground of action,
For the unattainable knowledge there is no consolation,
The ignorant and wise are both equally fool and wise depending on
our definitions.
So little we know that even I doubt if doubt itself is a doubting,
Nobody knows and nobody will ever know it - philosophy is nothing
but self-anointing,
Though I think it so, I know I cannot be sure,
One thing I know for certain is that everything is unsure.
The world is so quizzical that philosophy and life always seem out of
joint!
What I write, or what I say, make no point,
I never know which word will be next in my text,
I only know for sure that I will always be perplexed as the blind
world's Arcadian Rex.
Therefore I wish to know not,
Because all knowledge is valid and invalid,
When the language describes them always it describes them not.
In the nothingness where my soul is dipped,
I cling only to my doubt and try to be scrupulously honest to myself
that makes me dogmatic and stiff.
After all, what is truth or lie?
Is it not truth only masquerading of the falsehood and lie the means
to defy?
Aren't the lives of the philosophers and heroes,
Like Seneca or Nero,

Or Napoleon, or Hitler, or any other modern hero,
Or revelation of God, who is a big zero,
Utter lies written as truth in the annals, dramas, histories and poesy,
Aren't we all masked the way the liars like us to see,
The historians, the heroes, the lawyers, the priests, the philosophers
would like us to be,
I wonder if there is a choice for man beyond the question: "to be
what others say or not to be."

The first cynic sings

In the world where everything exists in order to die and rot,
In what others find worthless I find much worth,
With feelings or pride I do not use my time in seeking Devil or God,
For me all are hullabaloo around that may or may exist not.
The topics from Devil's blasphemy to virgin birth,
Interests me little like all other philosophical dirt.
The court of the royal, the camp of the soldiers, the church decorated
with the canonized saints, or the business in the mart,
Do not arouse my heart,
In gown, gain, glory my soul feels estranged,
For honour, pride, fame, my life I do not wish to exchange.
Like my brethren who have lived before in activities,
In creating one's own advantage have shown every abilities,
For harvesting personal profits kept things done or undone,
I do not wish to seek the filth of life and this is the reason why all
activities I shun.
When I see the human beings are acting in vain,
I feel nausea and pain,
When I see men and women running around in meaningless pursuits
as animals stinking and foul,
I feel ache in the abdomen and the bowel,
As in a sea-sickness the stomach rumbles and roars,
I feel vomiting when I see the human beings are busy as never
before,

When I see human hypocrisy being lived as life's finest art,
I feel a chilliness in my heart,
O! the whole field of human activities feels so emetic!
That even death seems more meaningful than living a life that is
meaninglessly pathetic.
O what a miserable misery!
The civic life's meaningless penury!
A hopeless squandering of wealth from life's frugal treasury!
As a saint or a cynic - a hermit in frairy,
Or the disciple of Diogenes - the money-changer's son who
produced false coins for the nation's treasury!
I find the life is a meaningless trial,
Where freedom is a liberation only through self-denial,
Living as a fakir in a pitcher,
I wish to live a life that is far more richer,
Than Alexander or his teacher.
I wonder what are man's own!
Wisdom, richness, natural zest that one owns?
The gifts of fortune that make them base?
The intelligence that produces the material goods and the virtues of
the life of debase?
Or the projects that constantly calculate the advantage
For one's own family, nation or race?
Or the hopes of beneficial transactions that their minds possess?
Or the fictions of freedom that they believe will liberate man from
the harshness of the life, as they define?
Or, the vulgarity of a consumer oriented world where their activities
are confined?
Here, there, everywhere- all around,
I see life follows man as a merciless hound,

Therefore rejecting all conventions of religion or race,

Manner or dress,

Without possessing anything that possesses man's soul,

I live detached from the world in the calmness of a cave, made in a

hole.

I live this life out of courage and not fear,

A life that, except those who possess rock like minds, would never dare.

I do not feel pale or struck by terror,

Because through self-denial I have learnt how to escape life's

errors.

The first blasphemer sings

Above Adam's sin and fall,
There is no greater glory for man to recall,
No heaven can yield a pleasure greater than this ambrosial sin,
Therefore I would better fall than be redeemed.
The fire that Prometheus flinched from us from heaven,
For which he was never forgiven,
Burns in our heart to incinerate the fabled world from which Adam
was for driven.
Pleasure is sin and in sin's pleasure,
Lies all morality's earthly measure,
Therefore I seek no other worldly treasure.
O Lucifer! who was hurled from heaven for sinning
Brought fire for the mortals who aspired for winning,
The world from the beginning,
Is a paradise for the sinners where there is no angel chaining or pining.
O amen!
The apostles say that such blasphemy will bring our end,
But whether God begins his silly creation or ends it, for me, it is the
same,
I am sure this downward moral towards which all morals trend,
At the end the Godly decree of the world's end will help to amend.
It will bring God to man's level,
And bring to the mortals the greatest reason for dance and revel,
Perhaps the pious will call us the children of Devil,

But who cares for those when we know that preaching is the highest evil,
Though someone with intellect spare and vast -
Murky with shadow that it casts,
Will like to see us thrown in the burning hell as the world's moral outcast,
As long as the prophecy that 'God is dead' wins mortals' hearts,
I soar towards the shinning world without God but with stars,
Rising fast and fast,
I seek the centre of the universe from which I am created in a cosmic blast,
And rejoice that, instead of man's, God's pyre will burn at last.
O immortal God ! Or His mortal deliverer crossed and pinned!
Hanging under the cathedral's vaulted wings,
In front of this cosmogony,
Poor is theogony,
In front of the anothrogenesis where man comes from stars,
Psalms and hymns for salvation from sin are only treacherous farce,
Poor is philanthropy when man is not emancipated from heaven's slavery and rods,
It is a misanthropy when man is seen as a sinner when he tries to find in himself his lord and his God.
It is said that since Eve's and Adam's fall
(Note that only the priests this fable are able to recall),
The mankind, that originated from their blood and flesh, had fallen forever in a hellish grave,
From where man cannot be saved without Godly whim randomly dispensing to the mortals His immortal grace,
It is said that it is the punishment for the fruit of knowledge that mankind has searched,

O providence! what a stupendous idiocy and curse!

O 'causa sine qua non' of all sins - the bellicuous angels of God!

O 'causa sine qua non' of all falls - Nimrod!

Stairs to heaven neither pass through the tower of Babel,

Nor through the bridges joining heaven and hell as says in the Holy Bible,

O tree from which all knowledge droop!

From your branches I desire to remain perennially hanging as a sinner who is not afraid to stoop,

In sinning I will be winning,

Hearing hymns and psalms while Beelzebub will be whining,

In Adam's fall I shall be shinning,

As a man made of star dusts I shall be rising, swimming and dreaming,

And as God- reborn in man- I shall be beaming.

Man has fallen for the apple and for the falling of the apple man has also risen,

Seeing the apple to fall the science has been born on the foundation of reason,

Though Adam from heaven is for driven,

The light of the knowledge that makes apple fall downwards instead of rising upwards to heaven,

Has brought us to the gate of heaven aglow with the stars outside the dark belief's spheres,

That are guarded by circles - some say twelve, some say seven -

But who does care,

About such silly affairs?

O! the light of reason that science has disclosed!

O light through the telescopes!

What I have known about the forces of nature,

Drive my spirit towards the universe's center for longer and deeper adventure.

O Lucifer! For whose sin man is thrown from paradise to till and plough,

O Prometheus! The shining mind's suffering hero chained as the prey for the bird,

The winged bird that flies over the earth,

Feasts on man's liver,

When man sweats and shivers,

Is the eagle of the knowledge, the Phoenix of our pyre, that lives in our hearts,

It is also the bird of paradise,

That brings man to the light where the thousands of candles of reason twinkle and hide,

And opens the gate of the universe beyond the immeasurable distance crossing our eyes.

O sin fall!

Let apple its power of reason install!

O heart rise!

See the glory of the human mind aglow beyond the gates of heaven and paradise.

The first hypocrite sings

The stars are made of matter and matter is of no worth,
As Bible says I also believe that from nothing the world has come forth.
Although as a blasphemer or a devotee,
Sunk in impiety or piety,
Man may strive without a pause,
When no one will never be able to solve the problems of universe or God - the mysteries to which no mortal mind has any recourse,
Why bother about the stars, God, or the universe's first cause or all explaining unified theory of force?
What is the point of making efforts that tax the brains,
Bring hard probation to the spirits for whom such matters are not supposed to be meant?
When there is no other goal for most men higher than reaching man's most desired station - i.e.
The earthly paradise where man seeks profit - be it, through spiritual renunciation, or mathematical formulations,
What is more to strive for the spirits untrained,
It is better to avoid matters that unnecessarily increase life's strains?
People call me a hypocrite because I balance my life between them both,
When there is need I denounce the material world on one situation and on the other make to Devil my sincere oath,
In one account I count my purse,

In other I credit and debit as Mr. Wilberforce,
Count on the coins keeping the philanthropic course,
And bring to the world Evangelist's spiritual force.
I shed sufficient tear- sometimes more when there is need for more,
And dry it as soon as I know that sentiment in others' eyes may be
considered as spirit's negative source,
I avoid corruption when I know corruption is watched with glaring
stare,
And look for opportunities when my way is clear.
I waste no time in conquest or advance,
When I know that it will only my problems enhance,
I take no chance,
In winning I pretend as if I have won perchance,
I know that this is the best way I may cheat and get things done,
O! My hypocracy is so refined that I belittle myself to none.
I am virtuous when I know that virtue will bring me medals and ranks,
I rattle and battle for moral cause with clink and clank,
Without causing anyone much pain or pang,
But that bring me from all corners of the world many honours and
thanks.
Smile is my triumph card,
At my inner nature where there is little moral substance,
I guard it carefully so that no one can get at it a glance,
I guard it so hard,
That even myself, who has no scruples - not to talk about moral
regard-
Can get to know it before playing out the card.
I smile enough when I know that it will do me well,
Otherwise I am a man of very ordinary nature prone to flattery and
swell,

However, before one divulges this truth about me to the outside world I know how him or her to quell.

I do not believe that I have any malice in my heart as long as malice is something that man should detaste,

But when it no more arouses any one's compunction or hatred,

I find malice serves the nature's best intent,

However, I do not like that one distorts my statement,

And thinks that on my part it is not well meant,

A hypocrite, who trusts and mistrusts himself, knows he existence of the malice as human nature's most natural trend,

Between the concepts of the good and the evil he perennially remains hanging in a suspense.

Hearing the songs of these philosophers he feels disgusted and enters a room where an existentialist has taken a refuge.

Flight from nothingness

I am alone.. starkly alone...within and outside myself. Everywhere the world exists as subject and object: I am on one side, and the world exists on the other. The link between the objective world and me seems to have broken. I can not enter that objective world outside myself, where everything are devoid of consciousness and meaning. I am the only meaning of my own existence - a consciousness that is in-itself exists as nothing. I exist in a vast sphere of nothingness, float in a vast sea of void, where I am never able to see my being in its completeness. Never I am revealed to me. The objects around, and the meaningless contingencies around them, shape and form me out of this nothingness and molds me into something that I am not. It deprives me of my freedom of pure nothingness, that exists outside the objective world , that exists as truly as I exist. I live under a perpetual fear of being deformed, transformed, metamorphosed as a creature, who has feet and arms, eyes and ears but possesses no vision and judgment, and generates no freedom and feeling of its own.

I try to escape, take refuge from this world that tries to form a monster out of me. I am frightened of the others- living and non-living- that are in themselves are floating in nothingness. They also seek freedom as I do, and wants to destroy other's freedom and annihilate the possibility that lies outside in others. They always form me in a mold, that I am not. I fear their gazing eyes, their constantly thinking mind, that interpret and impose images as me on me. I do not want to turn into objects of their mind as they want me to be. I do not want to be metamorphosed, without my own life, freedom, and own consciousness, that in turn is a nothingness. Instead, I wish to devour all others in my own nothingness. Therefore, I have taken this refuge where I feel alone and safe. From here I can see the world in my own way, as a free man fleeing into nothingness, trying to escape the monstrous human beings and the objects around. In this void I see a sea flowing outside me: It is time. I can not stop anything in it. All flows in this void without my willing it or not. It flows through me - through the nothingness- and pulls me into the void, where the objects lie scattered like shells or jelly fishes, or the crawling crabs with many feet, or the Precambrian creatures with many tentacles and glaring eyes - to mention a few of the images, in which I conceive this frightening state. I feel fear but I have no power to do anything against it. I only try to escape and overcome it by transforming the outside world as an object of my own reflections and consciousness. Like creatures crawling on the shore of time the objects, that I see, feel and touch, rise naked from this sea of fearful void, where there had been time, there is time and there will be time. They are always ready to swallow and devour the freedom, that I think, I possess. I know, like all others, I shall also turn into pieces of bones, smouldering parts in the glittering sand- as the dead shells are. Without any consciousness, without any freedom of my own I shall also lie dead - inert, lifeless in the shore of eternity. Foreseeing this fate I try to escape the howling gale that approaches to crush me, and turn my freedom, consciousness, and my existence into dust and sand scattering meaningless glitter in the shore of time. I am afraid of this fate ...

Therefore, I have taken a refuge of my own choice. I sit here and see

through the window, that is myself- the whole world flowing in time, while the sea undulates in the void. As I gaze, with the consciousness, that I bear, I build dunes, walls, and castles to defend my existence against the onslaught of time, that breaks all, tears apart all that I call freedom, and drags everything in the void - in the womb of a lifeless world that is detached and separate from myself. I know it is irreversible. I can not turn it backward to the state from where it has once begun. The moments fly, the speckles of dust irritate my eyes, the nostalgia for the past world flicker and I feel helpless. I can not destroy a single moment, or turn any moment to my favour as I want. I can not extend a single second, or dilate any moment in order to fulfill that I desire, or negate something that I do not desire. They penetrate the nothingness, and through consciousness enter deep in the void. I have only the choice to grasp this moment of freedom by self-reflection, and try to negate what is going on in the flow of time.

Song of the second Epicurean

In front of the burning fireplace where the friends crowd to enjoy a chat,
Relish the meal beginning with champagne, followed by salad,
lobster, crab and wine, and then cakes and cognac ... whisky and soda
after all that ...
The goal of life is not to win in Waterloo,
But to find peace and happiness in a world where there is always
something wicked to do:
Specially I think of women,
Who are prize-money for pillagers, soldiers and seamen.
While women's hips and breasts dangle as Bacchus's grape,
I seek the wine of love by seduction or rape,
I find no more sweet thing in life than this heart's dreamy escape.
When man is nothing but another animal created to reproduce,
Where shall I find life's more meaning and use?
With closet full of white-clothes, fine suits, black shoes in many pairs,
With luxury articles that keeps my skin and hair young, smooth and
fair,
I try to keep myself beautiful and neat,
And save myself from the philosophical cheats.
Under the fancy clothes where I feel naked and uncivil,
I constantly keep a balance account with Devil,
I like bull-fight, card games, and enjoy revel and dance,
And leave life to follow its course through luck and chance.
O sin! O wine! O womankind!
I may or may not be blind,
But what matters is not to resign.

The man is a carnivorous creature who needs wine and meat,
As water contradicts fire and heat,
Vegetables and milk similarly contradict man's nature - to say the least.
Like sharks and tigers he must live on the prey,
And fulfil the purpose of the nature by preying on others during night or day,
Beef, veal, mutton though may or may not be good for his digestion,
They are necessary as the women are necessary for reproduction.
Beyond all questions we can not avoid body's anatomical suction,
It will drag us to the flesh without caring for our philosophical reflections.
When the roasts and ragouts, fish, soups, dishes boiled or backed,
Give pleasure while eating, but afterwards stomach ache,
With digestion or indigestion,
That frees man from the brain's oppression,
Keeps the morality of good living safe and intact,
Why should we seek morality better than the pigs or the rats?
Apart from what is required for the gastric juice,
I see philosophy's no intellectual use,
Whenever I come to ponder on any thoughts verging in the emotion's brink,
It is always about the food I think.

The song of the second sceptic

The philosophers serve no truth,
They only speculate far and wide with a hope that their intellectual efforts will bring some fruit,
They pretend not to see the way all others see,
And instead remain blind in their own beliefs,
I find no worth in agreeing or disagreeing with them,
Because I am no worshipper of truth or falsehood - to both my attitude is the same.
However, to those who always must find something to call it right,
The best one can do is to avoid them without engaging in an academic fight,
When they see truth when no truth can be seen,
It is better to see what one sees than presuming that something else it is, or it might have been,
It is better not to justify one's own experience as false because so the philosophers say,
It will do good to remember that those great philosophers are nothing but their own hunger's prey,
As obstinate and cunning creatures they live on their intellects because they do not know any other meaningful way.
Like solitary fellows, who endure much suffering because of their belief or disbelief,
The philosophers give my sufferings not the slightest relief,
By dubious attempts when they truths attain,
For most human beings they are often the most simple and plain,

The facts of life that every mortal know to be certain.
They seem to be born with purblind eyes,
Seeing the earth they do not see the mud and dust but instead look at the sky.
Ordinary men and women who so little know,
At least know what they know,
But the great philosophers after reading hundreds or thousands of books immensely voluminous,
Feeling themselves thus highly luminous,
Scribing thousands of pages that illumine none,
Coming to the conclusion that their life's tasks are done,
When they come to the end of life they only produce a document of an intellectual cry,
That is lifeless and dry.
Among them those who are greater,
And can claim knowledge about all venerable matters,
Whose eyes blink tearfully in pity for the living creatures who live beneath,
While they see the world from the zenith,
Who have written great things reflecting their great minds,
Often never find the greatest wisdom of life there is to find - the wisdom of the common human kind.
On my part in the foolish world I see all those who are the wise,
The wisdom that one can not purchase with political bribe,
Or vindicate itself to the philosopher-cum-professor tribes.
O! I do not wish to judge this mistrustful and mocking,
knowledge-advancing, specie-preserving, institution-breeding types,
Or even wish to hurt their prides,
I only wish to avoid the places where these great philosophers thrive.
O! I do not bear any ambition for fame,

And desire to fight with those great or small for enlisting my name,
I mistrust all that on truth make a philosophical claim,
Rather I wish to bear upon myself as a sceptic all these
philosophers' blames.

The song of the second cynic

This world is wickedly inclined,
Every choice leads us to the evil of the mind,
Ambitions always usurp,
Mind remains always fixed to either honour, medal or purse,
Alas! many philosophies have also purpose to teach man to make
profit as if this life is nothing but a grand old bourse.
Time was, time is and time will be,
This is how life had been, life is and life will be,
I know with my cynical reflections nothing will nothing redeem,
But still the sorrow of life flies in rhymes.
In evil's call that makes man fall,
Confounds the mind in all,
I confess the feeling of the inanity,
Though, like Socrates, I confess that only thing I know is that I know
nothing,
I feel trapped in my inability,
I know not what is there to know,
In the wicked world, where people come and go,
In front of the questions where evil starts, evil ends, or when evil
with good swaps,
I feel helpless and dwarfed.
In this world, that I despise, there is no moral to find,
Everyone seems to live in the wickedness as hoodmen blind,
They neither listen to their own hearts, nor do they believe their eyes,
Instead, they cry for lies,

Philosophers, clergymen, and all, who teach or preach are like
morality's filthy flies,
The bearer of epidemics that sicken the souls when they fly to rise.
In this unvirtuous earthly station,
Where no sin can find its salvation,
Some take to woman and love,
Some philander in the city's hubbub,
Some take to drams as Sultan or Nabob,
Some cling to the heart as if it is only flesh and kebab,
Some run around in the offices and marts,
Pick dollars or dirt,
Some live in palace or filthy hovel,
And play golf, race on horse or peep in sex-shows after reading dirty
novels,
Some are ladies with affairs' lusts,
Some bring up thugs or clean up kitchen and dust,
Some are brides bearing other's child,
Some are children who are loveless and wild,
Some are Satan, some are hero,
Some are Apostles and some are Nero,
Some pray for sin in confession's cabin,
Some are Devil who offers salvation to the sinners wearing clergy's skin,
O what an evil world!
O Diogenes and Pyrrho!
It is a world where moral seems to be zero.

The song of the second hypocrite

Ave Maria! Ave Maria! For hours I pray,
I have been told that I need nothing more to say,
This will my desired path to the blessed city pave,
Where after the day of judgment the soul will be saved.
Whenever I go to the house of Mary where hundreds of candles burn,
I throw coins in the box and offer a candle that can earn
The divine grace of the mother of God's son.
I have another purpose that I dare not to confess,
Which concerns the nuns!
However, it is only a rumour,
Even to myself this sinful purpose I can not so easily discern.
Though in the luckless situations when loosing hopes and chance,
Finding no reward for my prayer I sometimes feel qualm,
I still read Bible, kneel on the bench, and sing the psalms.
In such a state to overcome the wailing in the heart when the soul
looks for some other balm,
Strange! The chorus in the church that keeps believers deep and calm,
Through unpleasant contradictions keep alive religious feelings and
charm.
Though I do not know what happens and how one may such
contradictions explain,
I visit cloisters, read classics, live in hell and the purgatory under the
transcendental plane,
Although sometimes I wonder if religion is luckless man's vodka or

rum,

Or the lucky man's divine lamb,

Or the blind man's alley where God is damned,

As a hypocrite I balance between the chant and hymn,

And the salvation and sin - mine and thin,

There seems to exist a gap between the practice that religiosity defines,

And the truth to which I remain responsible to myself and time.

When I see any fear or danger of death,

Ave Maria! Ave Maria! I pray in order to take a spiritual breath,

Knowing well that it may or may not help,

I test my own belief with inner cry and yelp,

Being at stake when I fall in doubt,

I damn the divinity with anger, hate and shout,

But if it happens that she answers my prayer from behind the invisible cloud,

And showers me with the splendour of wealth that no one would doubt,

As a favorite minister of her church I feel proud,

And in praise of her chastity and divinity I improvise hymns and songs when even it is appropriate and allowed.

Ave Maria! Ave Maria! Whose face is fair,

The goddess of love with the holy eyes and ears and golden hair,

In whom the Holy Spirit entered as a dove,

To give birth to the Son of God - the mortal salvation's only hope,

Who brings the blessed spirits to heaven through the holy stairs,

And gives to man the knowledge of the divine affairs,

Thy Son sitting on the right side of the Throne above,

Waits for the earth to quake, and crime and blasphemy to fill the cities' hubbub,

As a lamb and a lion assuring the world of His and His father's
love's and fear's light,
Down casting his eyes,
He waits for the moment when the day of judgment will be ripe,
And he will descend to destroy the world by taking his downward

Flight from nothingness continues ...

Thus I search myself, my freedom, my own world. Sitting in this place, where no one sees me, I think back of the life that I have left behind. I can see the contours of the sea, the forest, the lake, the castle, the gates, the garden, the dark black world, from where I have fled. I see the mirror, the reflections on the river, the rippling light over the stream scattering the moments as the time passes by. As I consciously contemplate my mind dissolves in the stream; my face becomes one with the masks of the others. The shadows and lights, carrying away the images deep within ... somewhere... in the depth of the vacuum...without any spatial beginning or end, becoming one with the void. I watch my flesh dispersing through nothing as someone who is not the same as I was. It flows, moves, oscillates, and swings. With the reflections on the waves time penetrates. I no longer exist as someone who had been, who had lived, walked, wandered as me. In the mirror I see me in the nothingness, in which I am totally absorbed. It is my way of crossing the island of solitude. While the fear rises with the waves, as the glittering flickers of thoughts, I move away and try to escape from the river.

I try to understand: Is time mind? Is this river mind? Is this conscious reflection only myself strewn on the surface as innumerable spangles dancing on the ripples, that in reality do not exist? There seems no way to know. All knowing seem to be dissolved in the nothingness. What I know remains confined in my thoughts that no longer can express what this knowing would mean. I remain invisible to myself and indecipherable by knowledge. In the mirror I have turned into a collection of spangles that has no definite meaning, no particular form, no identity, or any movement except the flow that is one with motion on the other side beyond time and space. In this mirror each time I look at myself, the images disappear. I can not recognize the rests that remain. The eyes, the noses, the mouths, the limbs, the chests, the bellies, whatever parts that had once defined my body, become so unfamiliar. It seems, with me on the other side of the mirror, I carry another existence, a new state, a new life. There also I flee, move, wander and search the part of myself that is left on this side, where I am "now" and where my consciousness floats! I have become transparent to the gaze of that other one. He is also transparent to mine. Thus as I stare at the mirror in the river, I see my own annihilation and emergence on both sides. The form, that defines me in a spatial boundary, disappears in a nothingness. I pass into another form, another domain, another existence, that is not yet connected with time. From here, where I am, I emerge in a state with no time, no past, no future - only a present, an unchanging void! I exist in order to look at myself as object on one side and consciousness on the other! The both states negate each other. And by negating and fleeing from each other they create the illusion of time and the existence that I call "me". In this irreducible nothing where all are absorbed in a consciousness, that is never able to define itself, or know itself as it is, negating the very foundation on which the consciousness arises. This side of the mirror, where I see the sea, the void, the island, the monsters on the beach, constitute the side of the contemplative consciousness. I am absorbed in a nothingness on the other side. Like me the others too are parts of the same object-subject duality.

The song of the third Epicurean

I am a mortal of careless kind,
For the learned and the learning I do not care or mind,
I am only concerned about the women whom I may share with one
or two,
As long as there is domestic quarrel in the families and adultery in
the world my purpose of living will do.
On sofa or armchair with women under and over,
Beside the burning fireplace when I hold my lovers,
And no one my scandal of seducing others' wives or daughters
discovers,
What else man should search for,
And for which needs to clamour,
Than this pleasure of amour?
When the husbands are away for business after they are wed,
The women's hearts like burning torches warm my heart on their
nuptial beds,
In the beauty of the flesh where the body caves in the weight,
Being united in the arms of the beauty as a creature caught in love's
bait,
I experience the ocean of pleasure while I undress and like an angel
she lies on the bed and for the serpent waits,
What more greater love there is to adore,
Than this love of the angel who is a housewife and a whore?
Ah! what is man without living in the verge of the peril as a sinner?

What are the happiness of the mortals who have not experienced
amours after drinks and dinners?
How sweet are these Sirens' arms that flay the beginners,
But submit in the joy of lust to the greater sinners!
How willful are the embraces of the mistresses or misses!
That warm the body under the blanket where the serpent coils and
hisses!
While the bodies on the bodies lurch,
There are no need for any philosophical search,
In pleasure's garden words are much.
Between the women and wine,
The maladies of the heart, that depends on how you define,
If I must choose,
I will choose the woman whose petticoat is loose.
Though I rather will have both than choosing between the either,
I will have the petty passion's whore instead of having neither.
Beyond this choice there is no need of philosophy that can be vital,
What more is there to search beyond eat, drink, and make merry
when love and living are only for the vitals?

The song of the third sceptic

Byron wrote: 'Let there be light! 'said God 'and there was light!'
'Let there be blood!' said man, and there was sea!
As a punishment for eating Eden's fruit this is how God man's fate
had decreed,
Although I am a sceptic, with it I feel I should agree.
Since the day God had damned Adam's eyes,
And thrown him from paradise,
Beside sending the serpent with the feminine,
To test his power of knowledge He had also sent hunger and famine,
Brought enmity and hatred among his progenies to examine,
How much he had eaten the forbidden fruit tended by the seraphim,
Death ponders over the skeletons,
And laughs over heroes even as great as Napoleon and Duke of
Wellington.
Everywhere where blood and sword preside,
' To be or not to be' is not what we really decide,
We only exist to toil for bread,
While the heroes and their heirs determine for us life's all other
important trades,
And living in their lists of pay,
The philosophers and clergies are the only privileged groups allowed
to speculate,
As long as they speculate that only in the monarchs the purpose of
God's creation is manifest.

The great God and His earthly agents of the mortal beings,

The eagles of power who are all seeing,

Unless one is agreeing,

Leaves for no one any room for mercy or feeling,

While from the unlucky throats blood gush and spout,

An eternal deluge this world devours,

God says 'Let there be light!'

And there comes an eternal night,

Man says 'Let there be sea',

And the world is flooded with sickness and moral disease,

There is no need for philosophical debate or shout,

This is the civilization is really all about.

In the civilization where man seeks immortality through war and conquest,

Where all happiness are cursed and man's ambitions for glory find no rest,

Caesar, and Agustus combat to amass power and rise as power's appalling sight,

Assault, slaughter and crush Egypt in order to rise to the temples' height,

And in vainglory stare as world's wonder in the philosophers' mind,

I abhor philosophy that glorifies this terror and might.

In this triumph and glory I see nothing but the misery of the mind,

The solitude and pain lurking behind,

In the omnipotent tyrants, whose swords are always unsheathed and whose faces are never impaired,

I see no godly stare,

To me their eyes only scatter daredevil's flare.

I do not believe that hands that destroy and unmake,

Can ever build anything truly great,

The restless hearts, who destroy and over the ruins their own monuments create,
Are the champions of the civilizations who live the life cursed on Adam and his progenies' fate.
I do not sympathize with such civilization that with the great monarchs' might the lost paradise tries to recreate,
For me the paradise is where the common man toils, trades, and procreates,
Where the shepherd boys sing in the glade,
The earth yields to the heart in the smell of the grass and dust ,
In the fragrances hidden in light and shade,
Where the teeming streams sing with the birds,
The sweet breeze feels the life's temptation without any fear of Cherubim standing as a guard,
Where in nothingness' stare brings no fear,
Where the Skye lights feels so dear,
In tears man sees the height so clean and clear,
O! Paradise is there where I am nature's close and near,
There is no need for me to fight or to fear.
Where the darkness is deep but like candle lights the heart awakes,
Where above the ocean and the earth mind revels seeing the starry flakes,
The paradise is not lost,
There is nothing to regain,
There is nowhere a fiend or God against whom man have to rebel.
I hail the human beings who in toil and task,
From morning to dusk,
Plough the field, sow the seeds, bring the life to sprout and rear it till it is ripe to reap,
O! Paradise is there where man feels the earth with hands and feet in

mud and heap.

I hail the unciviiized, the unspoiled, who loves the nature, and feels it with their lips,

Who plant the trees - not of knowledge but of life whose roots are deeper than any depth where the philosophers can dip,

O! Paradise is there where in the touches of the leaves, man feels to weep.

I do not wish to win any paradise with fire and flame,

I wish to be with the human kind who are nice and plain,

To the accursed race,

Where God withholds his glory and grace,

As God's chosen emperors and empresses,

Monarchs and queens turn their faces,

In the naked world where there is no need for dresses,

I seek paradise where the sun and the wind, the leaves and love,

Kiss with warmth the human bodies and faces.

I do not want to know from the philosophers what is the meaning of this life, or what it is not,

Because I know for sure that in what I touch and feel there lives my God,

Those who believe that God is there,

Flanged by powerful princes, commanders and soldiers planning strategies from His golden chair,

They are truly Devil's heir,

O Lucifer! let man forget their prayer,

Let mankind live in a love and peace without looking for heaven's stairs,

Let not your light bring the chaos of the night,

Let simplicity salvage man and bring him to paradise in himself of which he is deprived.

The song of the second blasphemer (*While drinking*)

When man drinks bear, whisky and wine!
O what a merry-time!
In this merry-world I give God a damn,
Same applies to His son and the Lamb!
O heart! My heart!
Lucifer's bird!
Take the bottles and pour it into the bottomless pit of the heart.
(*pours wine in the mouth*)
His mother is a Jew and father is a dove-like bird,
What more nonsense can be heard!
If anything I think is true and divine,
Lives in this flesh that enjoys the bottle of wine.
(lifts the bottle in his hand)
I need no transfiguration of wine into blood to enact the saving of
man from suffering and pain,
What enters as wine and pleasure I want it to come out as water and
pleasure of pissing again.
O mortal world!
Hear from me the sacrament's truth:
The excrement of Satan had fertilized the paradise's fruit,
The bread is only transfigured to flesh by massacres of crusaders that
 story is horrifyingly tragic,
There is no other divine magic.
Heigho! Heigho!

The life is wine and meat,

Whosoever says else is a misanthrope and a cheat,

It is more worth listening about potato and plumb,

Than hearing about Mary's child- that worthless bum!

If any one will be coming before the world comes to its doom,

It is the human spirit rising from its tomb,

O diddle diddle dawdle daddle doom!

This drinking and pleasure are all philosophies' summum bonum,

And ultimate wisdom's summa summarum!

Epiccuri de grege procus!

Which means, the swine from the herd of Epicure!

Dum vivmus vivamus!

Dominus vobiscum!

While live, live and let Lord be with you!

Trinkst du fur dein durst!

Pray for sin, and fall according to one's gout!

Vow to your soul the worldly virtue!

Sing about the world solid and true!

Ecco Homo! throw dice, and live according to exigencies and truth,

Make merry, eat, drink, and do not live like a fool,

Let the lamb eat grass, and the serpent dust,

But you eat whatever pleases your lust.

Thus I live while my mind is sunk in blood in water,

I have crossed a great length of distance by carrying my physical weight,

Like Lucifer's destiny when the night my destiny relates,

O diddle dawdle diddle daddle feet walking over the blue!

This pleasure of drinking that I know as life's greatest virtue,

Is the only aspect of existence that seems true,

Now the time is ripe for my soul to go to heaven,

And occupy the seat from where Son of God watches over the world

from his sphere beyond the circle seventh,
Amen! Amen! Vapours fuming and spouting!
The angels doubting!
I am mounting! ...I am mounting!!
All sufferings surmounting!!!
(Pretending to rise and fly, being excessively drunk he falls and
becomes asleep.)

Flight from nothingness continues

Only a mysterious film of nothingness divides us the one, who gazes at the suffering world, and the man who gazes at the self on the other side. Between these two worlds there occurs a strange metamorphosis! Something becomes nothing! Nothing appears as something! In front of the mirror the body dissolves and penetrates into nothing. From what I call inside, nothingness penetrates consciousness and the world appears as something. Thus there is always a dissolution in the other world, where there is nothing on one side and reappearance from the mirror in the stream of time. This is how I know I exist; thus I think I exist ; thus I am conscious of the two sides of the mirror where the river moves both ways - from matter to mind and mind to matter. However, only in the touch of the consciousness, what I call matter or mind, becomes matter or mind.

Once the matter is taken away it becomes nothing...pure nothing... the void... without any thoughts and words that are the components of the conscious world. Then consciousness is not conscious of anything ... mind simply dissolves. Without mind and matter all existence are withdrawn in a mystic void, from where both matter and mind have emerged. But the river never ceases; the matter never annihilates itself; the mind never becomes devoid of consciousness. Only in the whirl-pool of the ever amorphous present, shapes appear or disappear as new appearances somewhere else. Thus it makes mind conscious of itself again and again in new circumstances. This brings the illusion of time - the ever changing river - carrying matter and mind. In this river, like a projection from the void, I see him gazing. He gazes at himself. In dissolving in Him I become a part of the nothingness, from which He gazes at the world and me.

I have taken this refuge in order to gaze at Him, and be gazed at by His eyes, that illumine my consciousness. Beside this river the monsters also gaze all around. They are impure, imperfect and grotesque. Their existence are not yet organized and harmonized enough to bring forth the light of consciousness of the purer world. Every such existence is a source of fear. They prey on each other in order to live. This battle and struggle throw ghostly shadows all around. Under their gazes I am also driven to defend my existence and thus led to act against the fear by challenging the ones I face. I never feel free to be myself. I wish those fears will not threaten my existence any more. Therefore, I am fleeing.

Here I gaze at myself from a more secure place and see myself through the mind of the one, that illumines all minds. As I gaze deeper, I see the pyre in which the body of the beauty is burning. Like Ixion's wheel, the suffering of the flesh is rolling with the rising and setting of the sun in a burning circle of fire. Some call it the magic fire, that creates the illusion of time. Encircled by the fire she remains sleeping on the rock, and awaits to be awakened by her love. She again and again meets her lover, who comes to her rescue. She is the daughter of the god of heaven, who is kept sleeping on the rock surrounded by fire for the love she had carried in her heart for the mortal hero. It is a punishment for breaking the order of the heaven. As I gaze through the mirror I see the same mortal hero still wandering through the forest, listening to the birds and the beasts, searching the rock where the beauty is sleeping inside the ring of fire. He walks through the Medusa's world; sees the river and the dark sea from which all rivers spring. He is going home through the darkness of a hellish world. In that darkness he hears the voices from the tombs petrified by the magic look of the goddess of divination and augury. He is looking from the womb of the darkness of the world above which Pegasus is flying. He is dreaming to rise to the world in order to rescue his bride. I see him gazing in the light of the conscious mind emanating from the mind gazing at the sentient world.

On the side, where the time is strewn and scattered as in a temporal river, things appear separate from each other and create an illusion of the motions of the innumerable things floating in time. He wanders as a man of flesh and blood. He looks at the beauty of the world without knowing that he is a part of the beauty that illumines his mind. He sees the magic pyre, from which like a golden bird the soul flies to the height. On the other side, where nothing is disjoint, all are unified as a whole, and everything exist as present without acceding to the illusion of motion, Tathagata watches all in this light. A veil of illusion separates him and this world of mine with a film that floats as nothingness between the consciousness of the mind and the objects that flow as the river. On this river, where the words and thoughts float, I reflect in a pure subjectivity and exist in a domain beyond time.

Thus as he gazes at me and penetrates the veil of illusion, I find I have no name, I have no senses to throw away, or cling to! I see myself in the nothingness floating outside time, beyond the veil of Maya, in a pure world where there is a revelation of an infinitely unfathomable world, that is never susceptible to knowing and forming by the shapes of things, or the structures of thoughts. When these structures are removed I exist as him.

COSMIC JOURNEY
Beyond the life bound to Earth

Being disillusioned about the power of the mind, gained through earthly knowledge based on reason, he seeks the realm from where we receives signals of a higher consciousness which lies beyond the bondage of the existence bound to Earth and the life which inhabits it. This consciousness suffuses all in the universe and beckons him to search a realm which is not deniable by human concepts of time and space.

The Guode of the Soul, as winged Angel, lifts him up towards the cosmos to show him territories outside the Earth and human sphere of reality. While rising towards the heavenly sphere he discovers two contradictory paths: One lies in the realm of the scientific knowledge, and the other follows the religious and mythological world strewn with symbols.

Similarly, the cosmic beauty manifests in two contradictory aspects - both lying beyond the senses: On one side the beauty emerges through mathematical relations and cosmic laws, while on the other side it manifests as the cosmic mother and the divine bride of God, as conceived by the theologians and religious visionaries.

The guide of the soul lifts him to Heaven through the hallucinatory Paradise as seen by the pilgrim in Dante's "Divine Comedy" and at the same time imparts on him the scientific mind to explore the cosmos.

In this cosmos too the cycle of birth, death and rebirth continues. While the dance of death and birth perpetually renews every existence, all seems to be inseparably entangled together in complex networks of structures, which are beyond comprehension by human knowledge. This network, which has formed an infinitely vast labyrinth, has no beginning or end. Here death is an inseparable aspect of life. Without the existence of the one the other won't exist. In this labyrinth there exists no way out, or no way in. It appears as a timeless network designed by God.

97. The journeyman muses about mathematics and music

98. A vision of the cosmos unfolds

99. Cosmogony of Dante

100. Outside the planetary sphere

101. Flying by the constellation Lyre

102. Flying by the constellation Serpen

103. Flying by the constellation Dragon and Hercules

104. Flying by the constellation Lion and Great Dipper

105. Flying by Orion nebula

106. Flying by constellation Bull

107. Flying by constellation Pleiades

108. Flying by Demon Star and constellation Pegasus

109. Guide explains about the cosmic death and birth

110. Birth and death of galaxies

111. About the creation of the universe

112. The cosmic dance

The journeyman feels sick in listening to the existentialist, while a symphonic music being played in the background catches his ears. He hears the "Music of the Platonic Spheres".

The journeyman muses

In the turning spindle of Necessity,
From where the shafts of light revolve in the rainbow,
In the whirling whorls,
Where the endless wheels carry the world through the octaves of notes,
The cycles are interposed as before and after,
Where forms, patterns, speech coexist, precede and follow after,
As timeless aspect of time,
I hear the music that is not conscious of time.
Like the Sirens' songs from the rims of the Platonic wheels,
Which encompass the sphere with music of light,
Where the spindle of Necessity turns the rainbow in the sight,
In vibrant air,
I hear the waves appearing as the hidden world's beautiful flares.
I hear the chromatic scales,
The major, the minor, the dominant, the sub-dominant,
The fourth, the fifth, the triads, the harmony of the patterns,
Movements derived from the geometry itself,
Producing mathematical relations determined by internal symmetry
of shapes.
Where space reflects the property of the spirit explicitly defined and
unchanged,

The Phi, the Pi, the Fibonnaci series,
The numbers of the "Divine harmony",
The eurhythms governed by such undefined numbers,
Play the music beyond time.
As the transcendent light from a supreme mind,
Like Plato's Timaeus where in the nested spheres - cut away in
sections and rings-
The universe plays the harmony on the celestial strings,
Where Demiurge has composed the music assigning to the planets
and the stars their motions,
The principles of harmony are above all equations.
I hear the music of the stars, the planets, the cosmos -
Neither at rest nor in movement,
Neither in ascend nor in descend,
Moving always following transcendental curves and bends.
As the music rises to higher pitch,
I hear the deepest tone from the lunar sphere.
The stars, with the swiftest speed, play the keys of the highest tones.
What Pythagoras, Plato, Cicero had called the spheres of celestial
bliss,
Vibrating between man and eternity,
Though octave sounds do not comply with the scientific reality,
I hear in them the rhythms, that universe's perfection reflect,
And feel the coexistence of violin, viola, contrabass, flutes, horns,
drums in the pattern of waves,
My mind being engulfed in an eternal blaze.
The time that is past and the time that is future,
That in turn the eternal present contains,
When compounded with the motions in chains,
Create the harmony that is perfect in shape,

Transmit vibrations that are mathematically perfect and tuned to the light moving on the hyper-surfaces in higher space.

From the crystal sphere, that has many more dimensions than what man perceives in the earth-bound state,

I hear the melodies of eternity, the polyphonic chants, the tones in unison with the whirling world in flames.

In the interstellar space

Where the vibrations and the rhythms fill the darkness,

The strings in tension break into different components:

The movements in the mind carry harmony in the consciousness,

The musician of the souls tune the ennachords beyond the rules of science.

From the cosmic mystery where the proper motions are attuned to the music of time and space,

Reflecting the reason - the Mysterium Cosmographicum- in numbers, magnitudes and shapes,

The amazing order of the universe rises in the mind without sounds and waves.

Thus the mind hears music without any pressure in the air,

Listen to the polyphony of the past, the present and the future – far and near.

Vibrating at points in space and moments in time,

As proportions, order, symmetry, geometry, connectivity, continuity, dimensionality, and topology,

As music of astronomy, astrophysics, and cosmology,

The harmony of the spheres as mathematically ideal,

But not expressible by intervals of harmonic scheme of chromatic order,

Reverberate through the cosmos as a symphony of the eternal accorder.

The perihelia and the aphelia of the planetary revolutions,

The complex motions of the trajectories in evolution,

The arcs traversed in time, the surfaces spanned, and the work done,

Draw in thrilling precision the perfection of the music emanating from the sun.

Geometry of non-Riemannian kind,

Or pre-geometry without differential forms,

Non-descriptive, undefined with coordinate and measure,

Non-physical in relation to the possibility of visual openness and closure,

Discovered as pure subjectivity,

Formed through logical compatibility,

Hypnotize the mind with rhythms emerging from eternity.

The consonance and dissonance of the Pythagorian kind,

In the octave scheme, that the Greeks have defined,

Are the expressions of the pure thoughts reconciled in the domain of space and time.

Though according to the Euclidean scheme, the planets do not revolve,

The orbits do not attune with the Pythagorian forms,

The music of the ratios, the notes of velocities fall in harmony and symmetry

Where time is entwined on the surfaces of the topological forms;

Keeping time in association with space,

While space is time and time is enwrapped in space,

In wrinkles, rolls, and waves,

The music of heaven rises as mind's cosmic blaze.

In the music, that I hear,

I recognize the vibrations from stars,

In the forms of the moving spheres, which contain the orbits moving around the globe,

I can distinguish the different notes from the strings producing the harmony of the whole.

O Guide!

I wish to rise to the domain from where Apollo creates such beauty of the mind from his golden robe.

Bring me to the path where the cosmos unfolds.

A vision of the cosmos unfolds

In the silently shining, motionless path where all radiance are
remaining,
Where there is no end of the time without beginning,
The flowers of fire, the distant lilies, and lotuses of colourful radiance
- forming the ethereal petals - have emerged in starry splendour
from the points at height,
Past and future seem to be woven in the threads of astral light.
Undeniable but still unattached to human emotions,
Where the rays are renouncing the senses and breaking apart from
the carnal world that binds mind in time and causal motion,
Like crystals of the heaven emerging from an immense fire
emanating forth,
The stars form arcs and gates of light in east, west, south and north.
In this nothingness - the empty eye, that emulate the world that is
beyond the world of the living - the sense's tomb,
There are celestial doorways decorated with drapery,
In the curtains embroidered with brightening glimmer of the gem-
like radiant star there are celestial embroidery.
Their zigzag harmony,
Astral polyphony,
Bring to the mind a supernal world's fervent songs.
As the harmonies glide over pulsating light,
Through cracks, that asunder the masks of the hidden mystery and
open the shore flooded by the flaming tides,

In fleeting shadows, where the things are happenings without
seeming to be happening,
Tornadoes, typhoons, cyclones, tempest are summoning the smokes
to erupt, and create tides,
Where the new born stars pulsate,
Beyond the triumphal gates,
Bathing in stupendous light,
The nebulous clouds drawn under and below, left and right,
Steer the eyes where the mystery the marvel of the beauty radiates,
And in the mirror of time the innumerable stars the colors of rain-
bow reflect.
In the void, where the stars flicker as lifeless gems in communion
with a world that is beyond,
In the domain, where there seems to exist no sorrow or pain,
In a wordless world, that mesmerizes the mortals eyes,
A twinkling festivity rises, lightens, lifts the eddies and halos and
fills the landscape in a glow from the bottom to the height.
In this universe serene and clear,
Whose dimension is beyond the power of the mortal eyes to plumb
when they stare,
There are veils after veils,
That separate time and space from time and place,
Join the world of illusion with the world quivering over the timeless
filigrees and lace,
The hanging curtains that fill the distant world in an eternal haze.
In its shining depth,
Bewitching and infinite!
I see calm reefs, and waves,
Flashing streams of brilliant stars entering through and pouring out
of the celestial gates.

I sea the pearls, the birds, the cliffs, from where the space is plunging into a vaster space,

Moving towards and away,

In gleaming flashes of sails,

I see silvery decks of the sparkling boats in journey through time and space,

Lifting veils of darkness staring forth as burning gases from the tomb of the stars that are dead;

I see the fiery golden plumes of the Swan in journey over the stream of time sparkling like the gems in the hands of Fate.

In this celestial sight of plains, forests, rocks, and rivers glowing with stars woven in forms like gems,

Strung together in the immensity of the empty space,

All are quivering,

Though nothing is living,

All are trembling,

Without end or beginning.

Like in the shore of eternity all are plunging and upsurging,

Without any change, without drifting, without coming, going or returning.

In this unchanging harmony nothing is futile, ephemeral or frightening,

Though merely an atom in the infinite,

There is no crushing storm, no cloudy torments, no tempest in the mind that brings suffering, and tear.

In the open eyes, the shining stars reaching to the depth of heaven,

The boundary of the mind seems ineffable and vast.

Where Atlas, the titan, holds the heaven on the shoulder beside the garden of the gods,

The moments seem not to die,

In silence of the starry world, as a petrified figure, he stands in the sky.

In this garden trees, flowers, insects, that I know, and those I have never seen,

All await to die and be reborn...

Bound and finite carrying forms,

They breath in the fire illumining the celestial garden of the gods.

In this cosmic sphere I see Apollo moving in the chariot drawn by swans,

The illusion of purity and beauty of starry maidens wreathed with radiating jewels,

Who were not visible to my eyes before.

Over illumined clouds rising in the forms of pillars and columns,

Above the thunder bearing power of a burning urn,

I also see demons, beasts, and birds,

That pervade the world,

I see smoke and dust that reflect images of innumerable forms.

In an inner harmony,

In flashes of light I behold the inner union of darkness and light.

Here, there are shadows that divide the delusion between that are accessible to light, and which are beyond,

Through the webs, where like self-illumined gems, the stars shine in uncountable forms,

There seem to exist paths, that may lead to an everlasting immortal Home-

The land of never-returning,

The domain where things, that appear moving, move not,

Unperturbed by the motions of the sun and the moon,

The luminous chariots of appear ascending, or descending-

Though there is no ascending, or descending of the gods.

They ascend the Guide tells him about the Spheres of Heaven, that constituted the western concept of the cosmos, only a few centuries ago. The journeyman discovers those spheres, once described in the Dante's epic "Divine Comedy".

Cosmogony of Dante

While we ascend,

Look carefully at the orbs that curve and bend,

Behind these objects lie hidden spheres,

Through which Dante's lady of light had risen towards the Heaven

by climbing the golden stair.

In this celestial nature,

Where the angels guide the souls of the mortal creatures,

As we proceed watch carefully the fallen angels flying as modern

engines,

They pervert the world with evil and sin.

And tempt the mortals to eat from the tree of knowledge that the

serpent guards,

Don't fall asleep if Lucifer sings in the ears in Cherubim's skillful art.

Let us fly to the imaginary paradise,

Where the flowers and buds receive flames from the azure height,

Where the herd-boy meets the lover across the river of the night;

Using the wings of the birds of light,

Let us return to the Eden where the souls are in eternal flight.

To arrive there we must move in the reverse direction than what

Dante's pilgrim had done,

Instead of rising we must fall towards the planet, that circles around the sun.

As in man himself lies the heaven and the hell in the lower and higher parts,

Theology presumes the hell to lie below and the heaven above,

Man feels down going with Satan in the instincts based in the lower limbs,

While in the upper body, where the thoughts and feelings stream,

Man believes in the existence of paradise in a world of dream.

This concept is also extended to the material sphere,

Paradise and hell are projected as realms that one can reach by descending or ascending stairs.

Carrying such simple concept Dante's pilgrim had made his progress,

By rising towards the sky he had seen lighted worlds,

Where in reality there exists extreme conditions more frightening than the Hell.

Where in the sphere of the moon,Dante had met Piccarda and Constance,

The mother of Fredrik II, who fathered notorious Manfred, and an empress,

Seen the beauty wearing celestial pearls as her hair-dress,

Under her veil seen hallucination of a beauteous face,

He had seen himself in a Narcissistic world in error and self-embrace.

In the next sphere, Dante progressed to see the beauty

As a goddess of love who over everything shines,

And life's goodness defines;

Bathed in the light of Mercury, where beauty's radiance increases,

While his pilgrim had met souls as countless lights receiving divine graces.

Though full of heavenly bliss in perfect harmony of Paradise,

As warriors these souls reflect the light of emperors' worldly prides,
Who desired power and fame,
And failed to reach the higher sphere of beatitude belonging to the
divine dame.
Here Dante had seen Justinian, the emperor of Byzantium,
Who moved the seat of the Roman empire not far from Troy,
From where Aeneas had once fled in his journey to Latium;
Here Constantine had moved the Eagle carrying Caesars' names,
And had brought back the palladium, that Aeneas had rescued from
the Trojan flames.
Here the souls of the generals, who defeated the Vandals and Ostrogoth,
And established the reign of the emperor who took Caesar's name,
Fly the banners of the emperor who purged all laws of excess that
create shame.
In a sphere, where the summer is so hot that lead will melt,
And the winter is so cold that most gases will freeze and condense,
Dante had imagined the sphere of the providence,
Seen the souls of Queen Margarate of Louis IX, Queen Elenor of
Henry III, Beatrice of Charles of Anjou,
And talked to misquandering minister quarrelling with the nobles
about royal accounts and dues.
In the sphere of Venus, that is a sea of sulphuric acid, and a place of
volcanic hell,
Dante had imagined the realm of the divine female in her glorious spell.
With rays scattering as the morning and the evening stars,
She had grown more beautiful as the goddess of love born from the
sea of Cyprus.
In the heaven of Venus Dante had seen souls filled with amorous sparks,
Dancing as flames synchronized with the dance of the stars.
Here pilgrim had met amorous souls, who - though fallen- possessed

magnanimity because they had served the church,

And seen the soul of Folquet of Marseilles, the amorous troubadour and poet-

Later a Cistercian monk and Abbot of Torronet,

The Bishop of Toulouse, who persecuted the heretics during the Albegensian crusade in order to win the divine lady's heart,

And risen to the heaven by making use of the great merchant- son's skillful art.

Here the soul of Cunniza da Romano, the sister of the bloodthirsty tyrant,

Who took four husbands and two lovers also flew among the blessed souls,

By freeing the slaves kept by his brother and serving the church she had reached this pious goal.

In spite of the carnal sins and the excessive of desires,

The goddess of love had lifted her from hell and fire.

The way her divine love operates can be difficult to understand,

Redeemed in Christ's triumph here also flies the soul of the whore of Jericho,

Who once helped the people of Israel to regain their promised land.

She had hidden the spies of Joshua, the successor of Moses, and helped them to escape,

Therefore her soul had risen from the Limbo to the heaven to take a bright glorious shape.

Above the sphere of love lies the sphere of the spirits, who dance in circles as brilliant lights of joy,

It is a place for the theologians and thinkers, who had risen to the heaven floating on a grandiose cosmic buoy.

Here the souls of the wise are supposed to be brighter than the sun itself,

They possess intellectual power of illumination coming from the
Creator Himself;
While the divine female stands at the center of the circles as the
symbol of Theology, Revelation, Wisdom and Grace.
The most famous among these souls is Thomas Aquinas,
Born of the noble family, educated by the Benedictine, who entered
the order of the Dominican,
Writer of Summa Theologica - Christianity from the point of view of
the Aristotelian;
He was canonized as a saint after his death in a monastery of the
Cistercians.
His goal had been to reconcile and demonstrate the harmony between
the natural and the ecclesiastical laws,
And never found in the Christian theology any error or flaw.
It is the sphere of the souls of the commentators, the writers of
ecclestical treaties,
Who believed the heaven to be revolving around the Earth, by the
help of the deity.
In harmony with Aquinas' great clock chiming a divine music
arousing the faithful hearts,
Here the sphere of the believers of immortality starts.
Here the writers of the Seven Books of History,
The author of the City of God, or the composer of the Consolation of
Philosophy,
Teaching against magic and geomancy,
Receive the grace of God in a sphere of theocracy;
All others are supposed to end in prison, or pyres as results of their
heresies.
Besides these scholars of Dominican faith,
Who have merged science and superstitions to form a theology with

a Aristotelian base,

The souls of the Franciscans, who had proposed in love for the poverty the highest spiritual gain,

Also circled around the Bride of Christ - the seraphic love pouring from the divine flame.

In this sphere Francis, once the wool merchant's son,

Named Giovanni Francesco Bernardone when he was born,

Who renounced the worldly pleasure by casting off shoes, girdle and staff,

And went to serve the poor wearing his tunic girt,

Bore the wounds of Christ crucified on the cross,

And carried the light of love through sacrifice and suffering - believed to be the Bride of God.

The next is the sphere of the souls that flash as spangles on two huge bands of light formed like a cross,

Where the image of the crucified Christ appears to the eyes of the pilgrim puzzled and at loss.

In this ever-changing scene of shifting patterns, that fly by,

In the sphere of Mars, the sphere of warriors, is supposed to lie.

Here the souls wait for the Last Day of Judgment,

When they will resurrect with bodies and make the reign of Christ eternal and permanent;

After that there will be no need for making crusades to the Holy land,

Christianity will triumph across all boundaries separated by sea or sand.

Here Dante had also met his great-great-grandfather, who had died in the crusade led by Emperor Conrad,

And come to know about his warrior ancestors now flying as blessed birds.

Here Dantian hallucination had not ended,

Instead, his rich fantasy to the Jovian sphere had extended:
It is a sphere of the monarchs, who are just:
Like King David, who had moved to Jerusalem the divine ark,
And the emperor Constantine, the founder of Christianity in Rome
-defiled by sinful passion and lust.
Here a Great Eagle -composed of the souls of the monarchs- brings
forth the Divine Justice of the heaven before bringing them to Earth.
In this sphere the souls of famous soldiers form the verse of the
Book of Wisdom: DILIGITE IUTITIAM QUI JUDICAIS
TERRAM,
While the Great Eagle shoots up from the letter - signifying monarchs
a sparkling design spreading the military glory of Latium.
In innumerable sparks,
As thousands of lights rising up,
Here the Great Eagle had spoken to Dante about the Eternal
Judgment,
That comes from the Throne of glory of Christ that lies even higher
up in the firmament.
This vision was too much for the pilgrim's eyes at first,
But looking at Beatrice's eyes he could withstand the countless
heroes' flashes and bursts.
In Dante's heaven, between the Throne and this sphere, there existed
a golden ladder of light,
Along which countless souls descended and ascended far beyond the
sight.
In the sphere of Saturn, where the souls whirled along the ladder,
One could hear the thundering roar of the soul of Peter Damian,
which made everybody shudder;
Who warned the pilgrim not to try to know more of the heaven than
the blessed ones flying in this sphere themselves can understand.

Thus the author of the treaties on Divine omnipotence,
The power of God to act against all laws of nature had fiercely
maintained.
In this sphere Dante had also encountered the soul of St. Benedict -
The founder of Monasticism preaching salvation through submission,
A way of self- negation by practicing poverty, humility, labor and
religious meditation.
By destroying the temple of Apollo and the grove sacred to Venus,
He had built a monastery that became famous and equally heinous.
His precepts Regula Monachorum made the monks live like true
have-nots,
That had led the monks to try to poison him in order to free
themselves from the hands of this abbot.
Benedict had hoped that by his precepts he would help to create
proper conditions,
By which the souls would reach their salvation and true destinations,
Without such order and discipline,
He believed that it was not possible to climb the golden ladder meant
for the souls rising to the sphere of highest esteem.
He believed that only after purifying oneself with such sufferings
man may ascend to the sphere of Christ,
Where the apostles moved as spiritual whirlwinds in flight.
He had tried to stop with fervent contempt,
The usury, and greed of the monks for making worldly gains,
This was the reason why his soul had thundered and roared and
created such flames,
However from his wrath pilgrim was saved by the power of the
divine dame.
Above it is the sphere of the fixed stars,
With Virgin Mary, Apostles and Jesus with Triumph of love.

While they rose,

The souls of Church stretched their arms and heavenward strove.

Singing the hymn of beauty Regina celi,

They praised the Virgin Queen who is holy.

As a mother-bird protecting her nestling,

She protected the pilgrims - her beloved earthlings;

Here the heavenly lady and her son had filled the eyes of the pilgrim with a divine dream for long.

In this sphere Christ is the power of God and the highest Wisdom,

It is difficult to approach him before answering the questions on Faith, Hope and Charity asked by St. Peter, St. James and St. John.

In order to get the heavenly pass,

Here souls Apostlolian examinations need to pass.

Except those, who has taken to Christianity, this heaven is closed for mankind,

Where the divine lady and her son as the supernatural moon and the sun shine.

After Adam's fall, this is the only way open to reach Paradise.

Here the whirling souls coil around the tree of knowledge, life and light-

Made as an enormous cross - the symbol of death and ascension of Christ,

Around which all existence are bound to death and life.

Here Dante had seen Angel Gabriel, carrying a flaming torch,

Flying over the crown of Mary, the bejeweled queen emanating from the Rose- the seat of the Words of God.

In her garden of Paradise the Apostles floated as lilies, and directed mankind to the path of Christian Faith,

Only the blessed ones enjoyed the fragrance coming from the heavenly breath;

All others went to suffer in the poisonous river of Styx, or sleep
eternally in Lethe.
The souls whirling around the fixed pole,
Told the pilgrim that what man does, or does not do, really play at the
end very little role,
God chooses without any reason the blessed souls,
Who He wants to save from life's drum droll.
This is Sancta Simplicitas!
A great simplification of religion in which mankind is led!
As Nietzsche had said.
One can never cease to marvel how some can acquire such eyes to
see this paradisaical marvel,
For me this heaven is a real garbage and hell.
It is a fabricated paradise based on falsehood than truth,
Where the laity pays out of fear for the popes like Hildebrand - a
man, ruthless and brute.
Hildebrand had stirred the laity to riot against the clergies breaking
celibacy and living a life without Augustinian faith,
In his opinion the female had seduced Adam to eat the apple,
And thus caused mankind to acquire sin and fall as a result of God's
anger and wreath.
To arrive at the heaven there had been struggles of men of power
who were brutal and bullish,
Vengeance against the non-believers are crusaders', murders',
looters' ways that are no doubt blind and foolish.
No wonder that Dante had seen this paradise,
Because his family had been involved in the struggle against the
emperor and stood on the Papal side.
The visions, that sound like supreme insight, are reflections of follies,
Meant to farther propaganda of the powerful men exploiting the

Holy.

Let us now move through the same spheres and look at them with the visions of science,

And make a journey in the paradise of the promethean mortals, who have bade the heaven their rebellious defiance.

Outside the planetary sphere

Theology is a joke when it says hell is down below and heaven is above.
Christ sitting in Throne above the stars and Satan defiling the souls
on the Earth by offering material rewards,
Are eclectic apparitions that only exist in religious books and arts.
As we enter far above Jupiter and Saturn in the planetary outskirt,
Look how everything is so hellish dark!
Here lies the Kuiper Belt - the cometic region,
From where the dark frozen balls of methane and ice enter the
planetary spheres in elliptic orbits extending outside the solar system
from perihelion to aphelion.
The gassy comets, which are named after the centaurs galloping by
the riverside in hell,
Warmed by solar ray evaporate to form the blazing tails,
Like dark coal made of stellar dust,
They are carbon rich black rocks that pour steams from cracks on
crusts.
In the middle-ages the comets, which are spectacular to see,
Were blamed for all misfortunes that could be!
Before it was discovered that they were nothing but bodies made of
frozen ice, gas and dust,
They were considered to be supernatural evil angels moving fast.

The Halley's comet, which had appeared during the early days of
Christianity with glowing tail ablaze,
Was feared as the sword of fire suspended over Jerusalem before its
siege.
It was also the fearful flaming star, which had brought the death of
Emperor Macrinus,
And its return had coincided with the defeat of the Huns at the battle
of Chalon against the allies of Aetius,
It had brought victory to the Duke of Normandy in the battle of
Hastings,
And with its help the Turks had captured the city founded by
Emperor Constantine.
Though it is nothing but a gaseous ball,
The pope had tried to excommunicate this evil angel when whole
Europe in the hands of Mohammedans seemed to fall.
In recent times, as a consequence of the annihilation of the frozen
comet as gaseous vapor in the heat of the sun,
According to astrologers, has caused more theft, robbery, illegal
money lending and misappropriation of the public fund.
Apart from these, it has brought more arson, treason, perjury, usury,
sex and fun.
It has brought intelligent adaptation of the power of the fallen star
that every 75 years returns,
With the changing conditions of the planet where the power of
astrology is being replaced by bombs and guns,
It has given the earthlings more power to slaughter than the power of
the moon and the sun.
From this extreme boundary outside the limits of the planets,
Let us enter the realm beyond the sleep walkers' and crusaders'
spheres singing Dantian quintessential sonnets.

In the Christian cosmogony, the souls of kings, queens, powerful women and men, priests and popes have risen or fallen to different spheres in the Heaven following the pleasure or displeasure they aroused in the minds of the theological authorities. The most faithful souls and the most powerful rulers, who had promoted Christianity with using every means, had often received the highest seats in Heaven.

In the pre-Christian era too, the starry heaven was seen as the adobe of the heroes and warriors. Observing the correlations between the motions of the starry constellations and the coming and the going of different seasons, which brought forth different natural forces at different periods of the year, the cosmic arena was viewed by the people in the old civilizations as the adobe of gods and goddesses, who unleashed those forces. The roles of the heroes and warriors were to win over the wraths of the Heaven by controlling the sinister powers. Since then the starry sky has remained an arena of myth.

They fly by the celestial constellation, while the Guide tells him the mythological stories associated with the stellar world and the true nature of the stars.

Constellation Lyre

It is the Aeolian Lyre whose strings vibrate with the vibrations in the stars,

Where the frets of fire agitate through the cosmic seven-fold bar,

And enchant the world from the earth to the domain of the stars;

It is that Lyre of Hermes, which Apollo exchanged with his herd.

It is the instrument of Orpheus- the musician of death and birth;

It has been created by Hermes out of empty shell to bring music, poetry and art to human heart;

Its vibrations persuade the queen of death to let go Eurydice to meet her beloved.

It is also a cosmic constellation, that rises in the Northern sky as candles above the altar of Apollo,

That brings the tunes of the god of radiance soaring to the realm of the stars,

And illumines in the cosmic sphere the starry faces of the maidens of beauty and Orpheus' love.

In the summer night when Herd-boy plays his tune under the triangle of stars,

Weaving a veil of dream awaits for the appearance of the beauty,

It is the constellation, that has become the legend of Herd-boy and the Weaving girl.

It is here Apollo comes with his Muses flying with the swans,

And remains separated from the nymph he loves.

Like in Daphne's grove, through which the river Peneus - under the feet of Mount Olympus - runs,

Here the lovers remain eternally separated like the Sun.

While the hearts strung in music bridge the distance created by the celestial river,

The wings of the swan create a cosmic shiver.

Here lies the temple in which the blood of the decapitated Orpheus has flown,

While the Lyre has drifted and come to rest on the cosmic altar unseen and unknown.

Here one can see twirling rings of marvelous beauty with blue-white shine,

That create an impassable barrier that allows no spiritual lovers to bodily meet in time,

It is a window to a greater world where cosmic music meets the vibration of an ethereal brine.

Constellation Serpen

This constellation calls upon the vision of a fiery gate,
Through which Eurydice once entered the world of the dead.
It reminds one of a flaming world passing under a stream,
Where the dead assemble beside a whirling fire spreading fumes in
Devil's wings;
Here around the throne of Persephone, the queen of death,
Whose heart Orpheus won with his lyre's enthralling spell,
Hangs the infernal bells.
While, like glowing serpents, the clouds wriggle around the flaming
gates that rise like spires,
In towering pillars of black smoke,
The goddess of the underworld rises twisting and turning through
the fire,
In intriguing shapes creates strange visual effects of the realm of the
Hade:
It is infernally red.
The towering smoke, that one sees rising like a genie from a magic
lamp,
Is, in fact, an isle of hot expanding gas trillions and trillions of miles
long.
The mountain, on which one sees the Queen's throne,
Is so high, that even light will take years and years to climb and reach
her scepter's studded dome.
Here inside a hellish womb,
In a nebulosity of enormous extent,

Where curious formations shine in many different lanes,
The clouds expand resembling explosions of bombs;
While many stars, much bigger than the sun are born.
In the edges, where one sees serpent like figures, that fires eject,
A mist forms the material for life from the dust, that the stars reject.

Constellation of Dragon and Hercules

Heracles - the Babylonian Gilgamesh of the legend of the flood,
Bent on the knee over a writhing dragon's head sweat in blood;
Born of a mortal woman by the god reigning over the firmament,
Who ascended from the earth to the realm of the gods by climbing
funeral flames,
Once took burden of Atlas before the heaven's garden full of gems,
Whose bow and arrow brought Agamemnon's victory over Troy,
Wears on the head one of the largest gem in the constellation, that is
Dragon spun,
It is millions of times more voluminous than the sun.
It's density is very low,
Virtually a vacuum compared to earthly air,
Although very luminous,
It emits most of its radiation in wavelengths, that escape eyes' visua
layer;
Mortals are constrained to experience the beauty of the heaven in a
small spectrum of waves,
Illuminations coming from outside the visible spectrum appear to
earth-bound man as darkness' impenetrable veil.
The bright orange star that dances with a star of blue-greenish hue,
Expand, as if, to unite as two jewel-like celestial dews.
Gradually dispersing in space,
Becoming one with the vacuum by losing its mass every year,
At the end it will disappear from the sky-

The destiny that Gilgamesh feared.
Thousands and thousands of such supergiant-stars,
That in cosmos disperse,
Radiate luminosity thousands of times greater than the sun,
And are closely packed in space in the constellation of Hercules,
where a "keystone" is hung.
It is a globular cluster containing nearly a million of suns,
Where giants and dwarfs burn,
Die and decay pouring in the heaven the light of hundreds of
thousands of suns in return.
It is one of the finest clusters, that can be seen in the northern sky-
A blazing scene in the heaven thousands of light years away,
Observing from a distance, it appears as a blazing ball of rays.

Constellation of Lion and Great Dipper

Like a scorching chariot when the sun, drawn by Lion,
Creating turbulent wind, as Babylonian god Marduk, travels,
Rushes to slay Tiamat the bringer of Chaos-
The power of the sun in all directions unravels.
While with ferocity and swiftness, hurricanes and whirlwinds drive
his spear,
The monster of Chaos gnashes teeth and creates foam on the sea, that
is tumultuous and fierce;
The magnificent star Regelus - the Latin Rex, the Akkadian King of
the Celestial Sphere,
As the king of the heaven, revered by Mesopotamian, Persians,
Arabs, Judah and the ancient seers,
Reposes in the heart of the beast without any fear.
Like the magical Marduk, who triumphed over Tiamat by cutting
channels,
Bade the wind to bear her blood,
Split her flesh and fixed bolts to control all flood,
Made the earth inhabitable by man, whom he created from mud,
Regelus, burning at the heart of the constellation of Lion,
Is the magical star, that brings the power to control turbulence,
Creates the life giving water from the blood of the dragon who is slain.
Wining over the forces that bring chaos as the complot of the
treacherous Devil,
Slaying the evil,

As a soaring Eagle he asserts power over the serpent,

Whom the people in the ancient world believed descended from the celestial den.

The destiny of the sun-kings,

Who slay the monster and control the power of water, earth, fire and air,

Was believed to be hidden in godly altar above celestial stairs;

Where the Lion reposes,

Amidst the Zodiac signs, as a Sphinx poses,

The ancients believed that the destiny of the kings were already inscribed in the constellations' faces,

Like the king of Thebes, Oedipus Rex,

Who answered the sphinx and killed the hex,

Where Eagle, Lion, and Serpent- forming the mythological beast,

Keeps guard of the cosmic Pyramid,

They believed that along the ascending Dragon's stairs,

The destiny has laid the path of the Marduk's heirs.

Where the Eagle flies,

The mortal fights with the beasts in the forest by the riverside,

Where Gilgamesh swings his chariot in the sky,

And tries to escape the serpent-bound life where he has to die,

The Crab scuttles,

The Hydra attacks Heracles struggling against Fate,

The starry constellations the power of the divine world reinstates.

In the frozen north, where inhabitants of the earth have imagined in the pattern of the stars the rotating polar bear,

The constellation of the Big Dipper flings glitter in the northern stair;

Here people from the East have seen unfoldment of a secret flower carrying lustrous flare,

And the inhabitants of the West have marveled over the seven stars shining in frosty nights' brilliant glares.

Sparkling like gems,

In front of Valhalla's flames,

While Wotan's chariot drifting behind the clouds,

The gods move in the realm of immortality in steeds fierce and stout,

Valkyries ride white steeds beyond the sphere of the moon and the sun,

The daughters of Wotan wake the dead to life with the starry world's joyful shouts.

Where the twinkling stars as lucid songs of the heaven vibrate,

The celestial globe unites motions with rest,

Where in the wakefulness of the Valkyries nothing can be heard but silence,

Planets and stars disappear from appearance,

In a swirling harmony of ray,

The Celestial Dipper moves around the Wotan' Way,

The Chariot carries around the pole the dream of immortality, where nothing moves and sways.

Here the Egyptians once saw the floating Osiris,

The casket, in which he was sent drifting along the river,

A cycle of death and life moving around the Great Dipper.

Orion nebula

Where the marvellous spectacle, illumined by the diamond like stars,
That drifts as a great cloud, arousing a feeling of awe and wonder of
the universe,
Appears as a primeval chaos from a time not visible to the eyes,
There lies a nebula, awakening like a dragon from a sleep around a
cosmic hearth.
In its fiery mouth the matter pours in chaotic turns,
Nebulous gases condense, contract and form stars much brighter
than the sun;
Around orbs, that shine as diamond-like gems,
The gases swirl as eddies,
The masses are carried away in currents of whirling motions falling
in a nebulous den.
This thrilling view, that all awes surpasses,
Shows the mystery of life and death in the depth of space.
Here one can see all conceivable fates of the stars:
Known as variables, doubles, triples...multiples...
Orbs expand as giants, or contract as dwarfs...
Clusters remain wide and dispersed... or compact and condensed,
Visible or invisible as binaries ... pulsating and shifting ...
Burning, cooling and drifting...
Eat up the weaker ones,
Smaller than the sun.
Here stars die and disperse in space,

Illumine the sky with a nebulous blaze.

In this Isle of light,

Where fluorescing gases enter gloomy gulfs hidden under mysterious shades,

In the vastness of the radiant clouds from the living, or the dead,

Greenish tinge reveals the dark corners of the gulf unfathomable deep,

In a world intricately complex, in waking in the world man falls in a cosmic sleep.

A line drawn from the belt of Orion to Betelgeuse and Rigel lies the Dog Star,

Known in the ancient world as a hound that follows hunter in frosty nights along wintry snow-clad path.

Like a splendid star over shining over snow laden trees,

At Thanksgiving, or the Christmas Eve,

As a leader of the orbs in the heaven,

Orion's hound blazes as a star that first appears in the harvest month.

Though it is brightest of all,

Its shine evil omens recall.

When Achilles advanced to the Trojan plain,

To kill Hector - the greatest Trojan name,

Priam had seen this Dog coming at night,

As an evil omen it had burnt over the Trojan height.

Rising as shining Isis before New Year's day,

In the altar of Ra mingling with ray,

She is also the huntress pursuing the hunter as power of destiny and fate.

As harbinger of death,

Twinkling in tints varying from ruby to sapphire,

Known as Sirius, eight and half light years high in the brilliant attire,

Rising in the sky carrying inauspicious light,
That has caused Achilles' wrath and Ajax's madness as destined
from the power residing in the stellar height,
She is hunter and huntress,
United with the one who is being hunted.
The Egyptian conceived Sirius as Sothis - the soul of Isis,
A cow with a star in between her horns,
And called Orion as Sahu- the incarnation of Osiris,
Who dies in order to be reborn.
After he had fallen, and his head had been removed by Re,
Isis had made a journey to get back his life from the world of the dead.
Resurrecting Osiris as the Lord of war and feast,
Sothis had brought his consort to life wearing a head of a beast,
By a road ascending from the east,
And then followed him to the west,
Where he would fall and descend to the underworld to take a deadly rest,
Before resurrecting again from the realm of the dead.
It is an eternal drama of birth and death,
A perpetual search of the hunter for the huntress,
As well as love of the moon-goddess for the mortal men,
A play of destiny where every victor will be slain.

Constellation Taurus or Bull

The Bull, that Orion eternally faces,
In various cultures is associated with the spirit of rain,
That brings fertility to the soil that life sustains.
In India, the star Aldebaran is called Rohini - the Red Deer,
Wandering in the garden of the gods without any fear.
Beside the Rohini river,
It is seen to rise above the Lumbini Graden in the spring,
Where Tathagata, who eternally comes and goes, is born as a prince
in the house of a mortal king.
The constellation was named because it marked the Vernal Equinox,
Its meeting with the sun heralded the process of fertilization of the
mother earth,
Who revived her consort and lover to birth.
With its coming, the sun-king had to face torrents and tides,
Needed to plough the land,
Sow seeds by conquering the Bull of immense might,
Like Heracles' and Gilgamesh's laborious plight.
In Egypt it was seen as the Bull of Isis presiding over the cultivable
land,
Eldest of the animals in the Heaven,
Power of life enduring in all things,
A beast from whom immeasurable strength springs,
A redeemer of everything moving in the temporal stream.
It is the horned moon-goddess with a bright star decorating her ship,

Possessing the body of the earth from which Isis revived Osiris.
It is also the Bull of the Persians, whom Mithras seized,
And obeying the command from the sun flayed,
Thus delivered to the world herbs, grains and plants from its blood and flesh.
It is the Assyrian Winged Bull, that joined the heaven and the earth,
The figure engraved in kingly tombs as a symbol of divine power that descends in kings of mortal birth.
It is also an animal of Shiva, a Hindu deity of destruction and death,
Who creates and brings everything to life,
While he sends the world to annihilation through his flaming breath.
In the Minoan culture it was known as the Cretan Bull:
The animal who leapt in the sky to fight with heroic men,
Roaring in and charging the sky it is a divine beast, that is can not be slain.
Mino's wife, Pesiphae, met with the Bull,
And gave birth to Minotaur, who fought with the kings representing the solar-rule.

The constellation Pleiades or Seven sisters

In the Pleiades the Greeks had seen the constellation, which volcanic
eruption bring,
They were believed to be the harbinger of storms and tempest raging
over mountains, rivers and streams.
The Seven Sisters are also the angels rising at dawn in autumn,
And sinking below the morning sky in the west during the Spring.
After they depart starts the time to sow and dream;
Before they rise at dawn one needs to reap the harvest and protect it
from stars' evil beams.
As the stars in the morning horizon, they carry bowls of diseases and
plagues,
While on the contrary, they are also the stars of blossom in May.
Buddhists saw the birth of Buddha when the stars rose in the East in
a shining night,
As the flower stars of the East the constellation brought to the earth
the soul of the immortal light.
Persians wrote poems of immortality affixing Rosette Pearls of the
heaven along the Pleiades' path,
Hanging necklaces over branches of trees in rose gardens, they
sought love of beauty in Pleiades' hearts.
In the light in the silvery virgins' braids,
Poets and musicians of the ancient world had seen the heaven's door
guarded by these beautiful maids.
The Anglo-Saxons called them by the name Sifunsterri,
The Germans praised their beauty as Siebengestirn,

In the lands of snow and frost,

These daughters of Atlas were called Fur in Frost.

In the Minoan divine discs they were represented by seven dots,

That encircled the path of the journey towards the realm of the gods.

They are the beneficent sky spirits of the Vedas,

Who dwell at the centre of the universe,

Where the Supreme Deity heavenly order preserves;

They are also the goddesses of primitive tribes,

Who bring knowledge to cultivate rice;

They are the stars of agriculture, that wakes the seeds to life.

According to the myth in Greece one of the seven sisters veiled her face in grief of seeing the burning of Troy,

From where Aeneas had fled, and sailed on a tumultuous sea guided by the stars that burn and destroy.

These are the stars whose flames also beckon the world to surge with life,

As the queens of night,

Who bring earthquakes and tides,

They rise as maidens wearing wreaths of light.

They keep watch over the flames, that once kindled Troy,

And bring Odysseus' victory and joy;

Under this celestial sign, towards which all seafarers gaze,

In order to avoid the fearful goddess' wicked blaze,

A primal wheel of death and life revolves,

And the seven virgins fly as cosmic orbs.

Nearby, at the Pole, the constellation of Bear lies in a cosmic pool tranquil and unmoved;

However, there is no place where things can achieve a true rest,

All things must move in nature's behest.

The point, that seems fixed in the sky, is an illusion,

It is caused by rotation of the orbs once formed from the stellar dust,
Changing with the paths of the stars - as they must,
Every motion undergoes stress and tension of the forces striving to
tear the orbs apart.
Although stars fly and recede,
There exists no path to escape,
Travelling far one seems to return to the departing place.

Demon star and constellation Pegasus

Whom the Arabs named Al Ra's al Ghul - the Demon's Head,
The Hebrews called Rosh ha Satan where Satan treads,
Is Gorgoneum Caput of Vitrivus and Lilith, who took Adam to her bed.
The medieval astrologers associated with it a spectre,
And Athena wore it in her aegis as Gorgon's face,
That caries the mystery of the dead.
The Greeks revered Gorgon Medusa as terrifying enchantress
wearing beauty's mask,
Where love and death followed the breaking light of the dawn and
the twilight of the dusk.
While she kept upon her eyelids the agony of fire,
She created in the heart of the victims turmoil and despairs.
As shadow and light in which all loveliness shine,
She is beauty and horror, that is divine.
Paris, Achilles, Patrolus all had burnt in her fire,
She had also ignited Heracles' pyre.
In reality it is known to physicists as a stellar binary,
Where two stars are bound together in the celestial path generating a
variable light and scenery.
After every two and half days the light coming from the Specter's
Head fluctuates for hours,
Creating an impression of a ghostly realm lying beside the Devil's
Tower.
This fluctuation occurs when a star of solar size,
Obstructs luminosity of a bigger star to reach the eyes,

Thus in the ancient time it was viewed as the goddess who is cosmic destroyer and preserver,
Because they did not know the truth, that is known to today's earth-bound observers.
The eclipse of the star by its dark companion human fears enhanced,
And the phenomenon was viewed as Medusa's evil fluctuating glance.
The earth-bound mortals created by Prometheus from dust,
In whom Athena had breathed life and wisdom,
While Aphrodite had blown passion and lust,
Like Gilgamesh, have dreamt to build a tower reaching to the heaven,
And sought the domain guarded by the light of the Angels carrying the magical number seven.
The constellation carrying the Head of the Demon,
Inspires the earthly spirit to rise to paradise as Satan, or David's son Solomon.
To arrive at the realm of the Gorgon- the enchantress,
Perseus had to exploit the power of the transcendental wing of Hermes.
Near the garden of the Hesperides, where the Dragon coiled,
Wearing the Helmet of invisibility Perseus had gone across crossed the celestial domain where Atlas toiled,
Then looking at the image of the beauty in the mirror blazing and shining in the rays of the stars,
He had decapitated the head of the Gorgon- the evil enchanting monster.
Freeing the winged horse from Medusa's blood, that flew with the Muses carrying the spirits of the musicians and the poets,
Perseus had discovered Andromeda chained on a rock beside a sea monster lying in wait.
Where one sees Aplha Persi - the giant star with an actual luminosity exceeding fourth thousand suns,

The mortals for millennium have seen the way to freedom from the
hands of the witch-goddess who brings suffering, death and burn.
In this stellar sphere, where she wriggles as a serpent beside the river,
She is the mother of the horse, springing from her blood, that carries
creative spirits to realms that are deeper.
The Romans called the horse Equs Gorgoneus,
Striding on it Discouris guarded the Divine City,
It has brought to the world the knowledge of the laws,
And the principles that govern the functioning of the universe
without any flaw.
It also carried in its wings creation's natural propensity,
The desire for destruction and dexterity.
It is also the horse that once harnessed the chariot of Ishtar,
That the goddess had offered to the Babylonian hero, Gilgamesh as a
gift of her love.
Behold the transcendental steed flying above dusts and clouds!
As invisible spirit see its movements valiant and proud!
Rising with Lucifer,
The transcendental steed of Ishtar,
Behold in the realm of the stellar death and birth,
The paradise and the hell that looms over the earth!

The destiny bound in the cycles of death and birth

The tree of eternity, around which the dragon coils,
Stands as a symbol of immortality, where the wheel in the heaven
turns and toils;
Heracles once went to fetch the golden fruit from the garden,
Where the starry maidens water the soil.
While the dragon ascends the polar stairs.
Its branches spread from the earth to the heaven rising to the highest
air.
Around the motionless point, where the axis bearing the tree
penetrates the firmament,
Behold the constellation of Dragon.
This coiling of Dragon, passing through the pole, brings to earth
death and birth.
The spindle, that the Fate turns from the unmoving station fixed
amidst the orbs spinning around the earth,
Is spread over the tree of life, from where there exists no escape path.
When through the garden of Isthar Gilgamesh made his journey
alone,
He crossed the crown of the tree, which is also the pinnacle of the
mountain on his way to the immortal home.
In the paths along which the heavenly bodies rise, move in the Path
of Laws,
The orbs circle, turn, gyrate,

The gaseous structures fold, unfold, pulsate,

Expanding and contracting,

They travel away and return to themselves as destined by Fate.

The sizes and the shapes, that you see, are formed by the illusions of the eyes:

The white, yellow, crimson, vermilion, jade, green, blue, sapphire,

That colour the stellar atmosphere,

Define the ages of the stars after their births from cosmic dust.

Where you see them appearing as blue,

Gaseous burning balls scatter young stars' turbulent hue;

Those who appear white,

After billions of years of burning have avoided bursts,

And are objects that have arrived at an equilibrium at last.

In the equilibrium such stars balance the burning core,

With the energy that their outer shells outpour:

The turbulence of eddies, and pressure striving to tear open the stars,

Are balanced by gravitational force,

Which save them from ending up into a chaotic cosmic hearth.

Those stars, which appear torrid and incandescent,

And molten metal or dissolving ruby's effulgence claim,

Spew formidable amount of light from scorching flames,

Throw off vapors resembling radiating gold and gems.

Although they may appear supernatural,

They are in fact dying stars seeking sepulcher.

The stars, which twinkle and change fast from tints of ruby to sapphire,

Or emerald or amethyst in fire,

And sometimes sparkle as most brilliant diamond-tinged objects with iridescent hues,

Herald the catastrophic destructions as their dues:

They are the stars violent and troublesome,
That will fail to reach a stable equilibrium,
And are destined to end in creating luminosities of hundreds and
hundreds of millions suns.
What you behold, nothing is immortal and eternal,
Like the earth bound beings this stellar world too is subjected to the
cycles of death and birth.
These cycles create time and illusion:
What seems real is not,
What may seem unreal is,
What may seem to exist for ever is transitory,
And what appears transitory may be eternal,
What may appear as never-changing, never-moving and everlasting
may be dying,
And what is twinkling, flickering and pulsating and appearing in a
state to pass away, may be, being newly born,
What appears large may be small,
And what appears small may hold millions of stars that are large,
What is extremely luminous could be nearly a vacuum,
And what may appear very dim may be the densest part where an
inch of matter will weigh more than a mountain on the earth,
What appears most luminous is the source that do not attract the
light to itself,
And where light is entwined inside and can not escape the body,
there exist the profound darkness of an abysmal hell,
Thus everything is covered under illusion's veils.

It is a celestial wonderland where thousands and thousands of galaxies have clustered resembling the shapes of innumerable sponges, corals and mollusc from proterozoic and Palaeozoic era. Like snails, limpets, oysters, ammonoids, squid, they are sprawling on a cosmic shore. The Guide tells the journeyman about the Milky Way inside which they are flying. This galaxy itself is flying towards the center of the Virgo cluster, which attracts many clusters of galaxies around it. Each of these galaxies carry billions and billions of stars. This super cluster of galaxies is so big that light would take hundreds of millions of years to travel from one end to the other. Like the satellites of the planetary system rotating around the planets in days, the planets in turn circling the sun in years, and the sun in its turn whirling around the galactic center in hundred millions of years, the galaxies are turning around a central core. Many galaxies are being formed, many are dying and decaying. Some are exploding into space by scattering billions of stars in heaven. In this seemingly infinite world some galaxies have reached equilibrium, where the attraction towards the centre and the forces pushing the arms away from the centre are balanced and fine tuned. These galaxies - each producing many trillions of times more energy than the sun - are destined to burn in the sky for billions of years.

Birth and death of galaxies

The sprawling creatures, that you see glowing in the radiance of the nebulous light,

Are spiralling clouds of gases, where the stars are forming,

Or revolving in lanes of around millions of old stars.

In the field of nebulae, where you see the most crowding of immense dimension,

Is the Coma-Virgo section of the sky,

Towards which, the local cluster of galaxies are moving in the cosmic ocean.

Beyond the veil of the Virgin, holding Spica - the brilliant helium star,

See the ocean of the dark.

True description of the beauty of this goddess is certainly beyond the capacity of the human language to grasp.

There are millions and millions of such galaxies in the shore,

All of them would die in order to take new births.

The thousands of galaxies, that you see clustered around a centre, which is known as the Coma-Virgo centre,

Are only fractions of the true number of galaxies that there are.

There exist many more galaxies that emit in waves that are not visible to the eyes,

Only those that emit enough radiation in visible waves appear as islands of nebulous lights.

Each one of them contains many billions of stars- many of which are much larger the sun and some are of the solar size,

Every one of them is spiralling as if creatures in the universe bringing magical surprise.

The waves, that spiral through the clouds of gases giving birth to the galactic shapes,

Create numerous whirlpools in the Virgo-Coma cluster, and determine their destinies and fates.

This is only a window, through which you look at the universe, that is infinite,

There are many more vast clusters whose extensions and aggregations are hundreds of millions of light years in diameters beyond the visible sight.

These clusters, in turn, cluster together around a core where there holds no more the usual concept of space and time.

Before I tell you what is beyond that, and where lies its beginning and end,

I shall first describe their nature:

How they are formed I shall later explain.

Like sea gastropods of many shapes and sizes, that man finds on ocean shore,

Where the shapes of life sprawl in many types of spirals in different sorts of coiling of gnomic growths;

The galaxies too reflect the evolutionary patterns through billions of years:

Those, in which, the star formations have started look like sponges and fossils at the beginning of life;

Those whorls, that are tens of thousands or hundred of thousands

light years in diameter,
And look like peculiar snails and ammonites with two twisted
creatures spiralling inside,
Contain gases in their whirling arms where new stars are formed and
whirl around a core where the old stars reside.
There are also those that, like sea urchins developed in the higher
stage of the evolutionary process than the snails,
Look round or ellipsoidal,
They are the hubs of old red stars with nearly no gas in their spirals
and are more primordial.
There are many other varieties:
Some are like Siamese twins of two snails growing in logarithmic
forms with two heads attached,
Around which the gaseous arms are thrust in violent motions setting
the galaxies to coil:
They are the earlier stages of formation where the central cores have
not yet developed to look like whirlpools of stars which melt and boil.
Some spirals, whose arms lie in the plane of sight, look like Frisbees;
Some move, as if evolutionary cosmic misfits;
Some appear like eyes with black eyelids;
Some resemble carafes and cartwheels;
Some seem to be exploding,
Some interacting and colliding,
Some rise from a chaos unseen,
Some even can not be explained by imageries and words of human
beings.
The giant elliptical galaxies, like the one seen in the center of
The Virgo, are very strong emitter of radio waves -
Besides their visible blaze,
The strongest among them radiate in radio at a rate more than several

detonations per second of nuclear explosions of planetary size. Some are also called X-ray galaxies,

From centres hidden under luminous cores they emit enormous energies in X-rays fatal to the existence of life.

Some emit even more lethal gamma rays from their tiny cores - They are feared and adored.

The spiral galaxies are very unlike the elliptical ones, They emit radio waves mostly from the gases contained in their arms.

Apart from two extremely large invisible regions - one on each side of the galactic poles - far away from the visible domain where the galaxies lie,

Many elliptical radiate radio waves from tiny lobes at the centers - no one seem to understand why.

Like two invisible ghosts visible to radio eyes they seem to keep wake on the old dying creatures in the sky,

From whose center streams of gases violently fly.

This phenomena resembling like two jets in a line rushing out towards the ghostly lobes, as if, caused by an explosion at the center that man fails to explain,

Has kept human fantasies aflame.

The scientists wonder and speculate what might have caused the ejection of these cosmic flames.

No less weird are those huge spirals that are called Seyferts and emit high-energy radiation, from the tiny hearts at the centers,

Where gases flow out as well as enter.

At the hearts of the wheels of dimensions of the order of hundred thousand light years,

Glowing more intensely than million times the sun,

There exist regions as small as a few light years across, hat all human understandings stun.

There gases move many thousand kilometres per second forming filaments and blobs,
While around them many empty regions develop.
There seems to occur flow and outflow swept by supernatural storms,
Resembling, as if, cosmic hurricanes have formed.
Most puzzling among them are the ones known as quasars,
Though they look like ultra dense stars,
They are really masquadering Seyferts, that are only much more bizarre.
If you look North-west of the star Gamma Virginis - the Virgin star,
You will find the direction of the brightest quasi-stellar radio source in the sky,
That all human understanding defy.
It is a cosmic whirlpool possessing an extremely luminous core that outpours so much radiation that its glare obscures stars in the galaxy,
Thus creating the stellar appearance and giving rise to the scientific fallacy.
Moreover, it seems to develop ejecting jets in front of the human eyes,
In such a speed that this phenomena the laws of physics seems to defy.
This ejection of the jet and its speed that man has failed to explain on the basis of the belief that nothing can move faster than the light,
Make man wonder what is happening at this celestial height!
Many speculate that a black hole may have formed at the centre of the extremely luminous ball holding in its bosom an eternal night.
These objects are supposed to be so compact and dense that light curves and bends on its surface so strongly that even light can not escape,
Falling through it the relational structure of time and space change so drastically that one would come out in another universe with different

time and space.

The existence of these objects are fashionable to explain the immense output from the Seyferts and Quasars,

But do not believe in it,

You should consider such theories as human intellect's chance ridden hazards.

The journeyman wants to know," What is beyond the realm of the super-clusters ? Where is the beginning of the universe and if the universe will one day cease to exist?" Guide explains:

About the creation of the universe

What man has been able to conceive,

Only him, or her deceive.

It is believed that the world has started with a Big Bang some billions of years ago,

That satisfies nothing but mathematical solution and some scientist's intellectual egos.

It is believed that the universe started from a point where there existed no law,

And may or may not return to that point - depending on calculations' validity or flaw.

The galaxies are receding on an expanding surface which has more dimensions than two,

While the universe may or may not collapse depending on the invisible matter,

Which, may or may not, supply enough masses as contracting glue.

The picture of the universe depends on the values that one presumes at the beginning of time,

These initial values the fate of the universe define.

In the beginning it started with a zero size with infinite mass and infinitely hot;

As it expanded and cooled, it created gases from which arose these galaxies that you see flying around as nebulous spots.

Some physicists sitting on great professors' chairs,

Have ideas that will arouse even Devil's hair.

Like a horde of monkeys hammering away on a typewriter and pouring garbage as initial values from which the universe may have appeared by chance,

These professors believe that the universe has popped out of infinitely many possibilities and has no purpose and reason,

By pure accident it has come into existence to create this monkeys' prison.

Thus the conditions for life happened to be highly enhanced.

The universe - the way it is - exists out of chance,

Otherwise, there would be no existence of "intelligent" beings,

Especially the scientists who are all seeing:

The professors call it the anthrophic principle to exist,

Which they need to find an intellectual exit.

The universe of harmony and beauty, that brings to the wondering eyes flood of spiritual tears,

Is believed to have risen from random accidental process, that has also created mother Earth's "foolish" mystics and seers,

Who by lacking insight of the physicists see the hands of the divine world,

While the professors see nothing but monkeys' random hands to fear.

A part of the story they tell, of course, may not be completely untrue,

However, it is much more complex than the Big Bang creating different kinds of glues,

In the beginning there existed a singularity is a meaningless garbage, that gives only error's clue,

The theory of expansion starting at a beginning in time with reality may have nothing to do.

The great domain, that holds in itself the universes inside universes has really no beginning and end,

There is no concept of time, although inside it the universes fold and unfold by creating different curves and bends.

The universe is not in a stable state in a perfect equilibrium,

Its evolution can not be described by simple linear equations,

It will need non-linearity in higher dimensional space for its true mathematical description.

Universe is like a system where time and space change,

The matter and vacuum their relations constantly arrange and rearrange;

The matter dissipates into space,

Space folds, unfolds into matter,

The time goes over to space,

And space enwraps as time in dance of loops creating a labyrinthine maze.

The universe is not a sphere that expands and contracts like in a stable oscillating state,

It has much more complex destiny allotted by fate.

Carrying clusters and super-clusters each universe coils and moves away from its previous space-time state.

It dances away from a central attractor in order to return to it as spiralling coil,

And falling towards the attractor matter dissipates into void.

Thus the universe enfolds towards the attractor,

And in turn unfolds as it dances away.

As the new universe picks up the spiralling motion,

The space-time emerges in opposite direction,

And moves in a new space-time different than the old,

That has connection with other domains through topological loops I have already told.

It is like a non-linear dynamics where the space-time are generated anew,

In this eternity that never changes, everything constantly renews.
There exists nothing that can be called truly fundamental,
In the magical dance - universes' eternal hula-hoop,
All constants change through the coiling space-time loops.
It is a labyrinth so complex that by using the logical process of the mathematical kind,
It can never be comprehended by the human mind;
To formulate it as a set of equations may even be beyond the power of God,
Those who believe that it can be done, are ignorant and stubborn arrogant lot.
You should know that everything that move and change in all universes are connected and bound in an eternity -
The attractor, towards which and away from which the universes fall and rise,
Cannot be understood in its entirety.
Each point of space and moment of time exists in eternal past and future beyond the visible sight,
In darkness they are bound in domains of light.
Once matter comes into being from the void,
The light creates the illusion of space.
Mass can be seen as a phenomena of order and pattern illumined by rays.
Once matter moves in the speed of light,
Everything sinks in the infinite void and night:
The space dilates,
Time becomes timeless.
The structure of time appears in consciousness because the senses that perceive the world are related to the world's material content,

Which are caught in the flux of motions flowing through space-time curved and bend.

Only when in the consciousness order and pattern, creating the phenomenal world dissolves,

The mind is able to see the whole - but it may never this mystery mathematically resolve.

What you see as the universe, is the part of the whole connected to your sight by the rays of light,

More we speed in this height,

The physical time dilates more and the space contracts.

If we move in the speed of light,

You will see the eternal as void and night,

Where there exists no beginning or end, past or future - but only the eyes staring at the universe kindling the mystics' sights.

Hindus have called the cosmic rhythm of the creation and dissolution-

The dance of Shiva creating the ring of fire inside which he remains at eternal rest.

Like a dynamic whole without beginning or end,

He is immanent and at the same time everything he transcends.

Like what you see in galaxies,

He rests in earth, air, water and fire as spiralling eddies in streams, vortices and flames,

As the whole and the same.

Turning through himself as the energy that wakes everything to consciousness,

He reverberates from the highest structures to microscopic domain creating repeated patterns of order in time and space,

In winding paths he forms the world out of chaos as the god who is the source of all dynamics at rest.

All universes, all manifestations converge on him and diverge from

him,
He breathes the world out as the rays from the diamond beam,
And receives in himself all - seen or unseen.
It is possible to attain the consciousness of this still point free from turmoil,
Hindus called it the Diamond Body,
Chinese named it as the pearl of perfection,
That connects to the human consciousness through highest mystic reflections.
Through the expanding spirals through which universes emerge,
And the contracting spirals through which the universes in the void immerse,
A labyrinth penetrates,
That is depicted in all cultures and religions in different forms and shapes.
This labyrinth creates and dissolves, expands and contracts, reveals as well as conceals,
In it consciousness appears as spirit and will.
Often the mystics have represented the spiral as a labyrinth of intricate form,
That curves, bends, as if, depicting the spirit residing in fire, tumults and storms.
This labyrinth you will often find in the ancient world depicted on the tombs,
Invoking the spirit, from which the dead are reborn.
Such labyrinth represents the spiraling windings through space and time -
The ordering and the guiding power, which brings all to growth, and returns all to the cosmic brine.
On the heads of many sculptures of Buddha you will see this spiral and labyrinth engraved,
It is the symbol of order and inner tranquility -

Eternity in ephemerality - The sign of the creative energy, that with its radiant unfolding has brought order from chaos.
It represents the synthesis of Eros and logos.
Through acts of spiritual growth and evolution,
That brings matter's dissolution,
Through this labyrinth passes the path of journey towards enlightenment -
The pilgrim's progress to the peak of the labyrinthine hill - life's highest attainment.
In the Megalithic and the Neolithic world you will find stone structures with carved spirals guiding the holy-spirit along the labyrinthine path,
Which lead all creations from the relative and transient state to the tranquil sanctuary deep in the heart.
In India on talks about the eight-fold stages of the mind winding through the labyrinthine path,
In Babylon it represented the entrails of the demon in the great forest guarding the labyrinth of death and birth.
This spiral labyrinth, where as the divine and the mortal two parts of Gilgamesh met,
Is the symbol of a union between time and eternity,
The finite and the infinity,
The male and the female,
Yang and Yin -
Storm and tranquillity.
From the tiniest ephemeral matter to the highest forms this labyrinth passes,
Here, all beings are engaged in a battle with their other halves,
And strive for union with the Divine source of compassion and love.
Through the intuitive power of the mystics and the sages,

People of all cultures have known about these labyrinthine mazes:
Zulus drew it on sand and called it their royal hut,
Hopi Indians found it in the tranquil sanctuary under the Mother
Earth.
In seeking the power of the labyrinth folding and unfolding,
Making sand drawings Navajo Indians derived their power of
healing.
The Melanesians talked about the danger of the labyrinth on the way
along the journey in search of immortality over the water of death:
In the entrance the souls meet the female sitting in front of a
labyrinth spread across the path,
To test the souls she erases one half, which the new comers has to
reconstruct,
Before being allowed to pass.
Those who fail are devoured by the female,
Whose gape no victim can bypass.
Similarly the Cretan labyrinth was conceived.
Treading through the maze of paths - closing, bending, opening and
binding,
Like Theseus, who killed Minotaur, the half-bull-half-man monster,
The warriors and initiators are supposed to be led to regeneration in a
higher winding.
In Mahabharata this labyrinth was infused with special power with
the king at the centre,
Only the chosen victims, the most courageous and purest of the souls
were allowed to enter.
In the dynamics of the curved empty space,
Similarly the spiral maze makes chaos into cosmos that you see
kindled by the nebulous blaze,
It devours and regenerates.

416

Like Minotauer in Cretan labyrinth there seems to exist a cosmic mon-
ster, which devours the sacrifices as a ritual of regeneration in the higher
path of winding. It attracts, devours and releases the forms in the cosmic
sea that is nothing but a formless void. According to Greek mythology,
this monster was begotten by the goddess of the starry light, who was
the wife of Mino - the judge of the dead in the underworld. The god-
dess, hiding herself inside a mechanized upholstered cow, had met with
the cosmic Bull and given birth to the monster. This union between the
bull and the goddesses is the same union between the formless energy
with the form giving world. This duality has often been represented in
ancient religions in the form of the union between the male and female
powers: half-bull and half-lion, half- moon and half- sun, half-god and
half-demon, half-consciousness and half-unconsciousness, half-light and
half-darkness, half-heaven and half-hell, half-evil and half-good, half-
destroyer and half-creator etc. The monster, that devours all in the cos-
mos, is an off-spring of the Bull - the world in the aspect of form – begot-
ten by the cosmic energy – the queen of the starry light.

In this labyrinth the journeyman watches fearful scenes of immense beauty where the galaxies are dancing in rhythms: They are spewing out immense energy from the centres where the stars are dissolving in the void and reappearing as streams of energy that spiral outwards from the centres. From this streams of radiation, matter is pouring out and travelling through the labyrinth as whirling clouds of gases pouring out from the centres. Like the union of the mechanized world and the goddess, the energetic waves are attuned with the dance of death and birth of the cosmos.

The cosmic dance

In the dynamic objects, that you see expanding and contracting,
Inwardly spiralling and outwardly hurling,
From the cosmic dimensions down to the subatomic dust,
There exists a celestial dance in which all living, or non living, take their parts.
The whole is a continuum, in which the dances go on following spiral paths,
To form the structures and patterns which create the illusions of separateness of the whole,
In localized condensations appear as galaxies, stars, planets and the earth, that in trajectories move and role.
Like subject and object looking at itself and reflecting its image on itself,
This dance goes on perpetually as dance of the eternal Self.
Breathing wind and fire,
Inhaling the spirit from the whole that permeates the universe entire,

From points to points it animates and differentiates the whole as
appearances seemingly separate,
That create the illusion of time and space,
Where mind constructs the reality as a platform to observe the world
from the top of a minaret.
In the labyrinth, that entwines in paths after paths in spiral windings
through space and time,
To order and structure the world that shines,
The deity dances his dance,
Atoms, dusts, planets, stars all appear as patterns rising from a
primeval chaos and chance,
The creative vibrations that dynamics balance enhance.
On earth one sees this as the whirling dance of the mystic Sufis,
As they fall in trance,
Through their dances they attune themselves to this cosmic dance;
In whirling motions they lift the mind to the cosmos beyond the
domain of the moon and the sun.
In progressive whirling ecstasy the spirits of the Sufis spiral upwards
through the celestial orbs,
In search of union with the Divine they rise above the illusory world
that senses absorb;
Spinning as a planet in an orbit around the central sun,
That bring human suffering, sorrow, misery, joy and fun,
Their dances gradually spiral and expand.
When the arms, that in the beginning rest crossed on the breast
gradually outstretch towards the heaven and finally open completely,
and in ecstasy turn,
They feel at the heart the stillness of bliss around which the world
whirls as a ball of fire in the cosmic urn.
Although the spiralling power, animating the universe in dynamic

dance, is beyond feeling or seeing,

By this whirling the Dervish realizes the presence of the supreme power in his own being.

Therefore, in the Islamic domes one can see this Divine heart where the labyrinth is enclosed,

On it, like eternal pilgrim's paths, the labyrinthine windings roll and unroll.

In ascending dance the spirit dissolves in the void,

Through the spiralling coil;

In the descending path the spirit sinks in time and space in motions and toil.

Same happens with the dances of the galaxies, stars, planets and dust,

The ejecting jets and the radio lobes are nothing but the phenomena partaking in this rhythm of contraction, expansion, calmness and fury from the centre appearing as sequential bursts.

Part 3
REALMS OF SUPERMAN AND SPIRITUAL MAN

ENLIGHTENMENT ABOUT HEAVEN AND HELL

Realizes the meaningless of the human striving to escape the wheel of death and birth and achieve immortality and being freed from the ignorance, caused by insufficient knowledge of the cosmic mystery, he realizes the path of love and compassion as the highest path to pursue in life. he understands that in the universe all exist as parts of the great existence, which images itself in the same way in all. Gaining understanding that the universe exists because all should exist in harmony as a whole, where the power of life and death manifests as the foundation of existence of all, he experiences the existence of the cosmic energy that are embodied in all beings. This cosmic energy is the source of compassion and love. It is a purposeful act of the One, who reveals in all beings the urges to fulfil the meaning of existence by living harmoniously as parts of ALL. After receiving this enlightenment he returns to the modern life on Earth.

113. Enlightenment

114. Returning through the Dantian Hell

He feels enthralled by the beauty of light arising from the explosions and births of the cosmic objects. There exists no way out, or no way in the labyrinth. There is no path that would lead him further to any Island of Immortality, which Gilgamesh had sought. Real, unreal, conscious, unconscious, time and space, matter and mind, particle and wave, existence and non-existence, witch and goddess, man and spirit all are intertwined in a whole, where there is no beginning or end, no meaning of transcendence or emanence. Things are, as they are, as projections of the self through himself, entangled in a labyrinth, that appears real or imaginary to the mind existing outside and inside the mirror – as subject and object moving in a dialectical union. In dying things are being born; in freeing and rising things are being bound and falling. Journeyman finds himself flying in the maze as the eternal victim sacrificed to the monster, and the goddess. Here, blazing light is inseparable from darkness. There seems to exist no evil and good. The universe has emanated from the centre as the flower, where Buddha is sitting on the lotus of light, and radiating compassion and bliss. Realizing this all pervading compassion and love, which has brought the universe into existence, the journeyman feels the urge to return to the life on the earth.

Enlightenment

In this labyrinthine maze lies the blissful island,
Where amidst dreadful scenes love and compassion all fears transcend.
In flying upward man sinks,
In falling in gravity man rises from the abysmal brink.
Where in loops everything dance high,
Where the winged horse neigh,
Where in the dragon's swing everything is born to die,
There is the fall of the heaven on the earth from the sky.
O Guide! In the lanes where the gases fume and spew out smoke,
Where the star dust keep alight the celestial roads,
Where the dwarfs and giants rush in howling flames,
The beauty engulfs all like a supernatural dame.
Here the present, future and past whisper the secret of the eternal things without any name.
In the trembling gateways where the cliffs of gases stand and burn alone,
A transcendental mind shines within me as the eternal lamp without fire and flame.
It seems in dreaming I am awake,
In flying I have returned,
In the silence I have found the words that dwarf my feelings that senses benumb.

In this vision, where I have a premonition of a supernatural existence outside myself,
Where I am across the sea and at the same time trying to cross,
There lies the Blissful Island where there is no sea, no sense, and nothing to go across.
The paths that move, gnarl and twist,
Like the wandering shadows filling the wheel,
In the abyss of silence I sojourn to find my will,
Where amidst the mountains of gases the light drink radiation pouring out of perfection that change matter to mind,
And spirit to will,
I gaze forward and backward where backward is forward in space's and time's twist and twirl.
O Guide! Like half-man and half-divine I fly,
There is nothing to comply, nothing to deny,
There is nothing to proclaim,
Or nothing to declaim,
Everything is together in the boundless mystery of countless mountains,
The streams of lights fed by showers of ethereal rain;
Here all wanderings, and climbing in search of immortality seem meaningless and vain.
In this lofty sky where all seem so eternal and pure,
Wanton accidents, chances, irrational happenings have no cure;
Through things may seem impossible the world all possibilities implore;
In sinking deep beyond comprehension,
There is sunrise, light, and beauty that draw attentions;
In the labyrinth where time is woven as in a cosmic web,
There is a luminous silence, an eternal fear, a cosmic apprehension.

O Guide! There seems nothing to seek beyond,
All that outstretch in time and space, that is nothing and still moving for eons,
Which have enwrapped the world beyond which there is nothing greater to find,
Are nothing else than the illusion of the mind.
In this labyrinthine path, where in the shinning corner of the heart,
Love and beauty never departs,
Beyond the moon, the sun and the stars the unknown and the unfathomable as a luminous ball revolves,
In a divine loneliness I see the whole cosmos evolves.
O Guide!
Everything feels strange, appears hidden,
Everything seems chance ridden,
Not determinable but still determined by reason.
All that once appeared straight and true,
Seem complex, imaginary, unreal, illusory and untrue.
O Guide! Riding upon your luminous wing,
I have seen this cosmic world in dance and swing;
Like sitting upon a floating island I have gone far
To discover that I am one with stars.
This stillness around that never speaks,
Whispers in words that enter this world like lightening blitz.
O Guide! This silence and solitude seem to be charged with words,
That no speech can grasp,
The words that I have heard on the earth,
Express stillness of silence where everything remains unheard.
You have brought me aloft from the forest path,
To listen to the music of the stars,
Now my heart wants to hear no more,

All I want is to merge with the silence of this cosmic dark.

My thirst and hunger for knowledge, had brought me to the watery brim,

Where, like Tantalus, I once stood as the eternal victim.

O Guide! I do not wish to attain any further height,

I do not want to know any more- I have seen enough during this flight.

It is a blissful solitude, where there is no language and speech,

In this path lighted by the cosmic streams,

I stand against myself as if striving to win over myself in an eternal struggle- like in a dream.

Like Minotaur I remain concealed,

And devour my own part - strange!

Unreal! Unseen!

Like Gilmagesh in the forest, or Avimanyu in the ring,

I am sacrificed to the goddess wearing star-fold wings.

As Oedipus and the Sphinx,

I am the destroyer and the destroyed - one flowing away from and the other coming in the stream.

As a half- mortal and half- god I have risen above the mortal land,

Towards the shore where stars appear as sand;

Where darkness like Harpies sing the immortal songs,

I fly on and on...

O Guide! You have taken away the illusions from my eyes with the celestial flame,

And shown me the beauty of the supernatural dame.

You have brought me beyond the sense's grasp,

Where Isthar holds her golden cup;

Amidst the clouds of flames,

In the winding streams of the fiery fuming lanes,

You have shown celestial scene amidst starry crags, creeks, dunes and planes.

I desire no glory on earth,

No sorrow lingers any more in my heart;

With the strength of wisdom you have filled my mind's emptiness,

And elevated me above sorrow and happiness;

Here there is nothing to learn except the teachings of love,

More I have grasped, more I have become one with the stellar dust,

More I have felt my hunger and thirst,

More you have made me one with the void where galaxies fly from
the centre where the universes end and start.

O Guide! The radiant light!

Who brings the knowledge of the heaven to man from cosmic height,

I hail thee!

O glorious Angel!

You are the power of the inner sight.

You are Siegfried's guide,

You are beauty's steed carrying the mortal through the stellar light;

You are the bird of fire,

Rising from the pyre in radiant attire,

The horse of the heaven flying in ease,

Between the earth and the heaven you are mind's radiant bridge.

You, who have awakened my mind to this heavenly delight,

Now bring me down from this height.

I wish to return to the world where sitting on the crags in the
summer night,

The lovers sing songs of love like the weaving girl and the herd-boy
beside the celestial river bridged by the bird of light.

In this petrified world, in silence I hear the fluttering words and songs,

Coming from way...way...beyond,

Its center seems to merge with the very earth where I am born.

Bring me down to the world, where man wanders bewildered in the forest path,

Where the summer light ripens the fruits,

The earthly love merrily sails in breeze through forest and wood,

Let me descend to the world that shines as a blue sphere of love,

Through the blazing clouds and azure waves,

Let me go down to bring to mankind the Divine rays.

Bring me down on the land washed by water and breeze,

Where beauty of life springs from seeds,

Where birds sing and songs overwhelm all speech,

Where tongues tremble as sounds of magic,

Where rugged rocks, wind torn reefs sink deep,

Like the dragon, the storm clouds gather on the mountain tops before they take abysmal leaps,

Bring me in the world " there" beneath.

O Guide! In purest love for all that exist,

Let me descend through the labyrinth without entrance or exit.

O winged soul! Where man is destined to suffer in the mortal world's eternal story,

In selfless love let me plunge in the earth's fire without seeking joy or glory.

In love for life let us leave this lonely sphere,

And come down among mankind by swinging around the spiraling stairs.

Where amidst poverty, dirt, misery and happiness,

Man is bound in punishment in a world where thunders and storms rage in lightening madness,

The suffers in the village encounter the danger of going-across,

Let us start our down-going where man is crucified on the cross as Son of God.

I do not any more long for the stars,

Now I wish to the universal man, to whom I belong as a part.

Let us return the way Zarasthustra has gone,

And trace by the incandescent path above the sun.

In the eternally imperfect world that is driven by contradictions,

Let me seek in human beings my own perfection;

Let me descend to rise above myself as a brighter flame,

Let me go below the sky in order to rise above, and remain one with the transcendental flame.

Lower me down from this emptiness,

From this sphere above joy and happiness;

Bring me back to the corporal state where life is bound in joy and pain;

Where the power of gravity imparts strain;

Accompany me through earthly heaven and hell as my guide and a friend.

They plunge towards the local cluster of galaxies on the way to the Orion's arm of the Milky Way, where the earth is bound in the solar system and starts their descend towards the earth. While descending through the planetary spheres, the Guide tells him about the Dante's Hell, where Homer, Plato, Aristotle, Cicero were thrown because they did not believe the Christian doctrines. The blasphemers, hypocrites, epicureans etc. were doomed to the most tormented region of this underworld. Only those who shared Christian theology escaped the punishment in Hell.

Dantian hell

When one looks at Venus in the visible spectra one only sees a
featureless planet covered with yellow clouds,
But as soon as one makes use of the power to see in ultraviolet light
its atmosphere appears graceful without doubt;
Swirling in streaks from the equator to the poles like Earth's cirrus
clouds,
It features appear in the band radio-loud.
Thick noxious gases suffuse every part of the planet in a reddish
yellow glow,
Nothing can indicate anything else but nature's infernal show.
This volcanic planet is named after Volcan's wife,
Even in utmost phantasy one can fails to imagine any love, beauty or
life.
With this reality no description of any imaginary hell will ever match,
It looks like burning entrails of the goddess where only horrors can
fly and hatch.
It is far worse than the scene of the lower hell under Dante's circle of
six,

Where the heretics were burnt inside the Gates of Dis,
The Gorgon and Furies shrieked and tore breasts with nails ,
And sorceress went to the very bottom to fetch the souls of the
traitors from the deepest depth of the hell.
In the planetary sphere of Venus, instead of journeying through the
heaven one experiences hell,
A world more frightening than in Dante's and Virgil's tale,
And sees a wall of towers more horror stricken than over Phelgethon
the river of sulphurous fire- Phlegyas sailed.
After crossing the river, where Charon ferried the doomed souls to a
landscape full of howling,
Dante and Virgil had entered the five circles in the upper windings,
There they had met Homer, Plato, Aristotle, and Cicero - the virtuous
non-Christians-
Whose souls had no hope of encountering the divine Being because
of their pagan sins.
In the second circle they had seen the souls being punished by other
means,
There Dido, Helen, Achilles and Paris were whirled around in a dark
stormy wind.
In the third circle gluttonous soul were punished in filthy muck
battered by cold and dirty hail and snow,
Cerebus- the hound of hell- guarded the gate through which
sufferings flow;
While these souls had no chance of salvation,
The blessed one were supposed to resurrect in a godly glow.
In the Fourth they had heard those, who loved wealth, shouting
"Paper Satan, paper Satan Aleppe",
And hurling huge rolling weights against each other that hit the chests.
In the fifth circle the souls of the wrathful were bogged in a mire

beneath the poisonous river of Styx,

Dante and Virgil had seen them bubbling in its murky mud beneath.

Inside the sixth, across the river of Phlegethon, there were the tombs
of the Epicurean heretics,

And poisonous stench from an abyss where Pope Anastasius was
punished for heresy;

He was punished because he had denied Christ a virgin birth,

And meant that Jesus was begotten by a man with mortal's sin and lust.

In the seventh, where there was once a great landslide when Christ
had entered the hell,

There was a sea of boiling blood of the dead,

Where ferocious centaurs copulated with their sexual mates,

And shot at those who tried to lift their heads from the boiling mud.

There black dogs ripped off flesh from the body of the sinners,

Who were trying to hide from the pack of bitches looking for a
gluttonous dinner.

In this circle of violence with many grotesque features,

They heard wails and moans of the half-women, and half-bird like
creatures.

There were burning sand, where some were kept tied, naked and supine,

This was a punishment for blaspheming the divine.

In this circle there existed beasts of monstrous form,

With a face of man but body of scorpion;

Scuttling up from below with many legs and hands,

A group of sinners were squatting on this fiery sand.

Riding on the back of a scorpion Dante and Virgil had started their
spiralling descent,

In the eighth circle they saw flatterers, seducers and whores were
immersed in the stinking excrement.

Nearby in a ravine the Pope Nicholas III, who was famous for acquisition of lands,

Who channelled to his kinsmen public office, funds and grants,

Was undergoing a violent torment:

The sinner's legs protruding through holes,

Twitching and helplessly agitating burning bodies hanged by being tied around the soles.

In other ravines there were bridges from where the devils flung sinners into boiling pitch,

And poked at the bodies with pitch forks and tormented them in the ditch.

In another ravine weeping shades of the Hypocrites marched wearing Benedictine gowns -

That weighed them down.

Here the counsellor of Pontius Pilate, who gave advise to crucify Christ,

Remained crucified and transfixed on the ground,

And was thus left to undergo torment profound.

In the ravine where the souls of the deceivers were flickering as myriads of flames rising from below,

Odysseus was jointly punished with Diomedes - his Trojan war-fellow.

In the ninth circle they met mutilated, bloody shades,

Whose bellies were ripped open with spilling out entrails,

They were the sowers of schism,

Professing against Christian theism,

Especially prophet Mohammed, and Ali - his son-in-law - who assumed next Caliphate.

In the law of divine retribution - in the way the Christians have explained,

They were bemoaning their painful ends.

In the ninth circle, i.e. the last, they had heard a mighty blast,
It was the horn of Nimrod - the creator of the Tower of Babel,
From whose grip the Christians were freed at last.
He was thrown down below in a pit,
Where all religious traitors remained under ice as deep frozen meat.
Here they saw the one time associate of Archbishop Ruggieri,
Gnawing at the brain of the Archbishop frozen in a hole of an eternal
night.
He was Dante's political enemy, and therefore this punishment was
considered just and right.
Far across the lake of frozen ice was the place for Lucifer,
Each of his three mouths chewed one of the three greatest sinners
among mankind,
Among them was Judas- the Apostle- who betrayed Jesus,
Whose punishment even Christ could not rescind.
However planet Venus is more horrific than what Dante could ever
imagine,
Descending from the upper hell to the Cocytus, nothing similar he
had ever seen:
There are hundred thousand volcanoes erupting,
Through spider shaped systems of cracks and grooves innumerable
lava streams are flowing and intersecting,
The rings, like grotesque eyes, are spewing sulphurous vapors like
souls eternally tormenting,
The domes are collapsing,
The hills and ridges, shaped like scorpions and weird creatures, are
drinking molten rock and magma as punishment everlasting,
The chasms and toughs are swallowing the split open entrails,
Where burning sulphuric acid is raining in flames.
It is not possible to describe this fearful scene,
It is beyond anyone's imagination and dream.

IN A CYBERCITY

After circling around the visionary Hell, as described in Dante's "Divine Comedy", he returns to Earth and enters in a modern city, where its inhabitants have amassed weapons of immense destructive power. They have risen against Heaven and are trying to free the dwellers of the city from the fears of any heavenly power. They are equipped with missiles, bombers and nuclear arsenals as uncontestable superpower who can bring any other power to its submission.

Here he meets women and men worshipping the Devil and his followers, and sees the superman, possessing scientific knowledge behind the working of the nature, rising to tear down Heaven, and free man from the hallucinatory worlds created by religions. It is a city drowned in technological innovations, where people wander in virtual spheres. They have created a city which resembles more like the city of Maya (Illusion) where people communicate with each other at vast distances and fulfil their needs of love and pleasure by using technological means. They believe in a mechanical world that runs following natural laws and chance, where competitions and liberty to act according to one's free will are higher than anything else.

115. The city through which the roads to heaven and hell pass

116. Tathagata's meditation in the cybercity

117. A fearless hero wielding weapons

118. Beauty's invitation to return to the forest

The city through which the roads to heaven and hell pass

As they descend a lighted city with houses, gardens, roads, bridges, and cars plying in the streets etc. become visible. They fly over the city of the promethean women and men, who have considerable knowledge about the way the natural forces operate and know how to utilise these forces in serving the desires and the pleasures of the mortal life. The citizens are no more bound to the labour, tied to the cultivation of the land, as Heracles was. These freed men now live on the labour of the others, who cultivate land and produce food for them. These city dwellers are mostly engaged in scientific and technological sector. Some do not work at all. They live on inherited money, speculating in the stock market, or by making investments in high-technology sector, that brings high profit, or by owning the most lucrative houses, hotels and brothels in the city. These successful mortals import men and women from other countries, where people live verging in abject poverty. The immigrants serve in houses, hotels, brothels and do menial work, that the promethean men abhor. The dwellers in the city seek maximum freedom and pleasure, love speed of movement and maximum control over others and one's own situation through sophisticated method of communication. They strive to develop more and more efficient mechanisms to produce and market their technological goods at the expense of minimum labour and derive maximum benefits in exchanging them with the food and consumer goods that they need. In achieving this goal they are not concerned about the ecological balance that is fine-tuned in nature. In a constant striving for pleasure, freedom, economic benefit, power, and control of the nature that will make them invincible as the gods, they artificially invent products, that can be lethal to the nature, consume and pollute it to the extent that may affect the natural balance of resources.

They believe that everybody is entitled to use personal will to the best interest of his or her personal power and economic benefit. Each person must be allowed to do what they like as long as they do not trespass upon the same right of the others. Every individual should be free to negotiate on the best kind of contract that he or she can obtain from any other individual without any interference of any external law-making body or pressure of any organization. They believe in the atmosphere of free competition and free trade all economic commodities should be exchanged. The prices of the commodity should be fixed by the market demand and not on any other criteria except the law of supply and demand.

The most citizens believe that everything is a product of mechanical evolution including the habits, institutions, thoughts and beliefs of man. Mind is indissolubly linked with matter. It is only motion of substance of material origin in the brain that carries the sense impressions. There exists no innate idea anywhere outside the physical materiality in which one's body is confined. There exists nothing spiritual anywhere. All knowledge are results of sense perceptions. Everything man does and thinks are determined by the mechanical necessity. While the sensations are the raw materials, necessities are the forces shaping them into forms of understanding and knowledge. No knowledge can come from any domain of pure ideas or intuition. The reason only reflects a self-sustaining mode of the mechanical world, that combines, co-ordinates and organizes the perceptions in structures that form the basis of any truth. Therefore all truth should be derived from the experience and the physical observation made on the material world. Even the axioms of mathematics are simply inferences derived from the observed facts. Death brings utter extinction of both body and mind and there exists no supernatural world neither creating or governing the universe. All - from the material universe to the mind - can be explained mechanically without any need for invoking the existence of God. Man is his own God in the shrine that he has built with his own hands. In this shrine only the scientific truth is substantial enough to be taken as the guiding light for living. Only those, who do not have the courage to live in the face of this scientific truth, seek the higher domain and believe in destiny and fate. They should be allowed to perish in the hands of the stronger human beings, who possess the courage to face the knowledge of science with brevity. They are the natural rulers of the world.

For them the highest good is pleasure and the elimination of the fear of the supernatural. Accordingly all laws and institutions should exist in order to contribute to the welfare of the individuals. The society or state is nothing but a product of the self-interests of the powerful individuals. All human beings are driven by self-interests, desire for personal powers and material prosperity, that are kept more hidden with more refinement and learning of individual persons. In society power is for those who have the skill to seize it in a free competition and success means the achievement of one's purpose, whatever it may be. Goodness or badness receives moral meaning, that counts in life, only with failure or success. One should have faith in value only when it pays to do so in achieving one's ends. Like Prometheus, who often cheated the gods and lied in order to fool the heavenly beings to achieve his goal, these mortals too consider cunning, lie and deceit as necessary skill to achieve life's desired ends.

In trying to triumph over God, the citizens live with the Spites that gods had sent. Competitions for economic benefits and the power have made

them mischievous and deceitful like the Mycenean heroes: Brother kills brother; son murders mother; daughter conspires with her lover to kill her father; uncle kills the nephew; nephew hales the uncle in order to execute him; step-mother murders step-son; father violates daughter; brother runs away with brother's wife; employee conspires against the employer; servant participate in the plot to kill the master; friend kills friend; the murder of the son-in-law becomes a political ally and a new son-in-law etc. Jealousy, hatred, adultery, incest, deceit, conceit, lie, conspiracy, brutality, theft etc. fly over this city like the spites that had once come flying in the world when Pandora had opened her box.

The Guide shows the journeyman the laboratory where the pro-methean mortal is working day and night. He is developing new weapons that will make him the master over all other people in the world. He is pursuing to get rid of the dragon-power, that brings forth death, life and regeneration (in the ancient world the constel-lation of Dragon, which circled around an unmoving point in the sky (north pole), was seen as the origin of the dragon-power, which brought seasonal changes bringing life and death on Earth).

Tathagata's meditation in the cybercity

The world was conceived as mechanical. The concept of the reality was derived from the inter-relationships of the things that appeared and were subjected to comprehension by the experimental methods of permitting concepts that fell within one's conceptual framework and the categories of logic that contradicted and repudiated the validity of truth unless they fitted with the causality of the things. The world was seen from outside, described and defined by experimental methods that recognized nothing but the relationships of matter in space and time. The will was hypothesized as the procreation of matter and a me-chanical intelligence that is antecedent to the functioning of the will. It was called clarity of thoughts by which man wished to dethrone God.

They took world's command, played dangerous games of law of chance, made discoveries that removed the limitations of the perceptions, brought the remote parts to nearness, with prodigal cleverness liberated man from the boundaries of seeing and hearing. They freed man from feeling pity in accepting the higher order of things and brought an awareness of great independence. They extended the frontiers of freedom outward in the material world while the boundaries of the inner world shrank. The possibilities to explore beyond the realm of matter - the vast domain of experience of the human souls - were narrowed down with the progress that they called enlightenment. It was the freedom from the slavery to God and an awakening against religion, a voluntary submission to the Devil, who wished to make man more powerful than the angels of God.

All moralities were addressed with aversion to divinity. All behaviours were prescribed as brave and courageous that destroyed emotions through analysis of science and vivisections of the mind. The spirituality, and symbolisms were discredited as the timidity of the mediocre and the weakness of the hearts. They believed that the paths to seek truth and freedom rested in all permissibility of glories that heighten man to cultivate oneself. In painfully denying of everything except science and the judgments of intellects, that beget no distrust in the reality of the world as made of material dust, there was an attempt to triumph against heaven. The man conceived himself as object - an object of himself, mirroring no soul, but gazing at itself in the apparatuses. His existence was nothing but an appearance produced by random accidents and chance. They affirmed the freedom of the human will that as a machine that can take self command. As industrious scholars they wished to free humanity from the naivety and stupidity of the people still seeking religious paths. They were the bearers of the new will of man.

The guide shows the journeyman the laboratory where the pro-methean mortals are working day and night in order to get rid of the dragon power which brings the cycles of birth, death and rebirth.

The fearless hero wielding weapons to kill the dragon

Now I feel free from the forced drudgery, fruitless toil and the nature's contempt,
I can shatter, splinter, cut, kill , forge fearful weapons with which I can win over the forces of fate ,
I have gained sufficient power by wielding intelligence with strength,
The fearsome dragon, I fear no more,
No more feel stupefied by its formidable weight,
I have gained enough skill to join the bolts and lightening,
By making weapons that can kill and destroy whatever I seek to destroy.
I am the creator of my own destiny,
I am the source of my own power with which I myself wield.
I do not feel anymore wretched as a man who is wild,
I am not afraid of anything that I call vile,
I am relieved from the labor to make the ends meet for food and drink,
Whatever I cherish for my flesh and pleasure I can ask others to bring;
I am the master who thinks,
Sure in pursuit ,

I am able to bring the awesome power of the human mind to
overcome the nebulous fire in the ring.
I possess arms that can destroy this earth many times over,
This gives me pleasure of intellectual endeavour.
I know that I can get rid off anything that may fall in my displeasure,
I can quit anyone who may threaten my treasure;
I do not have to pine away in fear,
In heart's desires I can couch and rest in leisure and make others toil
in tears,
I do not have to roam around in search of an escape,
No one can harass me without worrying about the power with which
I can crush without feeling fear or disgrace.
I know how to curb and control,
How to scourge and flog and make things run and roll,
If someone willingly obeys me no more,
Or do not believe what I tell,
Nothing compels me to restrain myself from creating for them a
wretched hell.
Since I have left the forest,
Much I have learnt, much I have explored,
The doubts that gnawed my hearts and irked my soul,
I have fended them off,
In the flaring and flashing air glittering around in my weapons'
blustering roars,
I feel myself as the gods,
Though I am neither a philanthropy or misanthrope,
I believe that in my intellectual strength lies others' hopes.
The loathsome dragon that had pursued after me,
The monstrous power, swirling and whirling, that have threatened
me with its gape,

Like destiny whose claws had rushed over the flames,
Against whom, as defenceless, I knew not what to do,
Now I gladly wait to meet it in order to slay,
And clear the earth from the dragon's leys and create for mankind
the fearless man's triumphal way.
Where in rumbling noise it confuses the world ,
In the gloomy forest in shivering and shuddering creates alarms,
I have acquired the skill and craft to dispel its forces that bring
mankind harms.
In timid days and stirring nights,
In the darkness I searched for a gleam of light,
Strained my eyes to see an end to the blackness that covered my sight,
In willing to free myself from the hands of fate,
In the shinning shadows,
In the power of the human mind that is awake,
I have walked through the forest far and near,
But now there is nothing to fear,
Alone, destined to be free, I am now the promethean man, fearlessly
facing the dragon who is fierce,
I am forging the deadly weapons here.

The beauty asks the hero to abandon such unnatural pursuit for power.

The beauty's invitation to return to the forest

In trying to destroy the dragon you will destroy yourself,
The skill that is based on the intellectual comprehension
Is not sufficient to comprehend all consequences of human actions;
The weapons that you wield and forge according to your desires,
By consuming more and more destructive fire,
And you send off to destroy,
Will prepare one day your own destruction that you can not see in
your mind that is overwhelmed by intellectual triumph and joy,
Although it may appear that you escape scot-free,
The awesome weapons that you develop to make man free,
That reflect your intellectual skill,
Accomplish nothing but to kill,
Will bring unprecedented chaos and disorder of evil,
In the furnace of fire where you forge your will as stubborn steel,
Will spread spites and corrupt the human will.
In running from the forest, in pondering over the destruction of the
dragon, you create your bane,
Let us return to the forest from where we have come,
Let us go in search of love in a journey through the forest again.
In learning what you have sought,
You have gained only superficial understandings,

Resist the pride of what you have learnt,
And do not think that the moon and the sun,
Are just as they are there,
Made of matter and fire,
That can be fully discovered by studying their flares.
The reflections that you see of things are unlike the knowledge that you know,
Everything are strange,
More deeper you go.
All the fragments that you forge,
And the weapons that you brandish,
Show your temporary skill,
Return to the forest in order to be free,
The weapons that you produce today,
Will shatter others home,
The weapons that make others flee from their shelters will make you flee to the wilderness and make the civilization a ruin of stones,
Add no more destructive capability to your thoughts to destroy nature, that you believe as dragon's lair,
Subdue your passion to explore destructive arms that pollutes the air,
Instead heed to the heart that seeks love and care.
Do not imagine that you are so intelligent and wise,
That you need no guidance or counsel from the ones who your weapons despise,
Wander not in the savage heights of the mind where all darkness will appear as light,
Do not flare up strife,
Let not brothers slay brothers,
Do not seek to rule the earth from your mind's cloudy heights,
Let not the strongest of the race,

Forgetting the ties in the mothers' wombs peer out as a giants in
dragon's cave,

And emerge as the victorious and belligerent beasts instead.

With the cleverness of the weapons that you weld,

With the cunningness of man who can every opposition quell,

In winning victory in the war you may succeed,

As a master of the world you may instil in others tremendous fear,

And tame obstinacy of the others who may try to stir your peace that
no one dares,

Be off from this shameful path,

Do not spread more mischief and distress,

Unless you refrain from the stubbornness of your intellect that has
gone astray ,

And listen to nature's fear, call and concern,

You will be doomed to curse and death.

Leave your pursuit to gain formidable power to destroy,

Let us return to the forest,

Let us again go in the journey in search of love beyond sense's joy.

The modern man is a reincarnation of the promethean hero of the past, who has gain reappeared on the stage of life as the technological superman. He replies:

Scientific man's delight and downfall

Go off my sight, let me be alone,
I must endure what I must endure in order that the gods can be dethroned.
The earth sways under my feet,
The heart quakes,
Leave me now alone as the sun that rises high,
Let me rule the earth as the promethean man who is not afraid to live or die,
I wish to fight a formidable fight,
Do not come with your useless warning or advice,
I do wish to live in fear of death,
I shall welcome it when it comes to take my breath.
Away , away !
I do not wish to understand what you say,
I do not want to listen to anything that again will put me at dismay,
I have now found my way.
What is the meaning to be,
If man can not show brevity,
Laughing and dauntlessly can not live a life that is godless and free,

There is still so much to learn,

So much to find out about the way of life's combat,

No fear will anymore pierce my heart,

I have invented the weapons that every animal must fear,

I possess arms that can speed through the sky as lightening darts

chasing the opponents as timorous deer,

Everyone on heaven and earth feel threatened when they hear my

weapons'

roaring sounds shaking the sky - sunlit and clear.

Get away!

Search no love in a heart,

That seeks to free itself from the nature's black art,

With pain and laborious efforts,

I have found my path,

Where miseries do not cling to the heart,

Here I feel safe from the sly snare of love and hate,

I can keep guard of myself as a master who can abate any cunning of

destiny and fate.

Damnation! You may say,

But, the one who has understood that in the power of thinking lies

man's best way,

In logic and science, in own efforts have witnessed the power of the

mind's rays,

He values no more the blue heaven, the birds, the twittering of your

love,

Trusts no more the feathers that put man to sleep as dreaming hearts

sweet reward,

Believes no more in the journey of love as ethereal birds.

The one who rejoices the fire that has awakened him with its rays,

Like Prometheus free, swift in wings, inflamed in heart,

The one who derives power from the conscious blaze,
Dispelling the slumber who is awake,
In love's magic do not try to put him again to sleep.
Go away!
Am I accursed?
May be!
But what need there be to exist when man is not free?
If man by himself can not invent and perform wondrous deeds,
Achieve skill to overcome the timorous will,
Win over nature's treachery and guile,
In quest of knowledge,
Wherever life exists,
Go down in the abyss that is fearful and deep,
What is the meaning of being alive - only to dream and sleep?
I choose myself,
And with it I choose my downfall,
Which path, which other way than that endless sleep?
The dragon's path?
I seek myself,
In the fire and flow,
The glowing flames,
The fiery fury of the light that splendor spread,
The flickering flames billowing and pouring down from the
fountains' heads,
In the fire that devours and consumes,
Shattering fears,
In the wondrous glow and the gleaming radiance of the awakened
mind that dazzles like spears,
In the shinning road of knowledge I myself bear,
Under the radiant light I fill my eyes with the rays that tremble in the

heart and seek freedom in burning tears,

In the shining path of Prometheus I am a man to whom freedom is dear.

How delighted I am!

How noble I feel!

Long I have slept,

Now I am awake,

I defy all that I can not conceive,

I pay no attention to things that I can not grasp with the power to think,

I do not understand and grasp far-off things,

That can not be solved with mathematical precision and need efforts to convince others that there are laws beyond the laws of things,

Happily I challenge what I do not understand,

For example, for me there exists no divine punishments or penance,

Believing in outside power higher than man,

Man punishes himself or herself with fears that deprives man of the courage to face what one is,

There is no need to rear oneself up as blindfolded coward undergoing pangs that never come to cease.

I am not afraid of pains,

Instead of searching in the darkness in vain,

I love the pain of learning everything from the first principles that nature's mystery sustain,

I fancy no more in the blind beliefs of what others say,

I cherish knowledge that is tasted with proofs and not polluted with dubious constraints,

I do not trick myself to hide in cowardice in faiths,

I do not dally with ideas to cheat myself,

I grant me no liberty to approach truth without reason's guidance.

Thus I have explored in the depth of the matter,

Laboriously and artfully through questions, doubts and errors
subjugated myself to the path of knowledge,

I have contested, argued, challenged again and again myself and
pledged not to bow,

Before I have been sure about what I know,

I have asked, perhaps, many times more than I should ask,

And not spared myself the pain of pursuing the reason's task.

Thus I have explored in the depth of the space,

Seen the marvels of the celestial spheres,

As a courageous mortal bearing the fire of Prometheus I know that
there is nothing in the heaven to fear.

If I am accursed, let curse be my way,

Do not ask me to return to the forest where miracle and misery
confuse the mind and hinder the emergence of the illumination by
inner rays,

In this inner light I am ready,

Ready to go where this flaring mind will lead me to go,

I will not follow your treacherous road.

When others try to escape and evade,

Try to find way out of the reality through dubious debates,

As self-deceit gladly fly,

Believing that there is a world that can not be known they float in lie,

And conscientiously or unconscientiously deprive themselves of the
courage to live and die,

I forge my will and try not to escape or hide,

Although I never know who am I,

I know I am created by Prometheus, the bearer of fire and light.

I rejoice to see these sparks, these flashes, these fire that can dispel
nature's magical spell,

Make man the master of the world by lifting him from the misery of hell,

I wish to fashion this world anew,

In the lustre of the awakened mind,

With a glorious light that is shining and defiant,

I wish to slay the forces that lurk in the dark,

Subjugate the powers that challenge me in war,

As one doomed to death through curse,

I wish to make heaven crumble to dust.

Go away love!

Let me be alone.

In thinking about the war with the dragon I wake up in joy,

Everything in my life will go this way,

You will not be able to alter anything by what you say,

By destroying myself I will know my freedom,

May be that is my fate!

It is better to live with this courage,

Than to leave oneself in the savage world as nature's slave,

I do not wish to waste away my life by always nurturing fears in breast.

Go away!

Let me be alone.

Go far-off as far as you can go,

Do not return again before the curse befalls and consumes me in the fire's bowl,

With your soft lustrous eyes bear no sorrow,

There is someone in me that always contradict me,

Indeed ... indeed .. I would pretend that I have never seen love,

I have never heard her,

We have never met,

I have never wept,

Before all weak words in my heart tootle away,
I hope you understand what I say,
And go away!
Heed my words,
Forget my name,
Tell it to the world only after I am consumed in flame,
Accursed indeed!
Otherwise what leads you here!
Amidst wondrous deeds when I need no love,
Why your timorous hands come and touch,
Is it your black art and magic for which I feel disgust,
O heart! Keep guard,
As an oath of love take this ring,
And go ... go... before in my heart more solitude clings!

After she leaves the hero sees in his vision the breakdown of the Heaven in the sky, and emergence of the Heaven from the earth, where a superman is rising.

The dream of the return of the superman

In an endless quaking I see heaven being shattered in my heart,
Nevermore it will compel me to go forth in search of love.
Storms, troubles, endless swimming in the flood,
Whirlwinds flying off with the gusts,
Lightening fusing the corners of heaven and earth,
Wanderer moving through a tumultuous birth,
Earth's face being pierced by the lightening darts,
From the primeval ashes lights spreading in the inhospitable world
where everything must depart,
The swords splintering in clashes,
In courageous return the man conquering the Earth,
In light and flame,
Flashing and flaring,
Glistening as the sunlight's glow,
Alone invading and preparing for the rise of man from dust,
I am alone and accursed.
Amidst this I see brilliant glows,
Sparks and splinters of the burning souls,
Heavens' breakdown, the blaze of the fire, the trusty weapon's
crucial blow,

In this shower of sparks I see the superman rising from the dust
Who is me but still not me any more at last.
I am a stranger to myself without any home,
Shaping myself,
Fashioning my life again and again anew,
Stirring as the light in the gleam of the dawn,
Penetrating the darkness as shinning rays,
Breaking down the shadows of the darkness descrying the
disappearing ways,
Caught up in the tumult in a state between the sleep and when man is
awake,
Clearly knowing that I am not a man but a son of titan or god,
Who has risen to revolt against his father's weapon penetrating him
as rays to crush the despot,
O! I am awake to see the breakdown of heaven of the gods.
Frivolous pleasures I seek no more,
In the golden gleam of the light knowing who I am,
I can endure more pain and suffering than any man can endure.
I am free,
In this freedom my suffering lies,
I can not follow all possibilities of my freedom that I can descry,
I am entrapped in the snare ,
In an emptiness, and a loneliness that I can not describe,
Therefore I wish more to know,
In knowing I wish to fill the emptiness that always expands,
More I understand more I do not understand,
What a curse of knowledge!
What a prize for the titan or god whose eye sights the whole universe
spans!
I take the utmost troubles to reach the inmost thoughts,

There seems to exist an eternal drought,
There is no way to quench this parch of the son of a titan or a god.
More I drink to refresh my thoughts,
More thrusts for drink rise from an empty world that sinks
bottomless beyond the boundary that my mind can cross,
More I wish to know its end,
More and more it extends,
Sun that stands high!
Blue sky that gazes in emptiness at light!
Burning fire that inflames man's thoughts!
Scorches the hearts as a pyre of a mysterious god,
I feel confused,
In freedom I am in fetter,
In victory of knowledge why I feel so much conflict?
In taking responsibility of my own deeds do I myself punish?
Am I really awaken or still in sleep?
Through defiance do I really wish to revolt or submit?
Who but myself these questions would answer and resolve?
Everything, including knowledge itself, seem shamefully hostile,
O loathsome Lucifer! Light showing me the path of knowing!
Gladly penetrate... penetrate this abysmal soul swayed between light
and night,
Enlighten me through sufferings,
In this suffering let me find life's highest delight.
To redeem this pain I would never choose not to know,
O timeless sorrow!
In whichever path you would lead me I would follow,
If this is the way you would me kill,
In this courageous sacrifice of my will,
I wish to fulfill the meaning for which I carry this will.

As I look up I see the splendour is spreading,
Glowing, growing, burning, illumining and raging,
Everything is shinning where the flames are bathing,
In my eyes as a radiant sun the superman is emerging,
In painful trembling, quaking,
In a hail of light he is rising,
To awaken the earth he is gazing,
I am hearing his wondrous voice,
Deep within where everything is blazing,
Bright as a sun,
Always and everywhere,
With a force that is overwhelming,
He is moving between the mirrors stirring the radiant imaging,
He is becoming,
I see him as the One coming and going.
I hail Tathagata Thus Come Thus Gone One,
Shinning upon the Earth as the inner sun,
In the secret vision as radiant light he summons the man to sacrifice
In the tangle of the rays,
As the threads of the senses fade away,
As a brave and glorious figure without any constraint,
He rises in wisdom's strength.
I can not rightly grasp his glory that is raging free,
Unbound and enlightened he is coming to teach man the most
glorious path in which he will lead.
Through storms and clouds,
Lightening and thunders,
As enlightening power flying on his way,
Moving through the spheres of the planets and the sun and the moon,
In a winged steed leaping from the fire carrying the awakened mind

away,
As a bright soul he is descending through the clouds jubilant in the touch of the inner rays.
I hail this conquering light!
Asking me to make sacrifice,
The hero for whom I have awaited in this world for so long,
I hear him blowing his horns,
He is coming to destroy and create,
O! I hear his promise of a new Earth and the destruction that he pledged,
There will be peace on the Earth,
All will be noble through his blood,
Everywhere the world will turn as his wonderful work,
I fear not his flames,
I swear to sacrifice my life to the power that kindles and puts all ablaze.
O feeble desires! Go away!
I shall stand in front of this fire instead,
In the flaming wind that will sweep all away,
As a brave bold daring sailor I shall row in peace and move towards home far...far away.
As a stubborn and bold I shall wait where no will dare to wait,
I would not seek safety or rest,
Alone.. starkly alone ...in the frenzy to meet the fire in the glorious fireball that will leap on the Earth I shall leap and pass away.
When I close my eyes, see what I see over the mountain peaks,
Hear what I hear from the sky far .. far deep,
Heaven is ablaze,
The flames are leaping high,
The ramparts are falling giving out flashing lights,

Everything is being consumed by a wild fire,
I hear the horns,
The alarming sounds of the danger ahead,
The dark decrees of doom,
Calling for the faithless world's ash and tomb.
In a splendid radiance raging high,
In doom and downfall of man,
I see the return of the superman,
He is going to reveal to the world the sacred fire of the shinning sky,
Immortal glory of the man rising from dust to the domain of light
illumining the summit at immeasurable height,
On the Earth that is man's glorious abode,
He is going to pave the path of heaven - human salvation's golden
roads,
What gods cannot give he will bring to man,
With him the domain of the gods and the realm of man will merge
and become one.
As I turn my eyes to the sky,
As God and man - a loving pair,
I see him flying undivided in the two worlds joined as same - low and
high.
In powerful strokes but still in leisurely movement of the wings,
He is descending in the life's stream,
The time of sacrifice has come.

The promethean man and his pact with Devil

From the constellation of the Lyre,

The Swans and the lovers over the bridge,

The scintillations of the Sirius, Ras Algheri and the Demon Star discernible many light years away,

Orion's belt - many solar systems burning between heaven and hell,

The Scorpion's sting bringing cosmic life and death,

Immeasurably remote Hercules cluster burning with millions of stars ablaze,

Ophiuscus, Dragon, Alpha, Beta, Theta stars plunging towards the centre spewing out gases and rays,

Evolutions of the cosmos continuing from the vacuum and ending in the vacuum where all things take their rest,

In an infinitely remote world sunk in time and space,

The millions and millions of stars disappearing and appearing from the void,

Supernova bursting and dwarfs falling away carrying the stellar ashes in silent recesses,

In the visible universe the years precisely rotating, gyrating and wobbling with the cosmic turmoil bringing the precessions of the solstices and equinoxes,

Daylight and night repeating thousands and millions of years
millions and millions of times,
In vision and dream and through knowledge of the world Devil
makes the world so wonderful and strange!
With the instruments that I have invented I am able to detect the
splendid primeval light -
The sphere of radiation from which the universe has risen from the
night.
I hail Devil who has helped me to make progress in knowing the
mystery of the nature day after day,
Strengthened my sight in different wavelength outside the visible
rays,
Shown in mathematical formulation the path to grasp the infinitude
infinite reality made of fire, air, water and dust,
Kindled reasons and made comprehension of the world more than
fantasy of the mind and matter of the heart,
Shown the paradise of the promethean creatures made of water and
clay,
Taught the methods of lifting the body from the burden of the
gravitational weight.
I hail his intelligence with which it is possible to foresee the eclipses,
lunation, the sun and stars' daily paths- the entrances in
constellations and periodic transits,
The recurrences of the celestial phenomena including perihelion
shifts,
The appearances of the stars, their magnitudes in life and brilliance
before deaths,
The double, triple, multiple clusters scintillating in different waves
in different cosmic depths,
The collisions, contractions, dissipations and emanations of the

celestial orbs in the constellations,

The logical continuity of the universe ending in a catastrophic contractions or beginning in explosions,

The oscillations, the cyclic mutations of time and space dividing in millions and millions of nebular regions hundreds,

Or thousands, or millions, or billions of light years away,

The beings becoming from and returning to the invisible void,

The energy transmuting into and matter and energy fluctuating to potentialize as matter in time and space,

In this foreseeable causality with accuracy dependent only on the power of computability of the mechanical brains,

Devil has given the mobility to move beyond the boundary of the knowable time and space,

Rendered the forms, that never existed, visible in the mathematical space,

With conjectures and hypothesis proved that seemed impossible and disproved that anything exists as the hands of destiny and fate,

And thus glorified the power of imagination and freedom of the human race.

The forms that are immobilized and exist in the abstract domain of the mind are mobilized in the mathematical space,

In this illusory paradise where time past, time present, and time future are alterable by the choices in the logarithms reflecting ingenuity of the mind in the contemplative state,

Devil contemplates non-existent in existent framework of the reality in the mechanical plane,

Setting the initial time and the conditions of the space,

Changing the variables that respond to the changing boundaries - curved, complex, twisted or flat - as desired by the one playing the game,

In this world one can simulate tranquility and calm,
Or terrible tempests and storms,
Create splendid resplendence, and splendour much greater than
anything ever visible in light,
Or infernal obscurity, darkness, and shadows more fearful than the
most terrible nocturnal flight;
With delinquency of the mind one can fall,
With tranquillity, reflectivity and constancy of the purpose to win
paradise can rise,
With insufficient response and inability to comprehend the signs one
can end in the sulphurous fire of sensual delight,
With prudence, circumspection and foresight reach the firmament
floating in radiance and light;
Flying from Lyre to Vega, zenith to azimuth,
One can discover mind's illumination in the zodiac entire,
And move with the bird of light moving over the pyre.
By eating the fruit from the forbidden tree I am free,
I am made in God's own image- what more can I be?
By falling from the Paradise I feel I have become a greater man,
I can soar as high or low as I intend to soar,
Rise from the abyss of the dark, the flaming world where chaos roars,
I can win the Providence by intelligence and force as my cherished
sport.
I feel illumined in high and low,
Neither the hell nor the heaven is my goal,
I wish to find the Creator and transgress His power so that in my
world He wont have any role,
Against His Throne I have raised the impious souls,
Inspired them to revolt,
Aspiring the glory of the Almighty have hurled His angels in flames,

Bound the rest of the souls in chains, I am the omnipotent man - the hero of the mortal plane.

I have nothing to fear,

From the tracts of the hell, the fiery gulf, the doom and wrath of flames to the immeasurable space where eyes can not discern any boundary beyond the spheres of the fire and air,

With my intelligence all fallen souls I am able to steer,

From the ever burning sulphur, the tempestuous fire,

To the transcendental light, lightning and thunders of my challenging compeer,

I have risen as the invincible Promethean man from misery, suffering and tears.

God still tries to pervert the souls by evil means,

Creating doubts about my power he draws man to fulfill His dream,

To take vengeance I pursue Him with my intelligence till He will be extinct.

In stench and smoke I follow Him,

In the infernal world where His assault once the good angels' courage revived I search Him in the worst extremes,

Where the heaven is azure and under the vaulted dome leaving the Virgin's songs the angels had fled,

Where with victory and glory once the Satan his followers had led,

Carrying Prometheus' light I search Him in all places hidden and secret.

In the loftiest of the towers,

Or the darkened streets,

In the dampened mist,

Or the Empyrean light where the vision is led by the gold winged steed,

In the ethereal sky with silent twinkling beats,

Or the deserted streets from where all souls have taken their retreats,
In nightlong waking where on the window panes,
The dews of the night drip in pain,
The souls are engaged to find out what is real and certain,
With tedious arguments try to ascertain that can not be possibly
ascertained;
Where the houses sleep,
While the sleepless eyes formulate, discard, reformulate theories of
all - from the universe to the structures millions and millions of times
smaller than the tip of a pin,
In this Memory Palace I search Him in vain,
In my memory through mathematics I try to establish myself as a
powerful promethean man, who is above misery, sin or disdain.
I am the architect of this Palace,
This towering structure of the mind that can hold the adventurous
souls breathless,
Like Assyrian gardens, Babylonian glories,
Amidst the towering magnificence of the buildings rising hundreds of
stories,
Surpassing the power of deities and demons who descend and ascend,
I try to find out the hiding place of God from where He is supposed
to descend.
From morning to evenings I search,
Constantly revise the theories of the minutest particles and the uni-
verse,
With mathematical precision compute the time and space that is
curved,
Pin down the smallest structures on whose understanding the
understanding of the cosmos depends and to which it must always
refer,

In mathematical equations and on coffee-cups,

I bet against the existence of God and argue for everything as products of matter,

Rolling the shirt-sleeves search Him from the cosmic height to the hellish gutter.

In the consciousness' murky alleys,

In the dingy shades of the vacant space,

In the flickers of the starry lamps that hardly care to understand,

The blackened night's infinite pain where the man stares and stands,

Where the night's hours chime,

Trampling the time like gangsters out for hideous crimes,

Demons and Devil make contracts with man showing the shining knives,

And carry away the souls where God has to be thrown as destined;

I have contracted away my soul to Lucifer who has given me the power to decipher the language of the cosmic hymns,

As the promethean man born under the solar sign,

I am the tormentor of myself,

The liberator of the self;

For me there is no need for penance,

In humaneness I see in myself godly glory and eminence.

I am the victor over the gods and the bearer of the human hope,

The destroyer of the heaven of the prophets and the popes,

My world is above chance and chaos, miracle and magic, grace or disgrace,

Trapped within the labyrinth that I am myself;

In the snares of the flames of Lucifer I am the rebellious free spirit of heaven and hell;

I do not submit my will to the angels - the progenies of the divine,

Do not look for their miracles and mystic signs,

I know I am born of the elemental four,
And only intends to follow nature's material course,
Thus I drive my spirit to higher heights,
And see the glory and radiance of the human spirit falling through the night;
Prometheus' light has lightened my way,
In mathematics and physics I have seen the mind's highest rays.
There is fulfilment, security, illumination, meaning and happiness in this experience of myself as the free spirit not given, or taken, or determined by anyone by myself,
In this daemonic, chthonic power, in the shafts of sunlight, I have risen,
I am awake,
I am made of God's own image,
Like progeny of Lucifer unbound!
In the wonder of the knowledge I feel amazed!

From there he comes to the market place.

A city in pain: A labyrinth of damnation

Here Beelzebub like puppets in his hands makes man dance,
In old time on Candlemas Day, Rood Mass day, Lammas Day,
And the eve of the All Hallows people used to celebrate in this city
the festival of the witches in the presence of the Prince of the Dark,
who their powers enhanced;
By kissing Devil's reverse face under animal's tail,
In promiscuous orgies, that increased the fertility of the hunters and
herdsmen,
The devotees copulated with artificial phallus to enact the black
magic that even gripped virgins and nuns.
In the same place there are swelling numbers of brothels,
Appalling walls covered with nudity of advertisements,
Lightning flashes of the cafes, nightclubs and taverns,
The glaring strip-shows with music and dance,
The whirling hurries of the paltry loves, apathy, sleep and copulation;
Like powerful mechanical engine's prolonged exhaustion,
Wound, nausea and dereliction;
Like phantoms flying in the alleyways there are relations between
the consumer and consumed,
Hearts' remorse, disgust and incessant fumes.
Inside the city gate,
Wandering in slow moving shapes in gentleness,

In front of the banks, arcades, staircases,

Or inside revolving doors ,twisting passageways winding through the shops,

Where there are dark caves,

Where sellers stand upright or sit cross-legged,

Smiling faces please customers,

Ladies hold between colored lips their metaphysical warmth,

And circumambulate difficulties of selling products by using physical charms,

When the shadows wander by through the doorways,

In solitary suffering the citizens of this metropolis gaze at the windowpanes,

Without needing to know who pass by;

Like a number in statistics of the millions everyone enters and exits this city many times before they leave and die.

In this city in pain,

Vehicles, carriages, coffins mingling with the movements of the organs breathing, and activating hunger, thirst, despair and disdain,

From streets to streets,

In boulevards and avenues amidst bustling rush,

Carry shoppers, merchants, and goods,

With indifference transfer furniture, warehouse loads, as well as men and women with happy or unhappy moods;

Constantly changing the images rolling through the city in the labyrinthine maze,

In the glass panes on the windows, or doorframes, reflect an unreal world at the vacuous gaze.

Everyday in a laden boat here arrive sailors in search of hope;

From the abyss of the dark,

They come flocking across the gulf;

In squares, terraces and courtyards stand squeezed to see the city's
marvellous arts;
As tourists lined up as herds look at the ruins and ramparts,
Stand in front of cathedrals and churches,
Visit the dwellings and the tombs of the saints and the martyrs,
Loiter and stray in markets places;
In commercial districts, in galleries of arcades,
From Money Exchange to greengrocer's shades,
See phantasmagorias of Chinese lantern:
In Dragon's twisting paths,
In the blue beams illumining the skull,
Watch the masks of the unreal men and women walking along the
streets and the boulevards.
There is enormous flock of journeymen moving through this unreal
time and space;
They all move free with a will carrying languages and thoughts;
Like in an ocean deep, like strange creatures they reason, ascend,
descend through the market places and boulevards,
In worlds containing worlds within rush endlessly in a space
boundless and infinite;
Like mysteries walking erect in a vast universe sing, murmur, seek
redemption, happiness and escape,
In dreamy eyes in golden light in the arching marvel of the sky,
Where Prometheus and Heracles had once risen, seek to fly away in
dream through the streaks of rays,
Wish to return back into hundreds of years through the history, myth,
legends in the silence of the inner space.
This city lies on the shore of a strange sea that penetrates the
dreaming minds;
Its water are illumined by starlight;

It foams scatter everywhere:
From bubbles in champagne bottles and laughter of the night in
drunken sodden stairs,
To the morning bath in the fresh light of the day drooping in the
golden hair,
After bleeding in love in the dingy room's suffocated air,
It fills the blue eyes with bubbles of lights in which man feels
confession of guilt and sin and falls in prayers.
In the sunlight and the golden dust,
In meandering streams it crosses the hearts through asphalts and grass,
Passes by orchards and trees and the shops selling perfumes, scents
and Eau de Cologne filled in glass;
It meanders through the village life and the city breathing in the
rhythms of the shining marbles, glass panes and glaring voltaic lights,
Passes by the crowded streets, brothels and cafes woken up from the
night;
In squares swinging with military bands,
Amidst pensioners discussing while poking canes on sand,
Or discussion and disagreements of the loitering criminal gangs,
It breaks as waves of sounds burbling in a world, where outpouring
foams of beer on tables and chairs on the pubs,
While visitors move helter-skelter in hubs.
And here under signs of advertisement of the best selling drink, that
upholds the symbol of pleasure of the day,
The green benches in the parks stand to provide resting place for all
sorts of woman and man- including lesbians and gays.
In the quarter of the dazzling cafes selling beer and lemonade,
There are many alleys where the lovers promenade,
There are many shadows where the angels of Devil, like invisible
spiders floating in the webs of enjoyment, kiss the lips and necks,

And draw the travellers to gluttony and drunkenness;
There are many dark passages where the travellers can eat, drink, and
feel happy,
In sprawling dishes the demons offer them many grand old fashioned
debauchery-
And there are so many other ways of Devil's intelligent treachery!
Where stomachs churn,
Beefs, shrimps or lambs damp the appetite before the frying pans,
Vegetables, drinks, and numerous choices of fish and flesh moist the
belly surrendering to the habitual pleasures of eating out in
restaurants,
In the background where the poor and hungry squatter in the city,
The sailors anchor ships beside the life's darkened jetty.
In this city in pain,
Where they come to trade jewels, diamonds, and items of antiquity,
Taking with them blind passions, wounds and blood of the man as
victims of life's obscenity,
Bring back coffins stuffed with comrades who have perished in
freedom and promiscuity,
And float unconcerned in the streams of pleasures sunk in life's
ephemerality.
In this unreal city with bluish roofs,
Strange houses built with shining stones,
Beyond the boundaries of the doors and the windows, framed with
illusions of the eyes, acting as shutters opening and closing the
interior where man is skeleton and bone,
There is the limitless water of the sea where history rises and drowns,
Wreckage, inferno, and sinking crowns;
There is sunshine, deceptions, incineration,
"Yes" to life and "no" to all that bring veneration.

In glasses of wine, in cups of coffee and tea, in chatter and patter, in thoughtlessness or thoughts,
There are waves of nothing in everything,
There is the drama of the boat going down, shattering into pieces, wreckage,and tempest before awakening,
Like Hermes a mysterious figure rescuing the sailors before drowning,
There is a guide always returning.

The return of the man, who has made the journey from the village life to the cosmos, as a dual possessing a human nature accompanied by his divine guide, is another recurrence of the story of the eternally wandering man who starts his journey once again as the promethean hero appearing in the cybercity in a modern time.

He now appears as a new man, wearing a new mask, in a new set up of the stage of life. The city dwellers in the cybercity are the new villagers who gather in the market place where Tathagata, who has been meditating in the Time Hall of Illusion, holds a sermon for the human beings of the new age.

On the way they meet a sailor.

Sailor's recapitulation

Here life is a feast, wine and revelling in beauty in the libidinous
plane,
In Sabbath night in witches' arms a dancing sacrilege,
In wealth, luxury and mendacity a loathsome trade.
Here compassion, crucifixion, journey to the Holy land,
Are viewed as contradictions with science and reason of the reflective
man,
Here physics, philosophy, technology, mechanics carries evidence of
science as the only way to progress,
Chemistry, cosmology, mathematics the prejudices of the miracles
and witchcraft redress,
Here in reason, rationality and numbers man discover principles and
laws that can heaven and hell eradicate,
Here in the freedom of the spirit man marches forward to know
things as certain for himself,
Here I sail alone ...alone ... within myself.
In this city of modern age there are betrayal, and brutality,
Everybody are left alone to themselves;
While merchants, bankers, doctors, technocrats, bureaucrats,
squeezed the universe of pleasure in the luxurious drawing rooms,
Without clothes, without food, without shelters the weak are left
roaming in frost and cold in despair and gloom,

Nudity, and different pornographic poses have become a business in boom,

Erection, copulation, vulgarity, nausea, pelvis pain are served as best public entertainments in cinema, theaters and cafes that are in bloom;

Drums, dance, noise, debauchery, delinquency raise the demons from the tombs;

Orgies and all relations that were forbidden before pass as rights of freedom in liberated rooms;

Men marry men, women marry women,

And the maniacs, believing it as the work of the Magistrates of Satan, preaches the world's doom.

Man delights in the fatal powers of the machines,

Fanning the impious feelings yielding to the violence and terror of the sort man had never before seen,

To live selfishly with passion eternally without caring for any sin have become their greatest dreams;

In a ring of flames they hail the fire of flesh that burns from beneath,

In drunkenness of self-love orchestrate orgies to integrate the impulses of anarchy in the mass;

With canons, machine guns and mortars,

Manipulate rationality, morality, humanity and the ignorance of the hearts,

With propaganda in morning papers or evening transcripts or magazines devoted to the magnets, tycoons and stars,

And advertisements of all sorts that create ravenous drifts,

Paralyze the will of man who are forced to put their souls to Devil as bids.

Treachery, lechery, gluttony - everything that are possible when man has no faith,

Grow uninhibited in the name of happiness of the bankers, industrial and military men with stiff proud necks;

Massacres, cynicisms, prostitution, cunning and comforts march with science and technology in a monstrous race;

In damnation man finds the heaven in a blasphemous hellish landscape.

In this landscape floating downwards in the stream,

In alcohol, women, music and ferments of love and dream,

I have stretched the wings of freedom like a bird ,

Flying over the swamps and holes of the heart,

Fallen in the abyss of the mind that brings disaster,

Beyond the glaciers, the sun lit evening sky, the waves glittering as pearls,

Hurled by the hurricanes of the heart I have fallen in the black cave beyond the giant gulf,

Drunk, pale-eyed, crushed and wrecked by the ultramarine waves,

I am thrown in the bottom of the sadness where the Beelzebub sits as awake.

Seeing the passersby he asks:

Where are you going?

Like me are you also trying to travel through the untold space,
Trying to steer yourself across the abyss?
In the little moments of time trying to understand the man of
hundreds of thousands of years?
In the infinitesimal boundary trying to grasp the infinite?
In a drop, that glimmers for a moment and breaks in darkness and
light, are you seeking to create the holograms of the universe?
In chaotic spins and whorls of the wheel are you trying to go across
this tumultuous boundary of life?
Through the cluster of worlds are you trying to go across the abyss to
the village,
Where the mythical man is watching his journey in the multiple of
images in the mirror through and beyond time and space?
Do you also feel so alien in the world as me?
Seized by the tumults of terror are you also fleeing from the tyrant
and the man awaiting for the return of the superman?
In an emptiness, as a man deserted in wilderness,
Where a predatory light consumes the vision there is a strange light
that ruminates on the eyes,
As butterflies and birds it floats,
In the cerulean sky it wanders alone as an imaginary boat;

Haunting the darkness of the desires and dreams looms in variety of disguises;

Hovers contourless behind the shapes of things;

In dreams weaving threads of memories swarms as fugitive trying to escape the labyrinth felt and seen.

From the world in different space and time are you going to the so-called real world where I have been?

From the unknown and the obscure, that vibrates in the emptiness in a different light that can be seen in time and space,

Are you going to know yourself in a world where things carry name,

Seeking in words and languages the reality of the self?

In the innumerable worlds that exist as fragments of consciousness floating in time and space,

Where there is no centre or boundary,

Where everything glint as objects immersed in the many worlds without names,

Where things wind through multiple of projections of the mind in different levels of consciousness,

Where words turn into things and things turn into words,

In the mythical world, where deities transform as women and men,

In a magic or not,

In a strange light the images surface as symbols of the eternity reflecting the timeless God,

Are you going to the village where I have been born?

Are you going there where the mythical man is watching the life in a Hall of Illusion,

Rolling in the vision as, in a kaleidoscope, the fragments of imaginations,

That form patterns of thoughts by accidents and chance?

Are you going there, where beside a cerulean water in a vast rimless

look, like a boundless ocean looking at itself, an undefinable
intelligence is making voyage in the Time Hall of Illusion?
As fragments of the self strewn in many times and many places and
in many worlds separated by different types of awareness and concepts,
Where the mythical being is transforming from one to another,
Reflecting his self in the innumerable mirrors as many in one without
any name,
Are you going to that wilderness of images in the Time Hall,
Where wizardry, magic, telepathy bewilder, create hallucinations,
and dematerialize the world of time and space?
Are you going to meet that collage-of--Self, the waif, the poet, the
dreamer seeking refuge in an alien land ,
Moving as fragments bundled together in different spaces of inner
depths,
Who is striving to become one by striving for a total awareness of
the whole?
He is trying to take refuge in an imaginary shore beyond the domains
of the moon and the sun.
He is seized by the wonder and awe of the worlds that glimmer
behind the surface of the consciousness that the world of seeing and
hearing penetrates,
Disintegrated in different levels of awareness but still joined like a
knot He is looking at himself through the images,
Reflectiing in the mirror in the Hall of Illusion - the Time Hall of the
sun.
In the fragmental identities that he carries with himself in the wide
expanse of time and space as many other me's he is fleeing from
place to place.
In a series of moments where the eternity is embraced,
In fragments of projections moving in different planes,

As the mythical man sacrificed under the moon and the sun,
In labyrinthine alleys that pass through many locales of dreams,
As a journeyman he is moving through many paths,
As a being strange to himself and sprung from himself,
In a sudden upsurge of wonder,
Like a fugitive trying to flee from the wheel of time,
In fragmental bits he is searching an exit from the blind paths of things,
Arrested by the moments he is seeking eternity and freedom,
In a poem flowing through the world,
In innumerable sounds,
In words describing the faceless, shapeless mythical one,
He is waking up and falling asleep in a blind world felt, heard and seen,
As a sceptre of himself in different shades,
Making a journey through the poem,
In innumerable disguises as fugitive fleeing from himself and
returning to himself,
With the turning of the night and day,
In the rhythms of the sun waking the world and the moon bringing
man to dream,
He is coming out of himself and returning to the Self.
I am a fugitive sprung from him who is fleeing as a me-fragment of
the whole in search of an exit to escape,
Fleeing in a way that I do not know,
Under the big urn of the sun I am fleeing from time to time, space to
space, from world to world.
With a strange awareness of the man who knows,
It is here all will be sacrificed,
In a light, in columns of swirling winds different and strange,
He too shall be offered to the eternal flame;
I am fleeing from the tyrant and the exterminator pursuing me in time

and space.

I am seeking refuge from the frightening gaze of death holding the rim of the wheel burning in the light of the sun,

Roaming through the streets and the secret paths,

In loneliness haunted by the burning eyes staring from the dark,

From houses to houses I am seeking hiding places to save my existence from his cruel assault.

There is a constant fear of annihilation in the Hall of Time,

In the ephemeral world where all parts draw apart to join again and fuse together in the burning urn of the sun,

Where repulsions and attractions of the heart and dust fight against each other to annihilate and regenerate the ephemeral world in which all life are bound,

I am seeking refuge in world where there is no refuge to be found.

I am an individual fugitive fused with the primal one,

Fleeing from the surface of the conscious mind to the unconscious depth,

And vice versa, making a flight from the destiny and fate to the sun awaken mind trembling in trepidation to the god like resplendence of the inner illumination and rays.

Disguised under the sun born from the dust and carrying a spirit that is always unknown,

I am fleeing from the cycles of the endless sacrifices,

As a fragment fleeing to the depth and rising from the depth,

In a light that is nothing but a darkness that creates fear,

I am being pursued by the invisible killer.

As hands from the domain that seems beyond my understanding,

Like in a magic phantasmagoria constantly producing new images and forms,

Extending the grips to the one who is trying to escape,

In whatever way I choose to escape,

In all quickness he moves towards,

Returns as the exterminator,

In this strange destiny of fleeing to return and returning to flee again,

He lurches as the predator preying in a strange game of life and death.

Are you going to that Time Hall of the sun?

In the nameless world where in colors and forms things are invisible and diffused,

Where imaginations and fantasies open many possibilities of worlds where one may attempt to seek refuge,

Where as other I return to escape,

Where I appear as another again and again,

Are you going to that sunlit village where the mythical man appears and disappears as the fleeing and returning man in many disguises and innumerable shapes?

SERMON OF THE HERMIT IN THE MARKETPLACE

As a hermit, who has wandered in the mountain landscapes in search of the enlightened path, Tathagata addresses the new villagers who do not believe in any spiritual being higher than themselves. When the hermit talks about God, and the way a man of flesh and blood has become one with the Divine being, and now appeared as Christ-Man in the marketplace to explain about the existence of a supernatural world, the cyber-villagers do not comprehend what he speaks about.

Listening to the sermon, which the hermit delivers in an enigmatic language, and contradicts the knowledge of science and technology of the cyber-villagers, the crowd laughs and zeers at him.

When the Christ-man talks about the destruction and renewal of Earth, the crowd considers him insane and chases him away from the city. With it the Earth succumbs under a cataclysm and a spiritual age begins....

Address of the hermit from the mountain

In the time before the beginning or the beginning before the time I knew not myself. There were no myriads of things, no beings, no heaven and earth but only a sea that I shall talk about. There did not exist light, gravity, directions or percepts. In that void and nothingness there existed nothing that could be associated with right or wrong. Nothing was deep; nothing was high. There were no sun or moon, no life and death, no transformation of the shapes that bring association of time and space. The life was not an illusion because the illusion is something that the material world generates. It was not dream because dreams are governed by the intellects and percepts. It was a realm of the limitless.

I do not know how I shall describe. It is similar to the emptiness that penetrates the mind. It is an awareness of pure light that does not associate itself with the rooms or things or the time. It is boundless and massless, substanceless something that resides within itself. It is always there with ultimate fullness. Invariable, without end and beginning, containing the future in the past it is a world about which it is difficult to form clear understandings and concepts. Everywhere pervading but nowhere scattering the light or projecting itself on objects, it is the void preserving the structure of the universe in emptiness .

In complete harmony with itself, as a whole, without form, without any definition that can identify it with anything else but the being of the emptiness where rests all souls, it is the formless sea of the void that all relationships of the cosmos uphold. It is very difficult to comprehend because knowledge depends on something that it contradicts, opposes and annihilates before it becomes knowledge of things. Cause, causality, end, beginning, nothing, something , the attributes and essences of beings, man, God, nature's hidden marvels, the rivers and streams where the motions assimilate the myriads of ways, appearances and disappearances, eternity and ephemeral evidence of transformations and change that depend on each other and strive to go across, things seen with the clarity of the lights and things far beyond, all sorts of tranquillity and turmoil of the matter and mind exist as non-existence or existence in oneness in this whole.

I am a wanderer who has risen from this void beyond time and space. I am beyond and within the boundaries that define the qualities of matter and the domain of intelligence and awareness that extend within and outside the myriads of things. I have risen from the unaffected and motionless world as a stranger to myself. Assuming form in the world I am the incarnation of the being who has assumed consciousness though he is neither substance, consciousness or thought. I am the ultimate man who has sprung from the depth of the mystery that no one will ever understand.

Do not think of me as the man who is framed in flesh and blood. Though I stand in physical form I am a perplexing phenomena, a miracle that you need to understand. Though you see me in body I am empty, infinite and one with the great ocean. I have come here to reveal to you the endlessness of the being, the ultimate knowledge about the emptiness from which I come and to which I shall return. Although I see, hear and breathe know me as the ultimate man, the mirror in which all human beings may see himself and herself in an incarnation that can never be fully known or seen. I know it will cause confusion when you see me . But do not draw any conclusion about me because I am beyond all conclusions and judgments of the human minds.

The man, whom you see, who speaks about the unspeakable, carrying humanness who disguises himself with all human characteristics, beyond his mask he is the deep ocean - all streams merge in him. You may ask why is he here? Why does he masquerade? Why his eyes and ears are no more different than mine? Why does he feel pain, grief, trembling in the heart as all others who are alive and bound in the senses' chains? Do not be confused. Know that as the man he realizes

his sacrifice. He sacrifices himself in suffering and pain for the sake of the humanity. He is above all sages and all "superior men". All must sacrifice themselves as man life after life before they can be one with Him.

I know it is hard to understand what I am saying. I am the man whom you can never fully know. From the weakest to the strongest, from the tiniest to the highest I am present. I am identical to and different from all. I exist in all ages. I operate in errors, in free spirit, in impassive souls, in the myriads of will in turbid chaos. I am also in the minds of the sages who have their minds in full contemplative control. However I appear to be separate from myself when I reveal myself in form. I am the wanderer who has risen from the boundless ocean and beyond the characteristics of anything that will make me a character who can be understood and known.

You may wonder why am I wandering? Where had I been? Wherefrom have I come to spread the teaching of the ultimate man? I have already told you about the ocean from where I come. It is not an ocean you can measure or fathom with the senses or the mind. It is the dwelling of the light, the being who is never born. But how am I manifest then? How do I preserve body and at the same time remain bodiless? How am I revealed in the world when my existence can never be truly revealed ? It is a mystery that is truly difficult to comprehend. First of all know that I am not what you think I am. Then realize that I am not one. I am infinitely many in harmony with the whole. In myriads of existence where things manifest, I am not bound although through everything I penetrate. Once things form through appearances I am visible as something that appears by negating the knowledge of the existence that I am. There is no way of avoiding this contradiction in which all existence are bound with the great mind from which I come. I am not in the body where, you may believe, I reside. Beyond this body I have a different body in the realm of God. It is the body of the ultimate man. It is a mystery that is beyond the capacity of any language to explain. By the will of God this body is able to relate itself to the physical form floating amidst myriads of things moving by cause or chance. This relation is beyond comprehension of anyone. You may ask why do you see the ultimate man as a man speaking to you? If he is multiple and infinite how does he appear as bodily separate and distinct from others as an individual one? Know that I do not exist in one plane or in a particular level of existence or awareness. My existence is spread in many layers, many spheres, in realms after realms, in dimensions inside dimensions that are difficult to fathom with the limited awareness that man possess in the awaken state. This infinitely complex domain can be subjected to vision and awareness through a material body in the physical plane. However every awareness is qualified by the nature of the body to which it relates. Unless the ultimate man relates Himself to a body of an individual man, it will not be possible to bring forth concepts that may appear meaningful to man. The great mind, from which I arise, has therefore related Itself through a body to bring forth these messages to man.

The physical characteristic of this man is no different from you all. The mental realms that are related to the problems of the survival and needs are also the same like yours. But there exist innumerable realms of existence to which the body of the ultimate man is able to relate. He can move to the realm of the time and space in the domain of the inert matter as well as rise to the realm where he is the light of God. Know that I am the ultimate man. I have come to tell you about my wandering, my sacrifice, my suffering, my crucifixion in life. Try to understand what I say and for the liberation of mankind come with me to sacrifice yourself in the life's pyre in fire and blaze. With your sacrifice you will rise to the great mind from where I come. Sacrifice the way I have done as a wanderer wanderings from the divine domain to the sense-bound life in sufferings and blaze. Understand the meaning of the crucifixion of the divine in the tree of life - the cross, with four seasonal directions upholding the unsurpassable destiny of life and death - and follow me to sacrifice to bring forward the awareness about the path of salvation from the abyss bound in life and matter- bound human fate.

I am the ultimate man who shines upon all human beings as stars and also follow them to the abysmal dark. Hear about my journey how I have crossed the gulf, passed the hidden islands of passions of the heart and reached the forest path, seen myself in the lake of Eros as Bodhisattva who is searching in himself the great mind in the mirror of the illusory world, and watching his life in the blindness of the manifold world, through multiple of life striving to realize the freedom of the will and the union with the great compassion and love. Hear about the path of reason, knowledge of the self- gained through the knowledge of the chaos, and the dance and harmony of the cosmos strewn with the stars. Listen about the Minotaur destroyed, the freedom from destiny, the light of the illumined mind trying to rise to God. Hear about the will, the profound contemplation of the mind and the self-command, the journey towards the self, the man of flesh and blood gradually becoming one with the ultimate self. Listen how the ultimate man, as a stranger to himself, sprung from the great ocean, have carried the ashes of the pyre in his wandering towards the summit of the unmoved mountain, as a tormented man of flesh and blood has striven to unite with the tranquil ocean from which he has come. I have come to tell you about the vision of this ultimate man: The songs of the mountain, the fountains of love, the music of the divine drawing man towards the eternal path, the beauty rising, the light above the great sea before the eyes, the trembling mirror of the sky near the summit, and how I have felt seeing the abyss underneath full of pain, suffering and darkness in the valley through which the wanderers were still trying to pass. Hear from the ultimate man about the illumination before the summit, while the guiding spirit had disappeared, the hail of light, and the voice rising from the sea had called me to repeat the journey once again. I want to tell you about the cataclysms, volcanoes, eruptions and the premonitions of the destructions to come after which the valleys covered with ashes will turn into flowering valleys of great beauty no one has seen before. This is a sacrifice for the new will, new life springing from the sea from which I come. Hear about the sacrifice of the ultimate man in down-going to the abysmal suffering of the life on Earth in love for mankind to guide the wanderers in the valley to the mountain path. Hear me and try to understand what I am saying and follow me to the down-going for the sake of the suffering man.

During this wandering once more I was awaken in the village beside the sea. It was a shore where the suffering man dwelt. In the poverty of knowledge, that they called happiness, they lived in miserable ease without caring for heaven and hell. I had returned in the village in search of the spirit whose company I had lost in the mountain path and who had told me to go to the graveyard in the abysmal valley where he would resurrect to show man the eternal path. It was not any dream or a fiction. There seemed to exist an eternal purpose in this suffering . In contradictions, confusions, willing, doubting, trying to free oneself from the misery of the life and the dismal illusion of the pain and joy of the unenlightened minds, there were wars, sorrows, contempt and despises. In follies man sought pleasure; in willing to perish in passions man hailed the flames and madness by willing to win freedom for oneself by destroying others and doing to others great harms. The life was a suffering where every one was a prey of another. There the teachings of virtues were foolishness. Everybody devoted maximum efforts to win advantage that they hoped will secure them maximum span of life. None wanted to die. They wished life could be eternal. With hatred, envy, falsification, lie, and always looking for enemies everywhere they wanted victory and triumph over everybody. The life revolved without values. Nothingness, emptiness and solitude flew as poisonous flies in the market place where the life was a trade of flesh and blood, a hellish cross-road of travellers who did not give a damn about who lived or died. They practiced revenge, preached inequality of different races and men, soured the souls with self-conceits, worshiped fearlessness, violence and hate, and like solitary seafarers in faithlessness sailed to fetch pleasures against warnings and adverse signs of fate.

In this island there was a forest. In this forest, in front of the multifold mirror I had fallen asleep. In images and flying bits of illusions, that make the world, I had seen myself awake as many human beings in search of paths outside the forest and beyond the river and the lake. Through this inner domain I had risen in the celestial world and in love of knowledge aroused the free spirit of reason. I had seen man struggling with himself in search of truth, in dangerous paths seeking answers that will eliminate the role of destiny and fate. Like philosophers and martyrs, who had sacrificed their lives for the sake of truth, I had seen man questioning, doubting, in a protracted battle with themselves, in belief and non-belief, searching a proof of something that can not be proved. They were trying to overcome themselves by throwing away beliefs and faiths in predestination. By cruel ventures, which bind man in concepts that are falsely conceived, distrusting everything and screening everything that could not be related to the causal links, and the logic sprung thereof, in tortuous ways they were turned against the existence of the Self. For them there were nothing beyond the domain of matter and the laws of science defined in time and space. With suppositions, hypothesis, axioms, introspections, vacillations, and constant refinements of the logical methods of interpretation, inversions, introversions and narrowing the erroneous consequences of the conditioned reflections, they blinded themselves deliberately in their ventures of finding the right conclusions. Everything were judged with suspicion. Precisely where they understood nothing they reduced the understanding as the science of things - to get rid of the divinity and heighten the man as the courageous Godless being.

You may wonder why did I wander lonely through the streets in this world of the irreligious men? When they shouted God is dead, what did I think? When the city slept in the darkness, the souls felt comforted with the polluted river, when man was tied with a rope in a dangerous path with the superman crossing the gulf as an animal shuddering in fear and at the same time feeling the excitement of the adventure, danger and happiness of freedom of will, you may ask what did I say, what knowledge and awareness had it brought, how did I talk about virtue to these dangerous men? How did I myself go across?

Know that as the enlightened man I love all. I sacrifice myself for love of mankind in order to lift them from the darkness and downfall. When they play with dice, ask no one any favor but as free spirit seek no chastity but pain, in downfall, losing and perishing seek freedom's reward and gain, as the ultimate man I do not look at them with contempt or disdain. All human beings are born with the chaos of the will that unless illumined by the knowledge of the self may lead man astray. I had told them about the dancing stars, the rhythms and music of the universe and the chaos that brings everywhere the whirling disturbances trying to shatter everything apart. I had talked about the love and the compassion that flow in and from the sea where the unmoved moves and from which they bring forth the motions of matter and souls burning as stars and the ethereal bodies flying under the lights descending on the world. As you may understand they did not understand, could not always follow what I said. In the market place as faithless men they had listened and shouted again and again, "We do not believe what you say. We know long ago God is dead. Go away. There are many among us who feel hatred for you. We love this place where God is dead. We do not need to hear from any illumined man. For us there exists no ultimate man higher than us. With God he too is dead."

You may wonder why did not I abandon them and go away? Why my heart still felt a torrent of love in the valley of suffering and grief ? Know that as the enlightened man rising from the sea I am a tumbling cascade of love that seeks to plunge through the impassable paths. I always will to come where there is darkness and the shadow. Where sorrow and sufferings clog all paths I come trilling as the sounds carrying the light of love. Great love does not seek revenge or feel pity and shame. Nothing can humiliate the love that does not look with pity to anyone, to whom all are equal and same. It knows only the path of forgiveness. When they tried to drive me away, I trembled in the mirror of the heart as the burning flame living for eternity touching the sunlight and the shadows of the abyss truly seeking suffering in sacrifice for the redemption of man. It is truly difficult to understand this love of the illumined man. Journeymen follow me to sacrifice. You may be able to understand it at the end. This love does not go weary, never goes blind, or never delights itself in punishment of the spirits, who seek freedom and strive to know themselves. Most paths of life are treacherous and difficult to go across as I have already said. In every step there are trials and tastes. Believing or not believing in God are not really so important. They are only different ways. As God can never be understood the belief in the divinity without comprehending reality and attaining the capacity of the mind to penetrate in the conscious way the multi-fold planes in which existence is entangled or, on the other way, trying to comprehend reality by reducing existence to the space-time domain without knowing that reality of the multifold way and infinite domain of the mind are equally dangerous and full of errors. However for man there is no other way of knowing but through erring in life. All knowledge must proceed through errors by eliminating relations that seem false and incompatible with conditions and concepts of life.

Thus knowledge of the nature of life and things are essentially the knowledge of experiences and concepts that the life or things seem to be not. There is no way of knowing the so called things-in-themselves as they are. Likewise there is no one way to free oneself from the multi-dimensional web where every life is entangled and from where there is no one identity of man with which man can ever escape or enter the gate of heaven or hell. All human beings are in a journey together in this multifold world as one being searching to return home from where they have come. In erring one knows what one is not and thus becomes aware of one's own nature through negations and as someone who he might possibly be. There are infinite possibilities of this knowledge and inexhaustible paths of approaching the Self. Most paths are torn with contradictions and sufferings because this is the true way to know and become aware of oneself. Know yourself as the journey man and sacrifice your life for the liberation of man. Be aware of the wholeness and the innumerable paths in which all life are entangled and bound. There is nothing that can be called individual salvation. When true reality of the existence lies in the spirit, who is whole, you should know that individual salvation is only an illusion of the mind. Do not wander alone in the street in search of freedom that brings separation from the whole, creates deepest solitude and may result in self-destruction. Move forward and come home. I know it is not easy to understand. But follow me. You may comprehend this teaching at the end.

You may have heard from the madman shouting on the other end of the market place about the coming of God and the world's doom. But hear from the ultimate man the mystery that is much more complex and profound. God is dead and alive. He is both. He neither comes or goes, nor does He send the sinners to damnation or resurrects the chosen souls who have received His grace. He is the light and shadow, united in both. However, He is neither darkness or light, nor matter, spirit or ghost. This concept is very difficult. I do not know how shall I rightly explain. He does not appear as any particular person but is immanent in all. He sends His illuminations to the darkened minds through the ultimate man, who is neither a person, nor a spirit but a mysterious creation. This ultimate man is similar to and at the same time different from all. He receives energy from the profoundest source of knowledge where there is no concept of moving further or crossing any realm or going beyond.

I know that you will not understand but believe what I have said about my nature before. You may know me better if you follow me and make the journey. You certainly wonder about the journey after I had fallen in sleep in the mirror, that was the river in me. By now, you probably understand that I talk in allegories and cryptic language in order to by-pass the concepts that may distort the things that I wish to explain and which are very strange to be grasped by using the much used concepts. Languages distort the world and reflect the concepts and believes that man have constructed on the basis of the experiences that are simple to communicate by negating the world as they are. Therefore I distort the language in order to bypass the concepts that man are quick to define before I may have them defined. In this deliberation logic has its place when it self-contradicts and illumines through negations of what is said.

You may wonder after leaving the market place, which path did I choose? I cannot tell you exactly the way you may like to conceive. As said He neither is and is not. On one side of the river He is and other side He is not. On the banks of the river He is immanent as exist-ent and nonexistent as Bodhisattva, who is coming and going in the wheel. I went downward and went across the market place towards the path where I joined my companion, whom I had left in the forest. I am not the one as you may like to believe I am, as I have said before. I could move both ways at the same moment - one inside the realm of time and space and the other moving across the world towards the mountain way. If you follow me in this journey you may gradually un-derstand what I am saying. Do not jump to the conclusion that I had left for the mountains leaving the wanderers in the market place. At the end they followed the man, who immerged from me, to the sacrifice in the village and I followed Him towards the illumined way.

You may be curious to know what did I see on the mountain? As I said

I did not go alone. As I woke from the sleep I saw in front of me a glaring light on the mirror, whom I could easily recognize as the divine poet, who was the guiding light in the forest, where I was following Him as a shadow. I had followed Him as the dual united as one moving through the labyrinthine web. He had told me that I was the ultimate man born from the sea destined to move to the mountain way, I must climb higher to the mountain top to merge fully with Him and ascend the stairs of rainbows before I would be able to visualize His full splendour as the light of illumination. On this height all dualities would dissolve and from the summit nothing would return except the energy that can communicate with the man moving in the ultimate way.

As I moved higher my heart trembled in love as the sparkling lights in the golden glitters of the rays descending on the valley underneath."Thou shall choose my path. Thou shall be the holiest of man", I heard a "voice". The "voice" reverberated in the mountain landscape." Thou spirit is myself. Thou journey is my journey. Thou fire and ashes are the fire and ashes from the flames that I ignite. Thou body is illusion. Thou soul is created for liberation. See thyself as myself and behold in this mountain landscape how lights are vibrating in love and trepidation. Purify yourself in this godly illumination", I heard the voice vibrating from mountains to mountains and echoing time and again. "You ultimate man! Climb. Ascend to the height where you will be one with the splendid light", there were immense cascades of light that dissolved the feelings in a light, that I can not describe.

It appeared as the heavenly "voice"- outside my body, somewhere unknown from where it was communicating with my soul. I felt exalted. It seemed to me that I was hearing the "voice" of God. Truly I felt as if I did not exist in time and space and I was not what I thought I was. Indeed, I was unable to grasp who I truly was! There seemed to exist someone else who was bearing me as body and flesh against the gravity and weight. I found contradictions within myself - always lost as someone else, and always knowing that I was the spirit of the ultimate man in journey within myself towards the heavenly home from where I have come. I know, it is not easy to understand. But listen carefully. The language is so accustomed to falling back to the experiences, that are superfluous, that it is difficult to explain with language the experiences that sink deeper than the experiences in time and space. Although this experience can not be described in language the language is the only way to communicate and fathom the relations between the worlds known or unknown. It is a veritable contradiction. Therefore it is not possible to know who was me and who was the light, who spoke and who heard, who gazed and who walked, who was in me and who was outside in Him, who was moving and who remained eternally unmoved.

I saw a hermit on the way. As I said I do not know who he really was! He was wandering in the mountain in complete harmony with himself. He was out in the mountain landscape in quest of something. Hearing the mountains' voice he was moving along a path that was dangerously steep. Any moment's lack of concentration of the mind would have pulled Him down from the illumined precipice to a great dark abyss. Along this path living and dying seemed to hang in a thread. In reverence to the goal, the great sanctuary of light, towards which He was moving to, He had no fear. In His face there was no sense of anxiety that could disturb His concentration and deviate Him from his path even by the measure of a hair. With a god-like glance and lustre in His eyes and insatiable thirst for light He was climbing the precipice. Upward He was ascending. Like an exalted image of an illumined mind, glowing in the light, He was advancing. Like an elevated spirit He was surging as a river that was moving to meet the sea - far away, alone towards the summit from where He did not wish to return.

In this landscape from high rocks brooks were tumbling, the streams were plunging in impassable caves, and there were lakes that had risen from the river and taken rest in the tranquil mountain glade. There was a blissful freedom under the soft luminosity of the distant skyey arch bending down to earth feeling the giddiness of the soaring height of the illumined path. It seemed if one could rise to the top, all sufferings would cease, all desires of begetting or becoming will come to a halt, breaking the clear sky the great love will pour, in the trembling mirror of the heart the eternity will vibrate in the strings of feelings playing the unearthly notes. You may still want to know who was this hermit, who was the shadow, who was the guiding light, who was being illumined and who was He who was illumining the mind? Although I did not know through any language all the relations between them all, like you something unquenched and unquenchable in me also wished to know, "Who am I? Who is He? Who is the guide and who is that shadow being guided towards the light? " The glaciers twinkled in trillions of stars, scattering spangles in the heart the light leaped into the empty void, like dancing beats of flying stars a great love awakened the will, and the fountain of light again rose with the voice, "Trust me. Thou art me, one with the eternal Self. Through the process of thoughts, that flows in the river of the human will, and are conditioned by perceptions, it is not possible to know the relation between the guide and the guided, who are imperceptible and inconceivable by human thoughts. Relations between us can only be known through revelations as the ultimate mystery that will remain eternally unknown." "Who is the hermit then?", I repeated. As the music of a divine flute drew me upward to an eternal path, over the stones and pebbles where I stepped the fountain spoke, "O ultimate man! your vision and sight are still bound in the fallen state where human senses operate. You are looking through something strange and unknown, profoundly mysterious and eternal with a consciousness that are polluted by worldly visual images. The hermit, who is climbing towards the sanctuary carrying in the mind a strange mystic marvel, is truly a fugitive of your worldly state, who is contemplating on the eternal marvel. Strange to Himself, sprung from Himself, He is carrying the ashes of the world to the mountains. In the loneliest wandering, sleeping on stones, gazing at the stars, hearing the echoes of the tumbling streams from the mountains to the mountains, and listening to the whisper of the solitudes from glaciers to glaciers, gazing afar at the divine world, He is striving to know who is moving His soul as the great fountain of love. He is the man in the forest path moving on Bodhisattva's way. He is Buddha- to-be, who would again return. He is once the blind man who had gone across the river in search of the enlightened way. He is still striving to overcome the bondage of the ignorance, trying to see the true self beyond the mirror and reflections on the river becoming and begetting thoughts, that create the will and gazes at itself in the spangles of rays. He is incarnate and immanent projection of the Self among the living creatures, who has realized the bondage of the procreating life and is looking at the hundred fold mirror, and concentrating on one image, practicing self control to overcome the illusions of the mind trying to bring him astray. " You may wonder was He the ultimate man glittering, trembling and ascending towards the summit of love? Was He the unchanging man changing through all lives, with many masks, who was striving to overcome the bondage of illusions and ignorance resulting from images in the mirror entangling the will in the web?

Was He the journeyman still seeking the company of the divine poet? Was He living or nonliving, was He true or false, was He an image of the ultimate man still loaded with weight walking towards the weightless world hearing the muffled sounds breaking through the shadow under his steps? Was He me, was He you-to-be, was He him who is never known? Like you I also had wished to know. Like you I was also entangled in the web of thoughts, that are conditioned by the human percepts and determined by concepts built on phenomenal transitory world, that begets no truth but is founded on the illusion itself. Maya had still enwrapped my soul. Therefore being the ultimate man Himself I also could not know.

In this state I learnt about the secrets of the world, heard the words flowing from the mystic light. I had to interpret these words to make them meaningful to understanding by the mind constrained to exist in the material body moving in space and time. One calls it the consciousness of the being that reflects upon itself - negating and positing itself through a multifold patterns of thoughts entangled in the will and matter as a web. Here everything were empty, everything existed in the eternal present without any future and past. What was becoming was, and is, truly what becomes. On the lonely mountain bearing the ashes in eternity I was the hermit and I was also no one. Wearing the body of a man I was in a journey through the will as the creator and created bound as One. It was a fable of eternal existence. Here I had awaken from the sea as twofold-existence - myself and He - that reflected each other, who were separated in time and space but united in other dimensions.

You may wonder am I the one who was supposed to return? Yes, I know, you won't understand, but jump to no conclusion. Even the ultimate man can not explain everything that can be grasped easily by sense-bound human beings - as I have said again and again. Something you can not know unless freed from the bondage of Maya that the whole universe pervade. Follow me to sacrifice. You may be released from this ignorance at the end.

As I was climbing and coming home to the Self, wandering lonely towards the summit from where the rays were descending to illumine the abyss beneath, I was returning to me, in the most difficult part of the highest mountain with steepest cliff under which there were the longest crevices abysmally deep, indeed I had felt the presence of the sea infinitely deep. It was spread before my eyes as nothing above or nothing below. Upward, downward, everywhere rocks and pebbles were asleep as the tranquil souls; in high and low there were down-pouring and rising of the boundless love; backward and forward there were eternal reflections of shadows moving upwards or going downwards; in a maze of happenings where things already happened or going to happen the ultimate man was returning to and emerging from the same being sailing on the waves surging and sinking in the eternal man's vision of reality and dream. In this sky insurmountably steep, in this sea unfathomable deep, I saw the summit and the abyss united in the mirror where on one side there was the sky and on the other side the sea divided by the mountain ranges guarding the valleys underneath. On one side there was the hermit bringing the ashes to the mountains from the sacrifice in the pyre burning by the shore of the sea and on the other side the suffering humanity was gazing at the mountain summit waiting for the ultimate man to return from the world beyond the sky sunk in the invisible sea, beyond the rainbow's gates.

Here I had wandered long, heard the unheard, spoken with the unspeakable, in the silence listened to the mountains' songs. Here in stillness the words had come and in stillness had roamed in the wilderness floating with the mountain songs. Here more I had climbed more I had felt one with the light and the pebbles and stones. More I had risen more I had seen myself as bright as the glaciers in deepest contemplation in the lighted soul and as unmoved as the mountain rising to heaven's home. You may wonder why did I return? What made me leave the path to the highest summit to go downwards again towards the suffering abyss from where the hermit was carrying the ashes of the pyre to the lighted sanctuary towards which He had gone? You certainly understand the allegory where the sea rises to the mountains, forms the glaciers and from the mountains it pours downwards again bringing the rocks and pebble of the summit to the sea from where it had once risen from the eternal nothing - the void, that is my home. To know more about this down going you need to follow me. After that you will grasp the reason what makes the ultimate man to return.

"O ultimate man! You must go down as a shadow of man from the light that I am. Go to the grave to redeem the dead and awaken the corpse", like a commandment the voice rose again: "Humanity is not free. In down going to the suffering world help the grieving and weeping man in the abyss seeking to be free. In love for man follow this commandment from the light to whom you belong. A darkness will lead you away. The more you will go downwards the more you will loose the memory of this mountain place where the illumined souls dwell. But we will meet beside the grave where I shall resurrect and you will follow me again. As light to the shadow, go down to follow the destiny of life and fate for the sake of humanity once again." After this call for going down I saw my guide disappearing in the mist beyond the boundary of the vision. Then the thunder spoke, lightning cascaded, mountain top opened and ashes and smokes were hurled to fill the landscape. In the vapors of the eruptions as I felt chocked, a winged bird obstructed my way. In his talons he held the ashes of the dead. The mountains started to shake as if the Earth was going to see its end. Fireworks broke through the vents, cataclysmic storms swept, in horrendous outpouring the boulders rolled downwards towards the valley. "Go to the world in death and decay. Trust me. I shall return again", the voice of the fountain disappeared. Only His secret eyes burnt as the flames in the darkness. The wings of fate stretched its pinions beyond the limits of the vision. Then I was attacked by the beast with lightning. "Dear guide! Do not leave me alone! Retreat!" But before then a tumultuous cataclysm had engulfed the Earth and I heard Him no more. You may wonder was it real or a premonition? As you may understand it was a premonition of the doom that will come. Before this destruction comes I have come to tell you about the ultimate man and His teaching of the enlightened way. Listen carefully. Try to understand the allegories of this speech and realize that the great noon time of the awakening of the Earth has come. Follow me to sacrifice for the love of man.

Wanderers awaken! Sleep no more in the slumber of the heart. Dream no more in the illusory world. In eternity you are born, in eternity you will go. In love of eternity as recurrence of the ultimate man I come and go. Purified with the new will I am going downwards in love for man to the village to bring to the world the news of the down-going in love for man. This down going is a sacrifice of life for the sake of the renewal of the earth. Sacrifice your life in the altar of God, and follow me to the suffering and torment of life. Repeat the journey again without being moved by it. I need the company of the new man who will be able to bear the suffering as the mountains gazing at the radiance of the stars. Through these sacrifices in lives you will transcend higher towards the summit, and ultimately unite with the one, who is beyond coming and going, and all motions in time. O journeymen! Come! Let us go!

THE MOUNTAIN PATH
Realm of the spiritual consciousness

After leaving the cyber-village Tathagata meditates about the wandering of the hermit along the mountain path. In the mountain landscape he sees cosmos and earth have merged. As he approaches the summit the vision of the One, of whom all are parts, rises in his mind. He sees himself as one with the meditating cosmic being, who radiates compassion and love – the energy that sustains the existence of all. The wanderer, who is reborn as a man, and who has embarked on a new journey of life in the Hall of Illusion, merges with the universal being, who has lived, who is living and will live in the future. When he reaches the summit of the mountain he hears God who asks him to return again among the people wandering in different realms of the mind in the Hall of Illusion, that constitutes the nature of the world, in order to spread the teachings of an enlightened way.

Coming to the mountain path, the journeyman sees himself as the meditating Tathagata, who is sitting by a river under the tree of life. In the images reflected on the river he sees the whole transitory world moving with time. With it he gradually becomes a part of the realm of meditation, where Tathagata exists, and discovers himself as a part of the Divine world where water, fire, air and rock sing hymns of the cosmic being.

Hymn of Fire

The wind touches it,

The sounds high in the air crackles with it,

Saying "Thus there is "when it shouts with thunder in its mouth,

Like wriggling flying creatures flames anointed,

From a cavernous dark,

From a profound silence,

Thus it speaks of its lightened way.

Mingling with the flames,

Where the sun and the moon fade,

When it takes its breath,

What is inside flashes as outside,

What is outside strips off and goes off wandering,

Knows not where,

Amidst disorder, disaster, calamities,

It bounds, rebounds,

In a state of turbid chaos,

It flies, returns;

In perplexity observes its own nature bound between order and
chaos.

Like blazing flames rushing out of a lotus,

From points flashing inwardly where the poetry melts with the flesh,

As a fireball protecting a pearl,

Under a veil clasping with thunders,

With lustre rising high,

In an awakening splendour,

When from a tranquil state from sand and dust the forms transmigrate to the wandering river,

The flames around the wheel twist and writhe,

Beyond the layers after layers where no smoke or cloud penetrate,

It ascends,

Invisibly radiates,

With time, fleeing like spears, it pierces the flesh with its blaze.

As strange water that mingles with fire,

Through laceration, suffering and pain that brings revelation, heals and resurrects,

It leaves and enters the mortals,

Ascends as a bird of fire to the air,

And descends in the tributaries from the clouds moving downwards with scurrying down winds,

It is no being;

It has no name.

It rises from the one,

And subsides in the one without any form.

With its multitudinous forking heads,

Piercing through the clouds and membranes,

Moving between the cessation and the movement of life and death,

Forging the hillocks and hammocks with rocky beds,

In bewildering ways,

Moulding the masses that are igneous or metamorphosed,

Pouring along the volcanic runnels,

Evaporating vapour seaming from the porous magmatic specimen,

Wandering through the channels,

As unstable, flashing, spreading, supported by none by its inner force,

As a pure spirit turning into physical forms,

Drifting peacelessly, returning through the river,
It realizes itself as parts of the whole.
Through ignition and compression,
Through polyhedral masses,
Through columnar crystals rising as clusters in mineral forms,
By transmitting heat,
And cooling,
Dark surfaces turning reflective and things that absorbed transmit-
ting the lustre of polyhedral forms,
In boiling and rising,
In cooling and crystallizing, falling into larger forms,
Its energy transforms the invisible domain to the visible plane,
Hews and embodies the spirit of the nature in the world tossed by the
wind, storm and rain.
Its journey has no end:
In destruction and procreation,
In pain of separation from the integral whole,
In upheaval,
In growth, convulsion, metamorphosis,
From sedimentations to formations,
From rocks of huge geological dimensions,
Moving from the volcanic ashes to stratification,
And from maturity to decay,
Immobilized, remobilized, by terrestrial frictions and affinity to fall,
It moves, wanders, ejects, spews, glides, rolls,
In mirrors reciprocating in forms,
It interchanges from fire to rocks,
From rocks it emerges as fire,
In the interior undergoing transformation,
From virtual it returns as real in the burning pyre.

Dragging its belly on the bank,
Spreading its wings in the domain where the sun and the moon flank,
From where there is no going,
To where all goings and becoming are ways of returning,
Where something is always nothing,
And nothing always around something convolves,
Where by burning... burning... Burning,
The Boreal wind or the wind blowing over the Gulf,
Share their power with the fire that every other power exhausts,
It rises, illumines, fulfils destiny,
From the earth touching the heaven with flames feels eternity and
rejoice.
From jades, marble and minerals to ashes,
Like a magnanimous fire it exists,
In placidity, quietness, stillness and emptiness,
While moving things rest,
In rivers, lakes, fountains and forests,
Where in the currents of yin and yang the motion contradicts
stillness, and stillness contradicts changing state,
While spring summer precedes,
Winter comes after autumn,
In sequences of negations it leaps, burns, transforms, and evolves;
As a harmony of music preceding coming and going,
In appearance of the sequences of time it deceives.
From stillness it controls, unfolds, impels,
Turns the cycles and drives inexorably the clouds and rains;
With its flames winds rise from the north,
Drifting from the south it turns, spins and brings lightening cascades;
In an exalted journey,
Meeting the mountains and vales,

Where seasons arrive in succession,

In thundering crashes,

Flashing and tumbling through the vales,

Shaking soil in torments,

It penetrates, startles, rises, and collapses with unpredictable beginning, or end.

Thus illumining every valley,

And lashing with thundering gales,

It fills ravines and rocks,

Permeates every opening,

Modulates every shape,

Encompassing infinity in finitude,

Defines courses that shift and drift through the inconstant soil,

As if a dragon's coil.

Coiled up, carrying scaly patterns of the whole,

From clouds and vapours,

Streams nourishing the soil,

In silent depth setting forth movements that appear similar to the reptile that slithers and coils,

Where mountains and rivers conflict in search of a stable state,

With down pouring erosion brings down going of mountains with rocks and slates,

It disrupts the process of the formation of the mountains,

And brings down from the height the dust and mud to the river beds.

It is destiny,

It is nature,

Bound in separateness in conflict with and resolution in the whole.

Where insects chirp,

Virus and bacteria fertilize,

Villainous forces alter the patterns of growths in the soil,

The nature transmutes,

Evolution alters the conditions of competition,

It blazes and burns as ceremonial fire;

In the world of insects, animals and tribes bound to labor and toil,

As an emptiness and no-being bound to the world of beings and forms,

From high to below,

Between the heaven and the earth,

In reverberation of the clouds,

In wilderness blowing, breathing, inhaling and expelling the flames,

Striding over the sky,

Riding on itself in rivers and lakes,

Resting in a perilous journey,

And then wandering away as peeling cascades of light moving in unpredictable way,

Between tranquillity and turmoil,

Between water and fire,

It is the beast of the river and the bird of the sky,

Flying and falling between the abysmal darkness and the lightened way.

Tathagata's meditation

In the forest where spring blossoms and leaves fade in the fall,
Life and death return to all,
From dewdrops dripping on the grass at dawn,
To the emptiness reaching out beyond the silhouette of the mountains
slipping In the west,
In the sunrise and the sunset,
In the emergence and submergence of the night and day,
All things echo the ethereal shivers.
Here Tathagata- neither existent, nor non-existent,
From a vacuous sea appears in the forest in a boat,
In going beyond he comes,
In coming he goes;
Between the heaven and the earth,
Between the sun and the moon,
He moves from the village to the mountain summit towards the
emptiness where all things have their source,
And returns to the world from emptiness riding the dragon force.

He has an outward appearance that moves in a paradoxical path,
Neither searching nor meditating when he gazes quite at the earth,
Without words the highest state of the Bodhisattva's mind he grasps.
He clings to nothing, craves for nothing,
Nothing he discriminates;
With contemplation, introspection and intuition, his awakening mind
fulminates;

He regards the world as unreal seen as a vision,
Where all things change as illusion;
Living life after life he guides man in the path of compassion,
And helps man to vanquish suffering that rises out of delusion,
And lifts man to the domain of inner illumination.
In the object he sees himself as subject,
As a subject he sees himself mirrored in the object;
In both he is neither subject or object;
He becomes aware of existence through negation;
Between the two sides of the mirror he is one;
In disturbances he remains undisturbed,
In quietude he meditates in the ceaseless commotion;
In the relativity of going and coming,
He rests tranquil in the wheel of motion.
Without walking he steps,
Without stepping he walks in the insubstantial world,
In the impermanence and emptiness he wanders as substantiality and permanence;
All worlds exist as parts of His mind;
Awaken in the realization that all realms where causation have cause,
Consciousness form,
The being and the non-being of things flowing in the conscious stream shape the world where the reality form, change and deform,
There is no reality but the habit of the conditioned perceptions that are neither right or wrong.

Hymn of Water

In the journey of the ocean in watery wings like whirlwind the clouds
rise and travel towards the streams,
The galloping gusts of the winds,
The dusts and sand blowing from the wings,
Breathing over the plants and trees,
Covering the azure sky, from where penetrate the distant beams,
As if seeking to merge with the farthest limits they appear as clouds
of dreams.
Before landing and parching in a place they do not choose, or seek,
the fluttering wings fly over the distant lands,
What more, what more distance to fly,
They cry,
And fly over the deserts of sand.
Where evening dies,
And morning rises,
Rolling between night and day,
In the spring's and autumn's rays,
They go up and down to emulate the colors of the sunray.
Inside the limit beyond which the sky rises towards the limitless,
Spreading the wings suspended in the air,
In seas and breaths of birds and beasts,
Touching the blue sky,
In streaks of light flying with whirlwinds,
Flitting with cyclones and storms,
Without knowing where they are going,

They rise with the twisting winds,

And fall flying in the drifting streams.

Once they go off, they never come to the same place again,

They carry a soul of one that is extravagant and remote,

Far away, where the spirit of the earth dwells,

Congealed in the snow, in the crystal grains,

Inhaling the air and drinking the rays dripping in the dew,

This soul rides the dragon wandering in the four seas, the mountains and the lakes,

And displays the patterns that reflect the myriads of shapes of the living things scattered in time and space.

Where the waves surge to battle with chaos,

In fierce flames minerals melt and bring forth the jewels in the womb of the rocks scattering the lusters of the light like that of the goddess Eos,

As spirit of life, amidst dust and stones, it mingles and integrates,

As power of life, that no power of chaos can ever exhaust,

It wanders to the roots where from the seeds the plants grow,

As sap in twisted branches and trunks it flows,

To increase the verdancy of the nature it goes,

And as the liquid in the fruits it returns with its life giving force.

Emptying its breath in the wind when it howls,

Over cliffs and crevasses of towering mountains,

Around hollow cavities in the giant trees around which, like serpents, myriads of life wind around,

When it makes sounds of rushing water cascading from the hanging valleys to the world down below;

In whizzing, shrieking, crying, calling and chattering sounds of the birds and beasts a powerful gale of life blows in the time's arrow.

Immersed in shallow water and marshy land,

Where autumn and winter dissolve in inactivity,
In openness of abandoned landscape insects and fungus life's vitality incapacitate,
When nature moans in confusion and conflicts,
In quivering and tingling reverberations of the drops scuttling along the paths of insects when day and night decay,
In a music of emptiness,
When mind tries to affirm beauty on a grass blade,
Standing in a self denial,
Where there is nothing but nothing to affirm,
When all things are possessed by a power that no one can possess,
In a spiritual light, that unifies all things and forms without knowing,
There are mornings, evenings and nights.
It is its way, where all things go and from where all return.
With it the rivers turn to ice,
The violent thunders join, split, and rejoin....
Whirlwinds lash, frighten,
Riding the clouds the moon wanders around...
Life and death, beauty and beast, fly high beyond the humaneness in paths that are neither right or wrong.
The nature has made it- not any man,
In this ordered chaos,
In the unity of the Will,
In winds and with waves,
That invalidate and verify its power,
It stirs up, churns, brings an end to turmoil,
Glides to a perilous journey and involuntarily ends in wilderness,
Grasping for breath penetrates the vents,
As a response to destiny in dying it nourishes and in nourishing it destroys,

In its ultimate course as fate.
In hydrostatic pressure it remains calm,
In hydrokinetic turgidity it brings tides,
After causing devastations it subsides,
From the Arctics to the Antarctic in a dynamic stability it is partly
frozen and remains partly dissolved,
With its downward moving promenaries it erodes, deposits, increases
the shore that was once sandless and bare,
In eruptions, torrents, inundations, cloudbursts, and geysers,
In runnels, gullies and dams,
As vapor, cloud, sleet, snow and rain,
It wanders inevitably and thereby nourishes the destiny irrevocable
by man.
Man can see his images in it,
In stillness unfolding in stillness that seeks the stillness beyond,
In green summer field, like in a silent pool,
Man can visualize his own nature bound to the ultimate whole.
In it in striving it preserves,
In wandering it draws out its strength in reserve,
In austere autumn or joyous spring where the equinoxes cross,
Happily or in forgetfulness when it reflects the colors of the sky
bound across,
The life and death are destined,
In the towering statutes or the clouds that collapse,
Suffused with alluring charm,
In calmness remaining aloof,
Where nothingness nothing compels,
Merrily, happily, demurring, and undisturbed,
When images in feelings dissolve,
In a tranquillity in turmoil,

Watching itself from a domain beyond,

It eliminates present, past and future -ages become eons.

By the edge of a river calm,

It flies as a nebulous bird,

Going beyond the limits and wandering over the land and sea,

Like a creature trying to escape the hunter's dart,

Soaring in the wide empty nothingness extending to the limitless

space beyond,

In a labyrinthine abyss,

Balancing against the force of weight by flapping its wings,

In trying to go home it goes around the river and swings.

Where the waves are intertwined with the wind,

Ebbing webs, profusion of patterns image a disorderly order of chaos,

Fleeing from its own nature it seeks its forms by chance,

In frivolous exercise of the will, in a blind path,

It falls, decays, disperses, and dissipates,

And behind chaos leaves an orderly state;

In contentions and conflicts,

As if evil striving against good,

It returns, hurls, multiplies, breaks through foams and mutters to

glorify its strength in the face of the force that sweeps away all that

fail to hold.

Inwardly it draws away the dignified,

Outwardly it throws the myriads of reproachable forms that form and

transform.

Its true identity no one knows,

It is emptiness flying with no wings,

In the human feelings it impinges as true and false,

Stooping from mountains, stirring through the rivers,

As Feng Shui conducting through rocks and masses,

It is Yang and Yin - the destiny that moves as force that produces
changes for ever.
Like a tree, with branches shooting out from the trunk,
From where smaller branches spring,
It pulls itself up from the gravity pulling it downwards,
Twisting and turning and rising towards the upper air,
It scatters across bundles of beams plunging through the restless layers,
Like leaves shuffling the shadows and glistening in the air,
It penetrates downwards,
Articulates the transformation of shadow and light,
Causing vibrations brings springtime,
As mist from rivers and lakes evaporates,
As clouds assembled in the dreamy height awakes,
Carrying burden and weight wonders,
In drops of rain wanders,
In the wings of the nebulous bird in whirling wind flies away yonder.
Beyond the world bound in time and place,
Where the world within and the things outside,
Take in the unity the vital breath,
Where the creator and the created things,
In ceaseless cycles beginning and ending,
Are bound in the dust and mud of the mundane world,
Passing away it is reborn,
And being reborn passes away to the realm of rivers and lakes;
Where in the transformations of the things the world transforms,
In stones, rocks, in ceaseless metamorphosis,
Like awaken dreaming,
In the world ceaselessly revolve,
In streaks of clouds,
In feathers of bird,

In an awakening mind,
In curves and forms,
It reworks, remoulds, restores the wholeness,
In host of forms wandering between heaven and earth,
It emerges in the thoughtless form emanating from the realm of God.
As a nebulous bird going beyond the limits,
In search of a dwelling undisturbed by rain or storm,
Beyond vexing and toiling,
Beyond the reach of the hunter's dart,
Where in seeing there is no seeing,
Where in being there is no being,
Where in existence non-existence is involved,
Where in the webs of patterns of dazzling colours and lights,
The eye sights cross no distance but the distance that lies only the minutest time and space across,
In branching, lightening and cascading,
In thundering sounds,
It strives and elevates,
In striving to realize itself it engages in a battle with destiny and fate.
It flies above, under and through the settlements where people and tribes sailing on boats or walking over bridges move across,
Equally knowing or without knowledge strays, wanders, and gets lost.
Where in villages sounds of chickens and dogs,
Throwing of fishermen's nets,
Or, the noise of ploughs splitting open land to cultivate,
Senses' boundaries erect,
Barking and cackling determine peripheries of households and hamlets,
The hurling nets measure the power of the casts that man possess,
The furrows toil and labour to generate and equilibrate,

It brings the outpouring of the river,

Creates the emptiness of the valley,

Raises the levels in the lakes and the chasms,

Quarries hills, and fills rocks and soils with moisture from river.

Tathagata's meditation

As all characters of all generations,
Starting from the journey of the first,
All over again he journeys wearing innumerable different masks;
These characters have no name,
They participate in the eternal play as travelling, wandering,
Going to and coming from mountain hermitage,
Or the village homes;
As laymen or monks,
Searching immortality across the world,
They burn in the fire,
In search of the limitless light,
Leaving behind the untrue body fly with the angels in the celestial
night.

The causes of suffering is the very dialectics of the body and spirit
that no one can escape,
Here everything is balanced in the opposing scale,
In accepting evil and pain one may cultivate good,
In renouncing happiness one may realize the true source of happiness
and attain ultimate Buddhahood.
It is a state universal and transcendent,
Unlimited in time and space,
And everywhere perfect and the same.
It is the great compassion - the highest summit that all must climb

alone;

It is Bodhisattva's way that passes through the sky through Earth's dust and stones.

Wander along the river and dwell in the emptiness in the mind supreme,

Ascend to the darkness,

Stand under the pole,

Where beginning has no end attain understanding of yourself as a part of the starry souls;

Hymn of Rocks

Like the jagged mountains,
Straying away from harmonious forms,
Where movements of crust have stabilized,
But frost, ripples, wind, snow and ice are constantly wandering in the innumerable cracks and faults,
Taking advantage over others,
Quarrying the rocks,
Making the planes slide and shift following the basic mechanical laws,
Where the causal links are breaking and branching off,
Like a celestial potter's wheel,
Realizing the numinous patterns it branches off to create an ordered design that appears as the pattern of an eternal chaos.
Splitting something up into something else,
Creating something by destroying something else,
Stabilizing something by making others unstable,
Locating something by dislocating things from time and place,
Going forth in the spatial dimension,
While closing the boundaries of the openings that enters into the depth,
It carries a chaos of mutable patterns,
As the kernel of reality,
Joining order and disorder through life and death,
In coming and going forth in its wandering,
It carries with itself its destiny and fate.
In it the reality is only a subjective pattern,

A paragon that refers to itself,

As empty nothingness,

In it the movements and actions are interjections of extirpation and eliminations, and fusion and integration of complexities and perplexities,

Of the mind's real and absurd planes,

Between something and nothingness,

It is a paragon in a mirror blazing on one side while remaining tranquil on the opposite end.

Between the unreal and the real,

Being still...still moving,

Between knowing and unknowing,

Where with rocks and stones,

The mountains clumsily climb,

In yearnings to satisfy the conditions that the destiny will testify,

It wanders and climbs high,

In murmur of sounds,

Through misty gates and wilderness,

In arrival at the destination it arrives at the other side where there is only emptiness profound;

Seeking nothing, abandoning nothing, losing or gaining nothing it returns to the valley of mirth in the streaming life teeming with sounds.

In geological stratifications,

Where myriads of entomological organic substances are concealed beneath stones,

In cavities, hives and mounds,

Where microbes and germs,

Bacteria, bacilli, protozoa, Radiolaria,

Constellate, divide, grow and progress from life to life,

In continuation of the species,
In mutations of the genetic condition distinct from the mechanical
laws,
Still integrated with the whole,
With cataclysms, and accidents of life,
It mutates, transmigrates, populates,
Through eruptions, convulsion and metamorphosis,
It ineluctably constructs from the microcosm the macrocosm,
And as natural acts of its wandering it wanders through cracks,
creeks and rivulets.
In deserts and valleys,
Where rocks and sand encounter battle with the power that
accumulates and amasses,
In dunes and heaps,
Where withered and wizened edifices rest,
The flamboyant countenances of once glorious structures display
their perilous ends,
Peaks that once exhilarated the eyes,
Suspend in the air as terraced disorder heaped on disorders,
Where through haphazard changes of orientations,
The stones and the rocks their stabilities gain,
It wanders through the mass of confusion strewn in space,
Up and down,
Bound between infinities,
It creates and destroys mountainous chains.
This is its way,
In the physical forms lost and withdrawn,
Where falsity or truth,
Neither produces any error nor provides sufficient reason to prove
right or wrong,

On hills and mountains,
Through transformations and evolutions,
Ending and beginning in different orientations,
Correcting itself from the deviant mutations,
Ascribing to itself fluctuations, differentiations, and erroneous petrifactions,
It wanders through errors and rectifications;
Moving as nothing in various rocks in disintegration or formation,
That doing nothing does share the fundament of great mountains in transformations,
There is nothing that it moves or affects not.
Where yin and yang, like the moon and the sun,
Shining upon each other,
In the union of male and female,
Replenishing the four seasons,
From the subtler world, where things the links of causation evade,
Separate from the unreal the reality of the world in time and space,
Delimit the forms in boundaries,
In reversal of time previous causation erase,
In qualities inherent in things irreversibly stability and order with chaos replace,
Alternating between separation and union,
Security and danger,
Misfortunes and fortunes,
Predictable causation and unpredictable accidents and chance,
Exhausting many possibilities in particular forms terminate,
It wanders from the a-causal world to causation,
Though free, becomes bound in things;
Though beyond fallibility,
Through contingent causation ends up in errors,

Though beyond the realm of the sense bound beings,

Dwells amidst the factual domain of things,

And thus in the finite world its infinite boundaries circumvents.

When born it can not be known,

When unborn it remains hidden,

In observations it becomes indeterminable,

In superposition with the patterns when it emerges from the vacuous space,

It expands beyond the realm of things,

And as unreal, existing as the appearance of the world, in reality of things culminates.

Between fire and water,

Between pleasure and trouble that no one can escape,

Where from dawn to dawn,

Between gigantic mountains dragging veils of clouds,

Waves of sea rise,

As mountain mists, that catch the essence of the things in the domain of perceptivity,

Spreading finest feelings cups the radiant light over the valleys,

In rising it takes off,

Over green... green slopes,

Skirting, vibrating along the border of the virtual and the real,

It wanders off,

Goes, comes, abruptly changing directions suddenly escapes,

In relations to subject and object,

Matter and mind,

It remains always elusive and transient.

This is its way,

In quietness it speaks through metaphors,

In affirmation it negates,

Through negations it affirms,
In self-denial it grasps itself,
Through oppositions it responds,
In disagreement it seeks the significance of what it disagrees,
By saying something it distances itself from what is said,
In entangling itself in webs of thoughts it seeks to be free,
This is its way to be,
In this way of constant escape,
Between the real and the unreal,
It wanders to comprehend itself,
Taking refuge in the human consciousness,
Through numinous thoughts it wanders as a spirit that is free.
As shadow it walks,
Between flitting moments it stops,
To nowhere it departs,
From nowhere it reappears,
It wanders self compelled;
From the extreme boundary of time and space,
Passing from lands to lands,
Among people, events as a stranger who walks, stops and stands,
Somewhere in a domain between perceptibility and the imperceptibility,
It enters, exits, takes physical form and then disappears as formless in a domain beyond.
In recluseness amidst crags and caves,
Isolated from tumults, confusion and disorder of the wind and rain,
In the mountainous way,
Where the heaven encroaches upon the earth,
Where the goal is not fame,
The purpose is not to gain,

In a boundless illumination rising above the rocks crooked, chiselled, or straight,
Where the pinnacle of the heaven faces the Earth in all directions,
In a tranquil repose,
Before in aversions and dislikes everything is dismissed,
It reflects upon happiness, joyous intents, pleasures, desires, predilections and needs,
And conducts the spirit in a journey between the transcendental world and the sense-bound suffering, joy and grief.
Endangering its true nature,
Pushing aside its strangeness,
As a shadow in movement, transformation or stillness,
Awakened, enlightened,
Drifting in fire, water, rocks, dust and air,
Flowing through formlessness and gushing out of emptiness,
Dividing the great unity in patterns of forms,
It stoops, swoops, scurries along,
Flutters, moves,
And as beauty and beast - the dragon-bird - flying between earth and heaven sings the eternal songs.

Tathagata's meditation

He is no being, no one, with no name,
But still He is One without form,
Unveiled in multitude of forms.
Where the physical forms vanish He rises as the spirit of light,
As harmony of the world rising as the celestial song,
Where He merges with darkness to restore the attributes and
characters of the world that constantly change and reform,
He remains hidden as emptiness, placidity, quietness, stillness retired
and withdrawn from the fire, air and storms,
He controls, unfolds, impels all things on their course,
Still dwells in tranquillity that generates no force.

Know this enlightened state,
And do not seek to escape when you face life's trials and tests.
Go the way Bodhisattva has gone;
Do not withdraw in pain;
Do not hide in disdain;
Go forth in the roads where dangers may daunt,
The fears may haunt,
Follow the destiny of man,
Where the dragon breathes,
The serpent writhes,
One moment rising, next moment descending the will wanders freely,
Knowing that inner being is preventing or encouraging one to halt or
go on,

Follow the one, who is going,

Return with the one who is coming,

Although wishing neither to go or come;

Above all cravings and desiring follow the movements of the

enlightened mind's inner supernal sun.

Do not succumb to sorrow,

Enter deep caves without fear of death,

Walk over the fields filled with graves without losing the tranquillity

of the inner state;

In wretched circumstances remember you are the journey man

destined to move on the mountain way;

If you unify your inner visions where you see Bodhisattvas beckon

from many paths wearing many faces;

In multi-dimensional real- dream- mythical world where He wanders

in the human consciousness,

Harmonize your consciousness in the divine will,

Attain the spiritual intelligence that is immutable throughout all

existence;

Amidst evolutions of things and life,

Attain the enlightened state beyond living and dying.

Everything is spirit's abode;

Everything dying is being reborn;

Seeing withered carcasses, pyres and ashes,

Do not err and believe that beauty resides where things have forms,

And wither away when the body is cast off;

The illumined mind can differentiate the forms from the conditions

and cause,

In thoughts can penetrate the mystery of beauty that no eyesight is

able to penetrate,
In darkness he sees luminosities,
In myriads of things sees nothing but conditioned causalities,
In formlessness discover the true beauty of things.

Do not let your mind be agitated by the conditioned pain,
Embrace in your mind the unity of the whole- the stillness in
emptiness that is serene;
Control the perversities of the will,
See outside the absurdities of the acts that every life fill;
Develop attitudes and intentions to merge with great unity,
That also has dimensions outside the layer of rationality and so called
reality;
Lift yourself above the illusory state of human birth,
And meditate in the stillness of the heart.

Hymn of Air

It is the vital breath that nourishes the muscles,
In strides stretches with arms,
In order to excel everything it possesses, it destroys.
In it things float,
Death rests,
Dreams dazzle without worrying to wake up;
In transmigration it wanders from the unchanging stillness to anxiety
and joy.
Blowing over water it keeps surface disturbed,
Churning stillness it irritates,
Turning ripples, and creating innumerable images, in images of
things it all possibilities tries to exhaust;
In the essence of oneness, where sand and dust forms pervade,
It defines and embodies the spirit by nurturing patterns and in
unpredictable forms integrates.
The music of the heaven with it conforms,
Correcting patterns and accommodating errors, chances, and
fallibility inherent in the nature,
As spontaneously deviating wind it obviates reality and all
boundaries escapes.
As spirit of four seasons,
That fashions and governs the transformations,
Parting from its nature as it was,
Departing from deserts, sand and dust,
Initiating precipitation, dilution and stability of patterns,

It brings a confused disorder in return;
Among mountains and forests,
It impacts on the hidden order,
And completes its way - as destined by fate.
Always uncertain,
Always relative to the past, present and future,
Always being attracted and repelled,
Between occurrence and non-occurrence,
Between limit and limitless,
Between fullness and emptiness,
In levels of paths,
Where things are alive,
Though in reality they no life contain,
In limits that are extremely large,
And the boundaries that are infinitesimally small,
It wanders, seeks, delimits and expands,
Determines the indeterminable,
And in bondage adapts itself to the spirit, which is free.
As words it mutates,
As sounds it modulates,
As music it vibrates,
As nodes it leans on notes and reverberates.
Between the real and the unreal,
As odour stirred by the air and freshened by the wind,
Shuffling the noise, smoke, lamentations, black clouds,
In towering fumes of the windy earth,
It leans in happiness on grass,
Mingles with quietness in the dust,
Shapes, forms, colors the feelings,
And unfurls the trembling feelings as sails on the masts.

This is its way,

It strives,

And in striving it becomes,

Flapping its wings it moves neither to beginning nor to end,

Yet it advances,

Through stability it generates fullness in emptiness,

In ending that has a beginning,

It ends in itself by letting things evolve,

In a changing world where things revolve,

It neither comes from south or north,

From all directions,

It unfathoms the bewildered world where in heat and moisture the earth spirit absorbs.

It whispers in the leaves,

Sleeps in the watery mist,

From eddies in darkest obscurity,

To grandest storms battering with whirling perceptivity,

It takes off, uproots, tramples,

And then stops,

Disperses as mild wind,

Sinks in the whispering mist and fog,

And then sleeps with the tranquillity of the moments on skilful frogs;

Adjusting with the turmoil of the life with an understanding of the buoyancy of its lot,

It wanders, like in a dream, from the feelings of man to the pure domain of God.

As a nebulous bird coming from nowhere,

In profusion of images trembling in the blurriness of the flesh,

With eyes glazed,

And will floating over the forests, islets, rivers, mountains, oceans

and lakes,
Wandering while hearing beasts and birds,
Between name and nameless,
Where seeds turn into germs,
Plantain fertilize the soil,
Butterflies evolve from insects,
In misty spray,
In greeneries move away in myriads of ways;
In non-separation from the whole,
Yet separated by myriads of forms,
Purifying breath,
It falls, rises, comes, goes, stoops and flutters away,
In this way,
It withdraws itself from itself,
Then goes away,
Knows not where...
And carries away vibrations, breaths, agitations through the air,
In bedrock, flames, water,
Over mountains and the volcanic dust,
Over hills chirping with birds,
Echoes, cuckoos and swims away with the feelings floating in the heart.
It is its way,
One moment a dragon and a serpent,
Evolved from weight and mass,
Riding the crust feeding on mud and dust,
In another moment rising,
And wandering beyond the boundary of the sensing,
In one moment riding through calamities,
In another moment vibrating as ethereal harmonies,
In one moment fanning funeral flames,

And in another instant cleansing the desires and moving away to
wander in the domain where with desire no one can come,
It floats, flutters,
From shores to shores,
Journeys as the lord of beast,
And wanders away as an ethereal bird beyond the realm of fire or
mist.
It escorts those who are going,
Welcomes those who are coming,
Wandering in a boat where a person empties his feelings in the wind
and gust,
Or shouts to steer clear from the dangers of the lust,
It indulges in the senses,
And, while no worries beset, wandering alone in the heart, floats
away in the sea of nothingness;
Without opposing the inner thrusts, that pull the sails on the masts,
It draws the mind higher and higher from the realm of mud and dust,
When it goes forward it leads,
When it goes backward everything retreats.
Between the sun and the moon,
Above and under,
Between the past and the future,
Between thunderclaps and lightening,
And the blazing sun-disc scattering increasing radiance with mind's
ethereal heightening,
Between calamities, misfortunes and harms,
And emotions that, above all physical turmoil, embellish life's charm,
Where the human and the heavenly are identical,
Where in hunger, thirst, cold, heat the inevitable operates,
And in sounds of streams,

In the singing of the heart,
In a strange placid forest something inconceivable passes away,
Wandering in a grove,
Forgetting its being,
It speaks of its way;
In tunes and notes withdrawing in the heart,
It returns where its beginning is its end,
And from the centre - bound by east and west, south and north -
comes and goes away day after day again and again.
Remaining unchanged,
While awaiting extinction and disappearance of appearance,
It gallops over everything leaving all things behind,
It stirs, puffs, creates physical excitation of joy or pain,
Babbles in water as a bubbling chain,
In emptiness transforms, changes, creates membranes,
And through gain and loss of buoyancy against the physical weight
breaks away,
Evaporates from surface and as wind from the depth goes off in its
unpredictable way.
This is its way.
It can not be compelled to follow the human will,
It has its own reason without any reason to convey,
In all eternity,
It exists beyond living and dying,
As embodiment of nothing in myriads of forms that wax and wane,
In autumn's fall,
By mutating in the colours that the heavenly beauty recalls,
It produces luminosity that does not insist on reasoning,
But casts off,
Verifies no knowledge,

But clings to emotion,
Like withered carcasses, that does not look for meaning and cause,
It does not measure with decreasing dimension with increasing
stench and putrefaction;
It only wanders, moves, transmigrates without any pause.
It enters passes in mountains,
Dwells in gorges and cliffs,
Where the nature appears wretched with its power to destroy,
It preserves with cunning the shapes of the precipices from the
perilous power of nature's wind borne joy,
It climbs where rocks are confined,
Looks below and under where water tumbles in streams, while
streamlines are hard to define,
In confusion of murmuring sounds,
It forgets all that it wants to say,
In dumb nuance reflects and echoes petrified world's wonder in
pulsating breath.
It goes on wandering in vacant space,
In emptiness it enters the boundariless boundary,
Always free to cross any boundary,
It takes form by chance, and accumulates, disperses, or decays,
From tip to root,
As a dragon power,
It exalts the infinity in the finite forms,
As forms in formless,
It is existent in non-existence,
In existing it negates itself;
Thus in the mirror of the emptiness reveals its resplendent Self.
It is its way,
It embodies both of the dual in unity,

That has been before the heaven and the earth;

It has no state prior to it,

All generations of births from past, present and future are its parts.

Tathagata's meditation

There is no just one land and just one perfect way,
All existence flow through multiple of worlds that inside the
perceptible world dwell,
They penetrate each other in different dimensions of time and space;
The world in which man lives at present,
Is embedded in many other worlds spanned from future to the past;
Temporality is only a conception and man's mental construct;
Which govern the perceptions so that mind with the material reality of
motion and rest can adjust;
In a single life time of man many lives are spanned,
These dimensions penetrate various realms of consciousness that
unfolds as man more and more the mystery of existence understand.
All these worlds,
Like the one in which one feels, touches, sees and hears and calls his
or her own,
Are caught up in never ending process of formations and
disintegration,
Ending in cycles to the beginnings as they return,
Through extinctions and regeneration they can only be known;
Rearranging the past existence as life that is present,
In a constant flux causing the conditions that are destined to pass,
In the world with cyclic death and birth,
They penetrate through emptiness and illumine the consciousness
waking from the unconscious dark;

In these countless lands Bodhisattva appears as many Bodhisattvas in different levels of awareness as guide of man.

To elucidate the meanings,
And make aware of the truth that no words can expound,
To avoid the shortcomings of the meanings that with the follies of knowledge all knowledge afflict,
To undo the faults of the discursive reason that with causes and conditions conflict,
He preaches in similes and parables,
In all levels of existence he teaches in a way that can not be understood by reasons alone;
Go the way this Bodhisattva has gone,
Listen to him in all the different worlds where he appears as guide of man;
Be aware that you are another journeyman destined to follow his Enlightened path.

He is not any one man,
He is multiple in one,
Like a single intelligent being that manifests to knowing through inorganic matter and organic life,
Although existing in every dimension,
He is not in direct contact in time and space;
Through waves he communicates with parts that remain separate in the future, present and past between the celestial spheres and the Earth-bound base;
The intelligence of this whole,
Is greater than the parts that form the unity of the soul;
The place and time where and when he his teachings expound,

Are multiply interpenetrated from heaven to the Earth where man is
sense bound;

The light from his mind the countless shores illumine,

Beyond the limits of space and time in the mirror of things shine,

As someone never been seen and never known before,

He is everywhere, in all spheres, extending from the sky to the mortal
world where he is many fold. He is beyond the sun and the moon,

But still knowable through the lunar and solar lights;

He is beyond the laws of things but still in nature of things he is
immeasurably bright;

The lights that he emits form in the minds pure concepts,

Through numbers, principles and laws he emerges in the world of
percepts;

Take faith,

And believe him as the upholder of the events and causes;

Remove from your mind the sorrow and distress;

Be comforted and remain reassured of his compassion that upholds
the existence of the innumerable species and races.

I have seen him in myself;

Know thyself as manifestation of Himself,

And follow the path of Bodhisattva in the journey through the forest
in search of the Self.

Know that this suffering is the way to enlightenment;

It is an expedient means by which He shows man the greater way,

Come to know that those that seem inauspicious and portent,

Are the vehicles in the seekers' ways;

Concentrate your mind;

Be fearless and awaken in the journey on the boundless waves;

His doctrines are hard to understand;

But I have heard, practiced and achieved the goal beyond which there is not much more to understand,

There is not much to comprehend beyond the knowledge that in all living beings He is incarnate;

Through concentration of the mind you will be able to cross this forest bound by destiny and fate;

You will be able to see yourself from a higher state.

There is no one in blood and flesh,

Who can fully understand His incarnation at different states in varied times and places,

More one will exhaust the thoughts in trying to grasp Him as a living being,

More he will multiply in the vision without any limit of seeing,

In ten directions through numerous groves,

Joining through multiple dimensions all inflows and outflows,

As appearance and influence - latent or manifest,

Inherent in the cause but not determined by the causal effects,

Embodied in forms from the smallest parts,

To the dimensions that is beyond the capacities of thoughts to hold,

Like a single mind beyond all pondering and seeking,

As Thus Come One he is manifest among the beings.

ENLIGHTENED WAY

Tathagata`s teachings about the enlightened way

Delight not in the scented breeze,

shining rain,

Or the great light around,

Where the flowers tremble in the eyebrows as beauty's flames,

Quake not in the tremble of the suffering,

Let yourself be purified through the awakening enlightenment

through senses' pain.

Rejoice not in the brightness of the beam,

That illumines nothing but an illusion and dream,

In the color of gold,

Where the sun illumines the shores,

And attends with omen of death every birth,

Do not fill your eyes with the shining specter of the dust.

Know that through this forest path,

Pass many other paths,

Many other worlds are intertwined in this chiaroscuro of light and

dark,

Various realms in different depths move upward and downward,

Following the human mind's illusion, desire and lust.

The songs of the birds,

The music of the poets,

The wondrous vibrations of the Orphus' lyre,

The soft and gentle sounds in breeze,

That are pure and clear,

That seem profound and wonderful to the ears,

Are caused by the conditions,

Rejoice not in such chains of causation that bring numerous apparitions,

Free yourself from the mortal world's change, transition and repetition;

By seeking the way that Tathagata preaches,

Listen to what the Enlightened One teaches.

Like the sand in the river,

There are innumerable beings that precipitate in varieties of forms,

As no two corns are the same,

In the shore of life every life is unique in its cravings, and desires burning under the passion's flames.

Being formed and shaped by the currents,

That also the flaws of the streams to conduct the serenity of the sea conduct,

And in the frivolities of the waves churn and laugh,

Forgetting the ordering principles that dispel confusions,

Remembering no more the wisdom that brings the patterns of light in the dark,

Do not seek joy in swimming in the foams of the perceptions;

Seek deeper within in the immeasurable depth of the heart,

And follow the company of the Enlightened One - the eternal pearl.

Willing not to suffer is only ignorance,

To cross through the forest without meeting blindness is a foolish judgment;

Seeking beauty in the garden and the grove,

Amidst the splendid colours of trees, bushes and flowers,

Is like encircling oneself with dragon's unsurpassable power,

Advancing deep towards the lake,

Beside which in deep meditation,

Tathagata sees himself in the mirror of nothingness,

Where in the transcendental stillness and emptiness,

Inside the pearls and jewels,

The rays of gold, silver, amethyst, ruby, diamond, topaz, burn in the lotus of light where Buddha dwells,

Seeking the beauty and love of blood and flesh,

Is a misguided desire that may lead to hell.

Towards the way where Bodhisattva has gone,

Removing your mind from desires,

Dwelling in the emptiness and stillness,

Advancing deep in the transcendental power of the consciousness,

In meditation and through wisdom,

Cross this river where the destiny and fate again and again,

As dragon power return.

Leave this forest's illusory light,

That keeps man circling the lake of illusion day and night,

Willing to suffer the way Bodhisattva has done,

Unify the power of your mind to dispel confusion,

And follow the path along which Bodhisattva will again return.

You will see the wonderful varieties of life,

Find delicious pools to drink,

Pass by many comfortable dwellings,

Meet many females bathing in the streams dreaming for love,

Many jewels and gems will arouse the poisonous lust,

And you will often feel the human passion penetrating the flesh as darts;

But viewing the nature of all phenomena as born from the dual,

In the emptiness of the space,

Keep no attachment that can bind your vision in the illusory haze;

In the forest's depth,
Where the dewdrops dwindling as the jeweled bells,
Like a lofty dragon spirit,
Scattering the rays as spangles of gold,
Hanging harmoniously in the light like an ethereal music,
Where the wonderfully lovely petals the dream's deeper levels will
unfold,
Besides flowing springs or bathing pools,
Gaze at farther depth,
Where wanderer's vision opens countless lands,
And illumines the multifold world where man walks or stands.

Do not fall in doubt,
Wander not away from where He preaches;
Hear from his mouth the way that He teaches;
Explaining the reality, the multiple paths, and the way to transcend
the suffering through the awakened heart,
Where He awakens the Earth,
Listen carefully about the expedient means by which living beings
can free themselves from the sufferings of death and birth.
Do not be perplexed and confused by the host of troubles,
In previous existence,
In nurturing desires the paths that you have crossed,
Have led you beside the stream where Bodhisattva has ferried many
other lives across.
His light shines over the numberless multitudes of things,
That describe the distinctions between being and nothing;
Having been received in the material womb,
Where the realm of existence diversifies in multitudes of tombs,
Straying in the forest and puzzled by the mistaken views,

Unable to see beyond the erroneous pleasures that make man blind,
Where man appears in one place and at a time,
Striving to achieve freedom from suffering, confusion,
misunderstanding and the captivity of fate,
Encounters Thus Come One between existence and non-existence
between earth and heavenly gate,
From a realm of thoughts spreading his transcendental rays,
Bodhisattva watches you from his eternal way.
Go the way Bodhisattva has gone,;
He is myself but still distant and none;
Somewhere he flies as angel,
Somewhere he is a son of man:
He wanders in the forest,
Walks in the mountains,
Alone under the tree meditates;
Sometimes seeking, sometimes realizing the emptiness of all seeking,
Stands, gazes in the emptiness and lifts the mind on the enlightened
way.
He is countless and inconceivable in numbers,
Between existing and not existing,
He is incarnate in a threefold world to take on Himself the sufferings
and pains;
Drowned in the midst of existence that are consciously aware or
unaware,
He watches and guides man seeking to escape attachment to desire,
and striving to transcend.
Where false concepts create ignorance,
Ignorance brings desires,
Desire causes actions,
Actions form the consciousness and thoughts,

Consciousness brings forth in the perceptible world the names and forms,

The existence causes suffering, anguish and grief;

The journey through life is difficult, long and climbing towards the height is insurmountably steep;

The hearts that are not sincere seek in that situation an escape through devious means,

And invent corruptions through evil deeds.

The rulers and princes,

The warriors and wrestlers seeking hazardous amusements through acts that hinder them to engage in higher pursuit,

The hunter as illusory entertainments hunting without being aware that he is being hunted by the same dart that he shoots,

The men and women without making distinction of themselves from the life that is unreflective and crude,

Are engaged in raising sheep, chicken, and pigs, as their food,

Pursue the way of ignorance and torments by trying to escape by the way

That is lascivious, hazardous and the blind end of the sense's route.

Overcome the fear,

Rise from the distress,

Know your own innate nature,

Amidst causes and conditions where you exist,

Know yourself as one with the One who rests in innumerable beings who neither enter or exit;

In the village in joy and laughter, amusements and dance,

In the forest where from all directions the penetrating worlds inside worlds in myth, dream, and unreal the true nature of the reality enhance,

Do not associate with the princes and rulers who amuse themselves

as slaughterer and griffin of flesh;
Do not bow to those whose pleasure is to snatch and raid;
Where overbearing arrogance of the lesser mind stubbornly stamps,
Tries to quail and intimidate the seekers' quest,
Stand firm and show to the unenlightened kind the Bodhisattva's
compassionate way.
Remember everything real are unreal;
Do not try to comprehend phenomena that are beyond the human
concepts,
That, to be meaningful, with perceptions must associate;
All phenomena are empty, without any constant abiding,
They arise in order to be extinct,
The phenomena exist to reveal what exist beyond existence in the
realm of non-existence without any entrance or exit;
Where everything is born,
There is something unborn,
Like empty space - not moving, not advancing or regressing,
There is always a constant abiding of the empty world to a single
design with out any form.
Place your mind in this emptiness,
Learn to quiet the conditioned thoughts,
Concentrate to enter the tranquil center,
Through extinction of thoughts emerge out of the regressive barriers
that hinder to reach the domain of the transcendental God.
Wipe out from the mind all impurity of arrogance,
Have pity and compassion to all.
Listen to what Tathagata preaches and cultivate in the mind the
power to distinguish between honest and upright conduct,
And those that are deceitful and false.
Cause to no life any harm,

Strive to respect and revere without any claim of honour or demand;
Do not look with contempt to others that will make you regret;
With forbearance hold away from frivolous debates and keep in yourself the greater secret;
Practice perseverance and do not preach or expound before the earthly desires for fame have been recalled;
Wait, until you will receive the divine call.
Commit not the error to believe that by cultivating compassion you can gain emancipation;
Constantly guard against the illness of self-deception;
Do not adorn yourself with pride, precious objects, wealth and good;
Remove the jewels that reveal man's success and throw the scepter before going to teach anyone how to rule.
Firmly practicing the Bodhisattva's way,
Remain indistinguishable from the crowd,
Dwell in wisdom as the enlightened one amidst those who will fail to believe and fall in doubts;
When people will praise,
Explain and bring about the understanding that only casting off such befuddlement of ordinary people,
The true seeker finds his joy in the silent wonder around,
Walk, sit, lie in the garden and groves,
Where people gather to listen to the music of nature in wonderful sounds,
Meditate in the awaken state in the boundless compassion touching the ground.
Listen, observe in the body, bear in the mind the passing of time;
When clouds will bring thunder,
The lightening will strike,
The hail will pelt and bring hell down,

When pain of existence will press man in suffering profound,
Gaze at great compassion that is above wind, fire and misfortune;
Without being terrified hear the greatest sounds;
When beasts will encircle,
The sharp fangs and claws of flames will inspire terror,
Like snakes, vipers and scorpions death and danger will lift the
poisonous tongues or tails as menacing horror,
Do not scamper away,
From the pit of great fire emerge and gaze at Bodhisattva's way.
Knowing that you are being gazed at by Bodhisattva from his
enlightened way,
Quiet the striving to go in random way;
Follow the harmony that vibrates in the void,
Dissolve in the lucid self-illumination across the river,
As the part of the energy that in all things quiver,
Merge in the Self deeper and deeper.

Concentrate the power of your mind,
Try to gaze through the emptiness at the original state,
Meditate on the unmoving condition of the Self;
By conceiving yourself as part of Tathagata himself,
Overcome the principles of the nature,
The bondage of the wheel,
Become one with the ocean of true knowledge and merge with the
highest will.
Know that contradictions are essential in the world,
Without it nothing will stir or twirl,
The past, present and future will be non existent,
And without it there will be no goal, no path, no necessity of the will;
But know the oneness of the two,

In togetherness they appear as one in the constant flux,
The spiritual and the rational,
The instinctual and the irrational,
Are both instrumental in creating the power that this world propels;
Once you form the correct conception of the nature of this great
compassion,
You will be able to gaze in tranquillity at the heaven and the hell,
You won't be disturbed by this world, where ignorance and
sufferings dwell.
As the pain of hunger is a necessity to mitigate its needs,
The sufferings of life are essential in driving man to seek;
Do not judge this suffering as punishment,
It is bestowed on you to teach the significance of the suffering that
can lead man to a spiritual journey in a world that is inaccessibly vast
and deep;
The love of son and daughter and wife that you nonetheless feel,
That stir you so deep,
Is part of the expression of the compassion that pervades the great
mind;
Like bubbles in the ocean that reflect light and with tiny emptiness
the water replace,
Understand through this emptiness, that you feel, the great love that
pervades all and all sufferings displace.
From the shore of the great ocean to the lofty mountains where the
clouds hide the moisture of the earth that have risen upwards with the
scorching flames,
From the village- that is no where but within oneself,
Where man feels joy and pain,
Hearing the music of light and walking through the nature where
illusions fleet in the wings of freedom with a wish to attain,

Higher heights where the world is tranquil and serene,
In order to attain insight in the very life that makes man wander from
the spheres of water, fire and air to the tranquil realm where all
sufferings transcend,
The life is a perilous journey through flames.
Following the Bodhisattva's way,
Gain correct perspective of the direction,
And reconcile with suffering man's wishes and predilections;
Move towards your true home,
Gain knowledge of the world where there is no spring or winter,
Sun or rain,
And elevate yourself to the higher plane;
Seeking freedom for the benefit of all beings,
Progressively free yourself from the natural laws binding the power
of touching, feeling and seeing,
Keep the aim of being one with the One as your highest aim,
And discard all thoughts that bring personal gain.
Separate yourself from the ego,
Search universal relations to all beings,
Use the mind as the rafts to cross the river,
But never separate yourself from the heavenly river;
When the clouds will come and lean on your eyes,
On the waves pour away from the heart the inner light,
Knowing where to go,
Come close,
Awaiting liberation from time journey from villages to villages,
And as a messenger of light play the flutes in sunshine or moonlight
by the roads;
In the fresh wind coming from the far-off mountains that in an inner
serenity the eyes load,

Meditate alone by the lake where the beauty of the world as
blossoming lotus floats.
Seeing the beauty of the sun where the dews spatter and burst
creating vibrations felt by the inner sun,
Where in chrysanthemums and roses the flowers' splendid colors
plunge,
In the mirror, covering the vision, images quiver between durations,
Between emptiness and non-emptiness mind's dazzling power
reflect and return,
Without attachment remain illumined by the light,
And remain immersed in the world in a tranquil meditation.
In this emptiness that brings perfection and purity;
Know yourself as a part of the journey man guided by the
enlightened One moving in eternity;
Know that after many journeys you and Bodhisattva are going to be
one.
Awaken in the consciousness of the mystery of the One,
Walking towards and away,
As someone here and someone there,
Affirming the whole,
Reaching no final destination but keeping himself as the goal.
In uphill roads,
In boats,
Moving incessantly whose mission remains never complete,
Returning from home he goes,
In going he comes with the departing souls.

Wake from the sleep that you sleep in the world that is true when
seen,
And when unseen is untrue,

But remember that seeing is dreaming,
And through dreaming it is not possible to find the greater way that
pass through the celestial route.
You will see confusion and changes of directions wherever you go,
In the web of the dream do not search the true path of your soul,
Before asking what is right or wrong,
False or true,
Form the correct concept of the world that is real, virtual, true and
untrue;
Do not lengthen your journey by falling in grief,
In destiny's path, in complex webs, do not knit more illusory
thoughts that will bind you more instead of making you free;
Accompany me in the Bodhisattva's way,
Wander not in loneliness for something that attains no goal at the
end,
Move by keeping Bodhisattva's path as your aim.
Move through myriads of things and settlements,
Through forests teeming with birds and beasts,
But do not loose from the eyes the vision of the true freedom that
comes from a domain beyond sense's lights,
Where Sirens and Magpies thrive,
In the name of love ask for blood, flesh and sacrifice,
The hunters on horses come to impair the will to move in
Bodhisattva's way;
Loose not humaneness,
Plod along the path where Bodhisattva has gone scattering his rays.
Do not be confused by the errors,
Even the sages must err;
Through erring you will be able to cultivate the concept of the true
path;

Move along,

Follow the teaching of Tathagata who lifts all to higher ways;

You will find salvation from suffering in the path of the enlightened sage.

The arrows and snares of passions will try to throw you in terrible confusion,

But remember:

Between the sun and the moon,

Mountains and rivers,

The processions of the four seasons,

This confusion and chaos are the necessary conditions for species to remain alive;

Only look at this chaos with proper perspective with inner light;

Do not seek in lasciviousness and darkness of passion life's delight.

Where passions warp and ravish,

And remain never content,

In the name of enjoyment prostitutes its own nature to the power that do not preserve but only destroy,

Overcome the confusion of freedom,

That the needs for passion as life's only reason to exist employ;

Cherish respect for the integrity of all life,

And do not injure yourself and others in seeking happiness of flesh;

Realize the meaning of compassion, the path of higher delights for the human race.

There are many types and characters of men,

Some are boastful, insincere, jeer at all that with their concept of the world and life conflict,

Declining the heaven they live like passion's beasts;

They value the bodies as the highest values of all,

And try to thwart others freedom and bring others to submission by

employing physical skill;
Avoid these lower types of men,
Who seek in the fire of senses their banes;
Guard yourself from the errors that fan the physical flames;
Try not to defeat and consume others but embrace them as friends,
And seek the freedom of spirit in love and compassion knowing all
are parts of the same.
Do not wander randomly,
Do not move without knowing where you seek to go,
In stillness you may explore more;
Do not subject yourself blindly to the circumstances of the things,
And dissipate the power of the spirit amidst perplexity of not
knowing;
Situate yourself in the relationships of the things that evolve in the
bodily forms,
And the ordering principles of the spirit that assure security amidst
calamities and storms;
In the state of turbid chaos,
When things will bring tears and conflicts,
Humbly seek the guidance of Bodhisattva, the enlightened being,
Who moves everywhere to salvage man from suffering and lift them
from the violent eddies and streams.

Go the Bodhisattva's way,
Be awakened, be enlightened, by the inner rays;
Be one with the ultimate spiritual man,
Whose compassion and spiritual intelligence encompass all beauties
of heaven and earth and over all dimensions span;
Be sublimely disengaged from thoughts that drag the mind in the
whirlwinds of errors and faults,

Dwell in yourself as selfless light beneficent to all;
In the stillness of the mirror respond with the images without losing
the harmony and the sameness of the whole,
As a pure spirit tranquil and still - all mortal life's ultimate goal,
Keep yourself dazzling as Bodhisattva, the lighted sun;
Go again and again the way Bodhisattva has gone.
There is no fixed path that can be traced in time and space,
There is no entrance and exit that can be demarcated with boundaries
in space;
In a world that can be grasped as mental abstractions,
It is a path that returns from a stateless state to the images of things;
Here in this abstract space there is no limitation;
Here your existence is related to the mythical one:
He flies in the domain of the light with the exalted being - the
enlightened One.
Yielding to suffer in the world,
Like Prometheus rising to the heaven,
Like bird rising from the ashes of sacrificial pyre in the forest,
And descending from a domain beyond the sun,
In the vision of the enlightened one He flies in the world with the
promethean man,
Bringing the fire of knowledge and contemplative reflection and
making the heaven and the earth as one;
He is invisible and mysterious, with which your existence is one.
Go with Him the way the enlightened journeyman many centuries
ago had gone.

CONTINUED IN

DIALOGUES BETWEEN MAN AND GOD

Dialogues Between Man Existing in Flesh and Blood (Christ-man) and God

www.ScienceMeetsGod.EnlightenedWorld.net

The book is also available as audio-visual multimedia interactive book as well as standard e-book. For more information visit

www. BooksofExistence.no

www.ingramcontent.com/pod-product-compliance
Lightning Source LLC
Chambersburg PA
CBHW030938150426
42812CB00064B/3044/J